To Krissy, Wishing you lots of laughs, love + in your book + in your life. God Bless Patti Faloon

PITTSBURGH PIZZAZZ

A LIFE IN SHOWBIZ
• • • • • • • • • • • •

PATTI FALOON

WORD ASSOCIATION PUBLISHERS
www.wordassociation.com
1.800.827.7903

ISBN: 978-1-59571-868-6

Library of Congress Control Number: 2013901648

Designed and published by

Word Association Publishers
205 Fifth Avenue
Tarentum, Pennsylvania 15084

www.wordassociation.com
1.800.827.7903

CONTENTS

. . . .

CONTENTS

CONTENTS

CONTENTS

Dedicated to all the people I love—and there is a lot of you—and some I haven't even met yet...

And especially to my three kids:
Bill, Steven, and Lisa
to me,
The Greatest Show on Earth
• • • • • • • • • • • • • • • • • • •

A special thanks to Cheryl Stewar-Miller for her patience and kindness in helping me edit my book.

"Choose a career you love
and you will never work a day in your life."

—Confucius

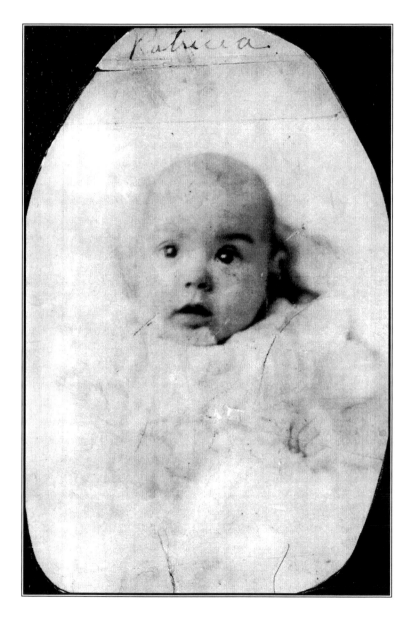

Curtain up! Light – the lights!

IN THE BEGINNING

Entertainers thrive on audience reaction. The first time I ever wowed an audience I was too young to under-stand what I had accomplished. After all, I was only two months old when my career got "launched." One wintry night my parents and uncle were driving in their roadster to visit Berkeley Springs, West Virginia, my mother's and uncle's hometown. The adults were in the front seat. There was no back seat to speak of, so I was tucked away on the shelf by the back window. Quite suddenly the roadster hit a barricade of some sort. The car door opened, and I went flying into an adjoining field. Fortunately my mother had wrapped me in several baby blankets to withstand the cold. The adults, who suffered cuts and bruises, were stunned by my "performance." I came through it all like a trooper—I was just fine.

I was born on October 4, 1929, on Greenbush Street on Mount Washington, in Pittsburgh, PA. I was twenty-five days old when the Great Depression began.

Greenbush Street was just a couple of blocks away from the police station. It was in many ways a safer time. I was about fifteen months old when I had my first "road tour." I wound up inside the police station. The police staff hoisted me onto a high desk. I'm sure I loved the attention. They evidently questioned me, but the best was yet to come: they also bought me an ice cream cone. This was a huge treat as we didn't have refrigerators with freezers back then. Not surprisingly, I managed to get "lost" again a couple more times. When the police caught onto me, it was all over.

At the entrance to Greenbush Street, there was a big, white, stately house. Its occupant—one of our neighbors—made history. On August 29, 1930, Sara Soffel was sworn in as judge of Allegheny County Court. She was the first woman judge in Pennsylvania.

My mother was only sixteen years old when I was born. My dad was twenty-four, going on five! They were young and exciting parents. Not only did my mother settle in Pittsburgh from Berkeley Springs, but so did many of her sisters and brothers. I had wonderful aunts, uncles, and cousins all around me.

Our next residence would be in Duquesne Heights, on the other side of Mount Washington. I remember that house literally clung to the side of a hill. Today when I enter the Fort Pitt Tunnel into downtown Pittsburgh, I often look up... way up! The house is right above the tunnel entrance. I don't believe we lived there for more than a year.

We moved often. Once again, we moved back to Mount Washington, this time to the bottom of Dilworth

Street. My sister, Corrine, was born in this house. A lovely woods and park were practically in our front yard. My father's sister, Aunt Pearle, lived in a big white house facing the park. The park had a baseball field, tennis court, and circular pool—maybe three feet deep—for little kids.

I was about three years old when, for some reason, I got in the middle of the pool and took my bathing suit off. Oh, the attention I received! There were a couple of adults and some kids around. Mother was visiting Aunt Pearle, and they could see me from the porch. The water was up to my neck, and I kept laughing and splashing. This would be the one and only "striptease" act of my life...that is, *almost* the one and only striptease act of my life. More on that later! Entertainers *love* reaction! I was sure getting it that day, and I loved it!

I can't remember how long we lived at the bottom of Dilworth Street. I was about four when we moved near the top. My baby brother Harry was born in this house. We rented, as few people owned their own homes—those were hard times. It says a lot about the optimism of the United States that Radio City Music Hall opened in New York on December 27 of that year.

PROSPECT SCHOOL

Despite the terrible economy, Prospect School was erected in 1931. This gem was just a couple of blocks away from our house and was practically brand-new when I attended kindergarten in 1934. It had beautifully smooth, varnished, blond wooden desks. There were hardwood floors, and a tiled, sparkling swimming pool, not to mention marble steps. It was like Eden to me.

When summer vacation ended, I was always happy to begin school. How I loved the music room in elementary school! I always loved singing "Oh, Columbia, the Gem of the Ocean."

There was also an adorable little theatre with a lovely stage elevated about two feet. I was given the role of a witch in one production. I enjoyed doing the squeaky, scary voice and the menacing gestures. I loved the compliments from the teachers the next day on my performance.

One day a traveling stage production came to our school. The theme of its performance was the circus! Our class tried out for different parts. I was so happy to be chosen as the clown. This was a prophetic role, as some fifty years later I would become a professional clown.

POP

If my father had ever had the opportunity to join a circus, he would have. He was a daredevil, and I was the apple of his eye and his clone.

On one of our family picnics to South Park, I remember him pushing me on a swing. The swing had very long chains holding the seat. "Higher! Higher!" I would encourage my father to push the swing. I do believe if my mother hadn't yelled at him, he would have tried to see if I could go all the way over. I was a willing cohort.

As a very young lad, Pop actually dove off Smithfield Street Bridge into the Monongahela River. Although his head hit a rock, he survived. For the rest of his life he had a deep dent in the top of his skull.

Pop had been a sailor for four years. He traveled the globe. When he crossed the equator, he took many pictures. (Pop always took a lot of pictures.) In fact, while he was stationed in San Diego, he was even able to get a snapshot of a younger Albert Einstein.

From one of his voyages he brought back a Capuchin monkey to give to his sister, my Aunt Velma. They called the monkey "Senorita." It might be a clue to where he found it. How he maneuvered the monkey's transport, I'll never know!

I believe my father would have loved to be in show business. He was my musical parent. He played a concertina, a hand-held bellows-driven instrument sort of like an accordion. He also played the harmonica and loved to sing songs.

To earn his living he became a policeman. One time he was assigned a motorcycle with a sidecar. After much begging by my sister and me, he let us ride in the sidecar. That happened only when it got dark in the evening, and we had to ride under a black tarp. We would peek out. What a bumpy ride around Mount Washington! Most of the streets were cobblestone, called Belgian block.

Pop would always find some interesting contraption. Somehow he obtained an old pinball machine. It was great fun. We could "tilt" over and over again and it didn't cost a thing. We wore that machine out. There wasn't another kid I knew who had a pinball machine in their dining room.

Policeman Pop, and his motorcycle

BERKELEY SPRINGS, WEST VIRGINIA

My mother, Pauline Nellie Hobday, was born in Berkeley Springs, West Virginia. Her father and my grandfather, Newton Howard Hobday, was an extraordinary man. He was fourteen years old when a tree fell on his leg. The rest of his life he had an open wound. He did lead a long life. The injury certainly wasn't a handicap for fatherhood. There were eight children who lived.

Grandfather was also an accomplished shoemaker. Attached to his house was his shop. I would stand and marvel as he put soles on shoes using all the complicated machinery.

He was the town's sheriff for a while. Also, he had a farm. I remember watching an assembly line in his barn. A moving chain would send boiled tomatoes up a conveyor to another floor where women would be seated. They would be peeling and preparing the tomatoes to be canned. Huge bags of salt would be stacked outside the barn. I loved to get a juicy tomato, dip it into the salt, and eat it.

Grandfather's house was on the main street—Berkeley Springs has only one "main street" to this day. The town has become quite a tourist attraction with its natural, warm spring-water baths, charming restaurants, and friendly locals. Many of Mother's kin stayed in Berkeley, but my mom couldn't wait to leave for the big city life. We made the trip back to Berkeley Springs many summers, and I loved it. Back then it was a daylong jaunt to get there. There was no Pennsylvania Turnpike. Pop was good at fixing cars, but what guts he had. I'm sure the youthful, invincible part of him played a part in that gutsiness. We would drive the car up those long mountains, and the car's radiator would go dry. Pop knew where the springs were, and maybe he'd have to walk a bit to reach one. He always had an empty container in the car to fill with spring water, and once the radiator was filled, we'd be on our way. Pop was an excellent mechanic in keeping the cars running. He "ran" a long time too! He lived to be eighty-four years old.

One summer we had a car with a rumble seat, which would accommodate the three of us kids quite comfortably. Pop would start singing, and we'd all sing along in the open air. One of those songs was "Be Sure It's True When You Say I Love You...It's a Sin to Tell a Lie."

Later on when I began taking dancing lessons, my Berkeley cousins considered me to be somewhat of a star. It was not true, but I enjoyed the famous tag they insisted on bestowing on me.

DANCING SCHOOL

We now lived on Norton Street in Mount Washington. I was about ten years old when Mom sent me to dancing school. I'll be forever grateful for this opportunity. Every Saturday I took my little suitcase containing dance shoes and rode the streetcar to class by myself. This self-assurance would come in handy throughout my professional career.

My cousin Olga, who was a few years older than me, had been going to the same dancing school. I loved getting her old dancing costumes and old tap shoes, even though they were too small for me. I would squeeze into them. Oh, the make-believe I did with those pretty satin costumes, this tomboy character—me—prancing around the neighborhood in flashy attire.

I did very well in all the dancing classes: tap, ballet, and acrobatics. (Today we call acrobatics "gymnastics.") I was a quick learner. We had a yearly show back then, and I was always put in the front of the line of dancers because I could remember all the steps. To have a solo number in the show cost extra money. We couldn't afford it. However, by being in the front, in a way I had a featured spot!

I was trained with live music. In the early 1940s a piano player always accompanied our classes. When the yearly show was performed, we had a full, live orchestra. No tapes or CDs back then!

In sixth grade we had a talent contest. I did a tap dance. Everyone got a delicious treat, and the winner would get two! It was a Dixie cup of vanilla ice cream covered with peanuts and Hershey's chocolate. I got two.

ACTIVE PRE-TEEN

We didn't have the Internet, iPods, text messaging, or Twitter. I always had friends to play with, but I could also play by myself for hours, making up stories and playing all the parts.

With friends we would make up shows and imitate radio personalities. Fanny Brice was always so funny, especially with her character Baby Snooks! Singing…I was always singing! I loved Gene Autry, the singing cowboy—"South of the Border Down Mexico Way."

With the woods being in close proximity to where we lived, that setting was perfect for reenacting scenes from *Tarzan*. My older cousin Merle would be Tarzan. I was "Boy," and with my limited physical attributes it worked out well. One of the most common clothing items for girls in those days was a short dress with a thin cloth belt. I would tie the belt across my sparse chest and tie it in the back. (I don't know why I bothered.) "Jane" was played by a beautiful neighborhood girl, Ruthie. We would make up our own scripts, totally believing ourselves to be the characters. Ruth later became a majorette with the local American Legion band. She was so generous in showing us younger fans of hers the many different twirling maneuvers she had to learn. I was able to use that twirling skill in many different routines throughout my dancing career, such as when I would use a cane in a tap routine.

I loved the ice-skating movie star, Sonya Henie. One of my "all by myself" projects took place at Christmastime. The picture-perfect holiday with a deep snow lingered for weeks. A week after Christmas I gathered as many discarded Christmas trees from the neighborhood as I could—at least eight. I dragged them to my backyard. The yard had a nice slope. I scattered and "planted" each tree in the deep snow. In my imagination I had skis on my feet. I would start at the top of the yard, and I *was* Sonya Henie, sliding down and around the trees.

Summers seemed so long when I was young. I was always, always busy. Many days I would ride my bicycle all day long, sometimes with my friend Mae. We could actually sail down the Mount Washington Roadway from world-famous Grandview Avenue at the top, where one can get a spectacular view of Pittsburgh.

At the bottom of the roadway Mae and I would continue riding our bikes into the South Side. There once was an incline there to take us back up to the Mount. This engineering marvel could take a couple of cars up to the top, and had a curve along its path. A sign now reads, "Knoxville Incline Station, 1890–1960."

There were times Mae and I would ride our bikes through the Liberty Tubes. At one time there was a narrow walkway with a railing inside the tunnel. It was quite a feat maneuvering our bikes on it.

Mae and I loved to swim. When summer was over, we discovered the pool at the downtown Salvation Army. In cold weather we would ride down the incline and walk across the Smithfield Street Bridge—even on bitterly cold nights.

One very hot summer evening as we were crossing the bridge, we looked over the railing. There were a couple of fellas in a rowboat. We waved and began chatting. They invited us down for a boat ride. There were mills along the river, and the boys knew where we could put on our bathing suits in some kind of enclosure. We did. I had my one and only swim in the Monongahela River. I dove into the water. When I opened my eyes under the water, I could see NOTHING! It was black. Imagine the debris, the germs in the river! Yuck! My skin and my suit were filthy. The mill enclosure had a shower, and I was able to wash away the dirt. Mae wasn't so daring—she didn't even go into the water.

Later, when Mae worked in a drugstore, there was a stock boy who would become very famous. Mae wasn't surprised. "He was the nicest young boy," she said. Donald Wuerl became the bishop of Pittsburgh and served for eighteen years. Later he became the archbishop of Washington, D. C. And in 2010 he was selected by Pope Benedict XVI to join the College of Cardinals. Someday he may become pope!

The front of our house on Norton faced a flat, smooth, orange-brick (not cobblestone) street. I would see how many ways I could ride my bicycle: stand on the seat, sit and guide the bike with my feet on the handlebars, ride backwards, and pedal off to one side with one foot. One day Mother was sitting on the porch watching me, and she pleaded, "Would you stop that?" I attempted (and succeeded) standing on my head on the seat with my hands on the handlebars. Mom stood up, shook her head, and went into the house. I really didn't need an audience for all of this—I just enjoyed the challenge of trying something different.

I would practice the same kind of antics with my roller skates, which were attached to the soles of my shoes, with a key to tighten them. There was a sidewalk in the front of our house about a block long. I had just enough elevation to keep me rolling. It would become my skating runway. I'd experiment with every conceivable way to skate—backward, one leg, squatting, spinning.

Being my father's child, I loved to take dares. My friends dared me to roller-skate down the long hill, on the sidewalk of the street. Back then, there were always a few houses that did not have paved sidewalks. I did it! Smooth, smooth, rattle, rattle, smooth, chug, chug, chug, smooth… There was a street crossing at the bottom of the hill with a curb I had to jump. My friends gathered to watch for cars. I jumped the curb, flew across the street, and wrapped my arms around the telegraph pole. I pulled splinters out of my arms for days!

It took me years—at a class reunion—to find out why I walked home from school in the snow…in my socks! I remembered doing this, but I couldn't figure out why. At the reunion a school chum told me why. She said at the end of one school day as we opened the door, we discovered heavy snow. Deep snow. I said, "No way am I going to ruin my new shoes!" So I simply took them off and carried them home. Mystery solved.

I can't remember the name of a particular male singer who sang regularly on a radio show. I do recall the words he would sing for a certain commercial for Scrapple, a food product. "Scrapple odle-lay-dee-ay, comes from Philadelph-e-ay. Try it once, and you'll agree, it's the food for you and me!" And then, wow, how he could yodel!

My friend Flo and I sent for a booklet on how to yodel. That summer the neighbors thought they were living in the Alps. We practiced constantly. "Oh-dee-o-lee-ay, oh-dee-o-lee-ay, OH-DEE-O-LEE-AY!"

In junior high at Prospect, I loved the swimming classes. Our teacher was all caught up in the Esther Williams craze. Williams was a swimming move star. We would do synchronized swimming to the Andrew Sisters' big hit, "Apple Blossom Time." I've never forgotten the words to this song. For years, when I'd be at the swimming pool, I would often swim and hum or sing the words.

MOM

Mom and I were the best of friends. The sixteen-year age difference meant there was not much of a generation gap. At one time in our lives we wore the same size of clothing.

She was colorful and innovative. She had a thick mane of peroxide blonde hair, which made her big blue eyes even prettier. And her clothes! One day I was with her when she was shopping for a new dress. The salesgirl kept leading us to the women's department. Mom said, "I don't want those drab, dull dresses!" (The word matronly comes to mind.) Then we went to a younger-female department. "Ah, some pizzazz," she said. "Some pretty colors!" I've inherited Mom's belief: if the world was supposed to be in black and white, why would we be given the choice of so many glorious colors?

Despite the freedom allowed in my childhood, there were consistent rules. We had to be in when the street-lights came on. Everyone had to be present at the dinner table. Our suppers were never dull.

But I certainly got a surprise at the dinner table one evening. We were having a spaghetti dinner, and my sister, brother, and I started to giggle, with me being the instigator. I would not let up...I kept it going. Mom tried to stop...mainly me. "That's enough now!" "Will you stop it?!" "No more!" Pop found a way. He took my plate of spaghetti and calmly turned it upside down on top of my head! I was stunned. That sure wiped the smile off my face. Pop was laughing now.

My mom was an optimist. I heard her say to someone once, "My kids can do anything!" In many ways I believed her, and it gave me confidence.

Of course there is confidence and there is stupidity. Another one of my youthful, foolish stunts happened on a vacation to Berkeley Springs. Lake Cacapon was large and deep. How deep, I did not know. There was a diving board about ten feet high. The locals dared me to dive to the bottom. I had no idea how far down I would have to go. To this day I can't believe I really did it. I dove, and it felt like I swam forever to reach the bottom. I remember seeing light about two feet above the black bottom. After that it was pitch black. I later came across a description for this: "euphotoic zone," meaning "down to two hundred feet, the depth to which light penetrates." But I finally did reach the bottom.... I grabbed some weeds and mud, and zoomed to the top!

WORLD WAR II

The year 1941 would be a significant year. I was eleven years old. We had our annual dancing show in May. I still have the lovely program. There was always a theme. This year it was *Dance of the Stars*.

Throughout the program there were titles like "On the Planet Venus" and "Satellite." I was in the advanced tap class and our number was titled "Symphony in White." Our class was the planet Mercury, with winged cap and winged feet. Another number was called "Out of the Moon," described as "fast and zippy." There were four of us in this intermediate acrobatic class. The finale was called "The Earth—Salute to the Red, White and Blue," the classic patriotic finale for many shows.

Little did we know how patriotic America would get about seven months later when the Japanese bombed Pearl Harbor. Pop wanted to join up right away. He was thirty-seven years old, with three kids, and the armed forces wouldn't accept him. Later that month, Germany declared war on America.

Mom began working in a defense plant during the war. The women in the mills were required to wear slacks on the job, which was unusual because women did not wear long pants back in the forties.

I was in junior high at this time. One day I wore Mom's long black pants, a yellow blouse, and an artificial flower in my hair. A flower in the hair was a fad back then. All of my teachers frowned at me that day. My sister tried the same bit the next day and was told to go home and change her clothes. The neat thing was my mother didn't seem to mind. Most of my friends' mothers were older and stricter.

My beautiful mother was a finalist for a Miss Victory contest during the war. The defense plant where she worked sent in her name and picture. I still have a couple of clippings with big pictures of her from the newspaper.

I even have the original script from a radio show for which she was being interviewed. It aired on October 30, 1942, on *The Polly Malone Show*, WCAE Radio. On the show my mother bragged about her daughter Patricia helping with the household chores. To this day I feel guilty about not helping her more. I do remember dusting furniture.

I was twelve through sixteen years old during the war. I was young enough not to realize the horrors of war and lucky enough not to have any war casualties among my family or friends.

I was a cheerleader and my acrobatic stunts came in handy. The other cheerleaders once played a dirty trick on me. One day before a game they asked me if one of the subs could go on in my place. I was quite reluctant... but they kept begging me! I finally relented. They knew something I didn't know: there were to be pictures taken that day. Years later I went to see a musical program at Prospect Junior High. In the hallway was a trophy case. You guessed it...there was the picture of the cheerleading team, without me. That might have been the girls' one shining moment—whereas I would have many more!

Prospect was kindergarten through ninth grade. A graduating booklet from the ninth grade: "Patricia Ebeling ('Pat')—Lifesaving, Cheerleaders, Navigation Club, Wants to be a tap dancer." I had done a tap dance routine on the auditorium stage. Above the stage was a very large, sculptured motto: "Where there is no vision the people perish!" With my visual imagination in show business, I would persevere for years to come.

Joe Negri, a fine guitarist and a regular on *Mister Rogers' Neighborhood,* was a neighbor of mine on Mount Washington. His mother belonged to an active, fun-loving Italian club. I agreed to do a tap dance for one of their parties. Joe's mother had me wear an orange, puffy-sleeved satin shirt that had been worn by Joe. Here's one for Joe's fans: His mother had him take dancing lessons!

That bright shirt makes me think of *The Lawrence Welk Show.* So many lovely, colorful outfits on his show! It's a different showbiz today. We see musicians in black jeans with holes...they could care less! Their pizzazz seems to be represented in loud music with electronic tricks and fireworks.

LOVE OF LYRICS

I like drama, but musicals were always my favorites. I love lyrics and I know the words to hundreds and hundreds of songs.

I was born in the wee hours of the morning. Whether or not this has anything to do with my being a night owl, I don't know. In the early morning my energy seemed to be nil. However, many nights my sister and brother would be fast asleep and I would slip out of the bedroom. Mom and Pop would still be downstairs and I would go into their bedroom. I would sit on the floor in front of the window. I would look out and sing and sing softly.

My father obviously loved music. Many songs he would sing and I would listen and memorize the words. Besides a pinball machine in our dining room we had one of those wind-up RCA Victrola record players. "Carolina Moon" was one of my favorites. I love rhyming words: "How I'm hoping tonight you'll go, Go to the right window…"

On weekends, we three kids would want to sleep in. Pop would be singing loudly, "You gotta get up, you gotta get up in the morning! Rise and shine! Up and at 'em!" Later in life, at parties, Pop would get requests for some of the special songs he sang. He usually needed a couple of drinks, and then could be quite entertaining. One of the novelty songs was "After You Get What You Want, You Don' Want it!" One song he would always sing to Mom: "If I had my way, dear, we'd never grow old… And sunshine I'd bring every day… You would reign all alone, Like a queen on a throne, if I had my way…."

SUNDAY SCHOOL

I enjoyed going to Sunday school at a Lutheran church. When I started my dancing career, the Reverend Statler came to our house and pleaded with my parents that I *not* go into show business. He felt there were too many bad influences. Looking back, I realize this was a sweet effort he made. I've had much happiness in my life, and through faith I have been able to handle the tragedies. I would be married in this church by Rev. Sattler.

FRED ASTAIRE

In September of 1943, I would get to see someone I admired and idolized. It was a dream come true. I stood maybe ten feet away from the great tap dancer Fred Astaire. Pittsburgh was a stop for a war bond rally. The parade, loaded with movie stars, came rolling down Fifth Avenue. It was a beautiful sunny day. The news reported: "A Hollywood Cavalcade at Forbes Field sells $87 million in United States war bonds. Among those featured are Greer Garson, Fred Astaire, and Harpo Marx." Also there were Mickey Rooney, Betty Hutton, Judy Garland, Kathryn Grayson, Dick Powell, and Kay Kyser.

The convertible car with Fred Astaire stopped right in front of us. We smiled and shouted, "Hi!" Astaire stood up on the seat and attempted a dance step. He slipped a little, and his smile was warm and endearing. I felt I could have reached out and touched him.

Fred Astaire, this sensational genius of a tap dancer, never disappointed me. Not just his amazing talent, but his private life was to be admired.

DANCING

My first years of dancing were at Martha Davies Studio. When I was fourteen years old, I got to dance with a group from the school at a local VFW club. I loved the experience.

I then began to study with Vera Liebau, who had an established studio with a good reputation. On June 15, 1944, I did a solo tap dance with a cane for the year-end final show. The tune was "At Sundown." Once again, there was a live orchestra. The show was put on at the now-defunct Nixon Theatre. The acoustics in this theater were superb. Many great acting stars appeared there over the years.

About four years later, in September 1948, I would see a live production of *A Streetcar Named Desire* on this same stage. The star was the great actor Anthony Quinn.
As for roller-skating, there was a wonderful rink on Market Street in downtown Pittsburgh. It was novel in

that it was like an enclosed bridge up in the air between two buildings. Trolleys and cars could drive under it.

When I skated there, I would try all of my childhood maneuvers. I would constantly get reprehended for skating too fast. I would pretend I was one of those roller derby gals, and I would zoom all over the place.

Each generation has its active hub. Market Street was abuzz with activities. The G. C. Murphy's Five and Ten was the width of a city block. There was a thriving Record Mart, where the tunes could be heard outside. Fresh food markets were possibly the biggest draw at one time. There were several saloons where I would eventually be doing my internship dancing.

Whether it was roller-skating or swimming, we would have a long walk to the incline. At the bottom of the incline we would have to walk across a long bridge. No wonder most of us stayed slim, active, and healthy. Throughout all of my growing up and school years, I do not recall one obese kid.

The roller-skating haven of happy times on Market Street would fall to the wrecking ball in 1961. (Later, in 2009, the city spent $5 million to overhaul Market Square. The area was to remain free of traffic.)

CAIRO STREET

I was sixteen years old when we moved to Cairo Street. This was the house I lived in when, on December 31, 1946, President Harry S. Truman officially proclaimed the end of WWII hostilities. Many gathered in downtown Pittsburgh to celebrate. The joy was contagious. It was glorious chaos.

We moved a lot, about every five years, and always within Mount Washington. The good part was, the move was always to a nicer house. On Cairo Street, my singing buddy, Aunt Grace, lived next door and Aunt Pearle was a couple of blocks away.

Aunt Pearle owned and lived in the same house as long as I can remember. I spent many happy childhood days in this big, white-framed house. Upon entering the front door there was a large living room. Under the staircase was a coat closet. It was actually a little room. The staircase had a nice-sized landing that would become a little stage where I could dance and pretend I was on a real stage. Aunt Pearle would applaud and encourage me. She loved live musical entertainment. She had been in many local minstrel shows. That era had passed.

After the war, Mom became a cashier at Stouffer's Restaurant in downtown Pittsburgh. Through her I got a job after school as a waitress. The constant jingle of tips in my pocket felt good. I became friends with an older waitress who introduced me to the joy of ballroom dancing at the Grotto Hall on the North Side of Pittsburgh. There was always a big, live band. I usually danced every dance with a different fella. Every type: fox trot, waltz, polka, and of course, the jitterbug!

THE MOST CONTROVERSIAL EVENT OF MY LIFE

With all the many hours I was spending at Moore Pool in Brookline, I caught the eye of one of the lifeguards. He would watch all of my fearless craziness off the ten-foot-high diving board. My swimming chums were boys. We would get on the diving board and think of every type of goofy dive to do. I once did a torpedo dive and survived! Hands at my sides, I dove in headfirst. I hit the cemented bottom so fast and hard I saw stars!

Al, the lifeguard, said he wanted to train me for the city's diving meet. I had entered the swimming meet the year before and won many ribbons for different styles of swimming. The championship event was held by the AMA (Allegheny Mountain Association). I felt flattered at the confidence that Al had in me. All summer he trained me. I guess word got around that I was doing well. A few days before the meet, the *Pittsburgh Press* came to take a picture of me doing a swan dive off the high board. Wow, what a picture! Pop carved a wooden replica figure of the dive. The write-up with the picture emphasized my young age. A sixteen-year-old had entered the diving contest! There were four entries for the contest. One of them was an older (maybe thirty) lady who had been the champion for several years. She was to be married and this was to be her last meet.

On the day of the meet, under pressure, I did all my dives perfectly: swan, jackknife, half gainer…and my favorite, the one-and-a-half somersault pike. It always felt so natural and rhythmic. Perhaps those acrobatic lessons lent to the smooth transition.

The concrete stands were overflowing with nearly four thousand people. Many of my friends and relatives were there. I was considered the underdog, which made them cheer all the louder for me. It became a contest between me and the champ. Talk about a hometown advantage! With three of her dives she hit the water with the seat of her (bathing) pants. Not a belly flop, but a bum flop! The spray was magnificent, about six feet high! I felt I deserved the gold medal I got that day. The crowd went wild! We all seemed to enjoy the underdog victory.

However, that evening we got a phone call at home. I had to give the medal back: the "champ" claimed she should have gotten extra points for attempting more difficult dives. Everyone said, "Don't give it back!" I did.

The following year I would enter again, reluctantly, because I would then be a professional dancer with little time to practice for the meet. I got another silver medal, and I deserved just that, then.

I would do exhibition diving around the city pools. The newspapers were always flattering to me. One write-up with a picture read: "Miss Ebeling, who is a singer and dancer as well as swimmer, will do exhibition diving." I loved when articles would call me the Esther Williams of Pittsburgh. I never missed any of her beautiful aquatic movies.

I only have a few regrets. A big nightclub attempted to cash in on the fame that Esther Williams had with her marvelous synchronized swimming movies. The club planned an extravaganza-type of water show. I was asked to be in it. I declined. Just the thought of getting my hair wet constantly was one reason. I was into learning and creating ideas for floorshows. The aquatic show was not that successful—just a short run—or, I should say, "short swim"! But it would have been another kind of experience.

SOUTH HILLS HIGH

Growing up with all the familiar faces at Prospect was so secure and comforting. However, going to South Hills High presented a scenario of strangers.

I couldn't wait to get out of school and start my career. I even went to summer school so I could get out a half-year earlier. By going to summer school and advancing to another grade, once again my new classmates were strangers.

Our Class Day program was in February 1947. I would be eighteen in October. Ironically, the senior program was titled "The Family Album." I am listed in the program: "'Sunny Side of the Street'—Pat Ebeling." This would eventually be one of my routines when I became a professional singer and dancer.

I would need a job to pay for the costumes. Typing and shorthand were my best qualifications. I got a job easily as a private secretary at A. M. Byers Pipe Company on the South Side.

The job itself bored me. Often I would type and write poetry or songs. I couldn't wait to save enough money for my eagerly anticipated career.

CELEBRITIES

• •

Instead of going home after work, I would often continue into downtown Pittsburgh. This was when movie theatres not only showed a popular movie but also had a live stage show. I remember seeing the beautiful actress Arlene Dahl. She sang. At the end of her show she brought her husband, Lex Baxter, onto the stage. What a gorgeous couple they made! These live shows were at the Stanley Theatre, which in 1984 became the Benedum Center for Performing Arts.

The late great Danny Kaye did a live show in this theatre. My friend Mae and I (we were about sixteen years old at the time) sat through the same movie twice and three of the live shows. After the first show we managed to get seats in the very middle of the first row. I don't recall the movie at all, but Danny Kaye was wonderful. Such finesse he had with a song, and he danced to "Ball and a Jack." His cleverness and wit are still unmatched.

During the third show he looked right down at Mae and me and said, "Are you girls still here?" We grinned, nodded, and applauded loudly.

There is no way the intimacy of this theatre could compare with the big stadium-like halls of live shows today. They try to create intimacy with huge television screens that project close-up pictures of the performers.

Around this time my friend Claire and I went to a bigger arena in East Liberty called the Duquesne Gardens. We had neither the intention nor the money to be able to see the show. However, we had a plan.

We stood in a long line at the stage-door entrance. We watched as the limo approached with the celebrities inside. We could see Bob Hope in the car, and with him was the up-and-coming Doris Day. They seemed to be chattering away. As Bob Hope strolled down a path lined with fans and headed for the stage door, there was utter silence as everyone stood in awe. Just before entering through the stage door, with his well-known sneer and strut, he quipped, "When you got it, you got it!" Everyone laughed. Even though we couldn't afford to see the show, we were thrilled to be so close that we could have touched this great showbiz icon.

On October 24, 1947, I went to New York City. Helen, a good friend of my mom's, was taking a trip to New York. Her son, who was a high-ranking officer in the army, was to be in a big parade that would head down Fifth Avenue. I was invited to go with her. Wow! What a thrill! Back then, traveling around the USA was not as prevalent as it is today.

By now I had been a professional entertainer for about nine months. Many a comic I worked with at the time would often get a laugh by asking the crowd, "Anybody here from New York?" If anyone dared say yes, the comic would shrug his shoulders and say, "Big deal!" It always got a laugh. For me it *was* a big deal.

The parade was wonderful and exciting. What captivated me was the movie and live stage show at the Strand Theatre on Broadway and 47th Street. The movie was *That Hagen Girl*. It was one of Shirley Temple's grownup roles. The leading man in the movie was Ronald Reagan.

After the movie was a live show. The music was provided by the Ted Weems Orchestra. Listed as "America's Newest Singing Sensation" was Gordon MacRae. I thought he was cute and a wonderful singer. The females in the audience were screaming for Gordon, akin to Frank Sinatra. I would become a lifelong fan of Gordon MacRae.

Also on the bill was "Radio's Funny Man of WHN," Morey Amsterdam. Morey later had great success on TV on *The Dick Van Dyke Show*. Within a few years of seeing him in New York I would work an after-hours, private club date with him in Pittsburgh.

Scanning a sixty-year-old, yellowed newspaper page, I see there is a history of show business legends: Howard Hughes's controversial movie, *The Outlaw*, with Jane Russell, was showing at the Broadway Theatre on Broadway at 53rd Street. At the Paramount, Times Square: in person, Charlie Spivak and his orchestra, Al Bernie, and Tip, Tap & Toe. Listed as an extra was someone who would become a star: Mel Torme. On the bill at the Apollo, "Harlem's High Spot for Colored Show," was the first lady of song, Ella Fitzgerald, with Buck & Bubbles and the Cat Anderson Band. And, how about this? "Attend the 'early bird' show for 55 cents."

GETTING STARTED

I was about sixteen years old when Mom and I went with Aunt Pearle to see her daughter, my cousin Olga, dance in a private Elks club. Olga opened the show with a tap routine and closed it with a lovely Hawaiian routine. She wore a different costume for each number. And after the show we saw her get paid. Wow, this was for me!

I was seventeen years old when I joined the American Guild of Variety Artists (AGVA). It was the spring of 1947, the era of nightclubs: saloons, joints, dives, bars, lounges, cabarets, and supper clubs, to name a few. There were many private clubs like the Elks, Eagles, Moose, American Legion, VFW, and the Shriners. There were country clubs and stage shows. Some of the clubs offered one-nighters and some a full week's engagement. The coveted gigs were banquets, company picnics, and corporate shows.

AGVA remains a very active union for the live entertainer all across the country, with headquarters in New York. For several years Penny Singleton of early TV's *Blondie* was the president.

When I joined the union, I changed my name from Patricia Ebeling to Patti Eberle. I also took care of three essentials: wardrobe, photos, and music arrangements. Volkwein's Music Store was a buzzing business in the heart of Pittsburgh in those days. On the first floor a live female piano player sat on a raised platform and played requests. I was mesmerized. Upstairs one could buy entire orchestrations for hundreds of songs for small bands or large orchestras.

As soon as I had my 8 x 10 glossies, my costumes, and my music arrangements, Pop began driving me around Pittsburgh to all the agents' offices. There were at least twenty theatrical agents, most of whom were nice and encouraging.

My very first costume was a top hat and tails. I admired Fred Astaire and this was his signature outfit. I was able to buy an expensive black top hat. It had to fit very snugly on my head so that I could tap dance without fear of losing it. The top hat even folded flat. It's the only piece of wardrobe that would forever fit me. And my head's the only part of my body that hasn't sagged! All these years I've been able to use this wonderful top hat for kiddie shows doing "Frosty the Snowman." It's so small that it fits most kids' heads. Popping out from the flat position, it appears to demonstrate that "magic in that old silk hat they found"!

Mom would stay up nights sewing sequins on outfits she would make herself. One particular outfit that she worked on for hours and hours never made it to the stage. Experienced as we were, we found a bathing suit that we thought would work out great. For many nights my dear mom would sew tiny sequins over the entire suit. When she finished, I tried it on. Oh no! The material was some kind of jersey, causing the suit to pull in and shrink unevenly. All that work for naught! My mother was so wise and never wasted time with regret. "Okay, that didn't work out! Forget it—move on!" This attitude has worked well for me many times, in large and small crises in my life. I would think, *Can I do anything about this? I can? Then do it! I can't? Then forget it!* What a wonderful inheritance.

For stockings, the elastic mesh pantyhose were popular. I would dye the stockings to match my outfits. On my early shows Mom always chaperoned me. On one of these jobs I forgot to put on the pants that went under the short skirt. It was a good thing I was wearing the mesh pantyhose. Still, Mom said she cringed every time I did a spinning step!

I loved being able to try whatever struck my fancy. There was a revival movie that was a tremendous success, about the great Al Jolson. Al Jolson often worked in blackface makeup. (Minstrel shows were popular at one time, where white men would paint their faces black.) Inspired by the movie I did a song and tap dance to one of Jolson's greatest hits, "Swanee." Mom made a white satin costume with colored musical notes sewn on it. This would be the last number of my evening because…are you ready for this? I put on blackface makeup for my finale! The number went over well, but not great. I decided to drop it. I was relieved because it was a mess to clean up.

I would continue to be successful in getting lots of jobs. Eventually I found one of the best showbiz wardrobe makers in Pittsburgh—Maleta! Oh, what a lively, artsy, talented woman she was. She knew my body—the good points and the bad. She was expensive and used the best materials. The outfits not only looked good, they held up well.

For my "Begin the Beguine" tap number she layered a fuchsia satin under a delicate but sturdy black lacy material. Two gloves in the same material went up my arms. I wore a big red rose in my hair. If Maleta were here today making costumes, I'm sure she would be making those fabulous costumes that you see on *Dancing with the Stars*.

There was a tap number that I did to the "Twelfth Street Rag." Mom sequined a bodice with gold and used a gold satin material to make a short skirt. Maleta made a brilliant satin, kelly-green jacket with short tails to go with this. I would wear a matching green derby hat with this outfit.

The most fabulous outfit Maleta made for me was for an Arabian acrobatic number. It was made with pink satin and delicate sheer pink veiling. She copied the bodice from an outfit that Yvonne De Carlo wore in a movie. Yvonne De Carlo later was the character "Morticia" on the hit TV show *The Addams Family.* The music was a special orchestration of "In a Persian Market."

In the beginning Mom worked into the night sewing on costumes. I would need at least four to get started. On the show a dancer was expected to do two numbers. If there were two shows, that meant four changes. One of the waitresses where Mom worked had a brother who made theatrical wardrobe. (This was pre–Maleta.) Character dancers were popular at the time. We had him make me a cancan outfit with the skirt lined with lots of ruffles. When I lifted the skirt to twirl my leg, it was very effective. When I went for alterations, both he and my mom tried to talk me into enhancing my chest. I would have none of it! Oh no! Not me!

MY FIRST PROFESSIONAL JOB

On April 14, 1947, I got my first booking from an agent named Eddie Hileman. He was a down-to-earth, rough-around-the-edges type of man, a description that would also describe my first professional engagement. The place was a small club named Ziggy's overlooking a railroad track. How should I describe Ziggy's? Let me just say that a boyfriend who drove me to the job said to me in disbelief, "You're not going in there!?!?!??" I did, and he waited in the car.

I would come to know that type of venue as everything from a "dive" to a "joint" to a "dump"! To me it was my debut! The audience was very happy and I was very happy. They showed great appreciation for my talent. For years the musical fanfare that the band played for opening and closing a show was "Billboard March."

It was on this first show that Mom and the fella who made the cancan outfit tried gently to get me to use some padding. I adamantly said, "No!" There was a tall, broken mirror against the wall of this dingy dressing room. While I was dressing for the first number, I gazed in the mirror at my boyish chest. In my anguish over wanting to make the best impression, I gave in. Mom had packed my suitcase with white tissue paper between the costumes. I grabbed the tissue, crumpled it up, and stuck it into my bra. After that night I agreed to buy "falsies" for all the costumes.

From the beginning I took good care of my wardrobe and props. After dancing in the many cigarette-smoke-filled clubs, I would take the outfits out of the suitcase as soon as I got home. I would hang them out to air a day before putting them away in a special wardrobe cupboard.

I would continue to take refresher courses. Ballet tap was popular. Paul Heinrich, who had taught me earlier, had night classes. I was surprised to see a schoolmate from high school taking the course. She was a very pretty girl and all through high school we had something very much in common: un-endowed on top! Now we were both in this class and both "endowed"! She said to me, "Isn't it amazing how after high school I've finally got a bust!" I said, "Uh-huh!"

MONEY

Here are a few items to demonstrate the cost of living in 1947:

- Average house price: $1,823
- New house: $6, 600
- Average wage per year: $2,850
- Average new car price: $1,300
- One gallon of gas: 15 cents
- One loaf of bread: 13 cents
- One U. S. postage stamp: 3 cents

I could do two shows and make as much as I did working for a week as a secretary.

EARLY SHOWS

I started in show business in 1947, the same year Jackie Robinson, baseball's first black player, got started. He made his official debut with the Brooklyn Dodgers.

Tom's Café in downtown Pittsburgh near Market Square was my first weeklong job. I did two shows a night. The gig paid $45, less 10 percent to the agent. The 10 percent was the standard agent fee for a good while, but slowly the percentage grew bigger but then so did our wages.

The drummer in the band was very kind to me. He demonstrated some tricks I could do with a top hat. He showed me how to make the hat flip with one hand. I could then twist it with my thumb and fingers and still retain control of it. With the hat on my head I could stretch my arm in front of me, then tilt my head, and the hat would roll down my arm to my waiting hand for me to catch. A crowd pleaser!

I encountered many generous entertainers. On a blustery, snowy night after a show, a magician and his wife insisted on driving me home so that I didn't have to take the trolley. Up, up, up they drove to Mount Washington. Many treated me like family. So many kindnesses I would never forget!

The "Old-Timers" were happy to take me under their wing, and I was eager to learn. As I was dressing for a tap dance number, one of these ladies said to me, "Aren't you wearing a dance belt?" I didn't know what she meant. She explained that a dance belt was a wide elastic band that one wore under one's panties. It fit tightly around the belly and waist. "It keeps your insides from jarring and juggling," she said. I would buy one and wear it for the rest of my dancing years.

During another full week of shows, Mom accompanied me to the North Side to a nightclub called the Churchill Tavern. Dick Smith, the bandleader, announced the acts for the show. "Pretty Patti Eberle is going to come out and do a great tap number for you. The last time I looked in the dressing room, all she had on was the trumpet player!" I looked at my mother, wide-eyed and embarrassed, and said, "Oh, Mom, did you hear what he said? I can't go out there!" Of course, I did!

Mom was constantly working on different costume ideas. She was able to embellish the long, light-blue sheer gown I wore to my senior prom. She sewed sequins on the entire dress so that I could wear it in a unique ballet/acrobatic routine. Pop was happy I chose one of his favorite songs, "Peg o' My Heart," for the music for this number.

I performed amazing feats in this gown. There's an acrobatic trick called a "walkover." To me it was always a graceful movement. I was able to do several of these while staying in one spot. Picture a pinwheel: I would start with both hands on the floor, doing a handstand with my legs in a split position. I would stand in one spot and spin over and over like a windmill, one leg after the other. This particular trick came in handy when I had to perform in tight areas. I could even do this with one hand, the other hand holding a maraca!

A smaller club in McKeesport once threw me a curve. I was to perform on a table not much bigger than a card table. In all honesty I enjoyed the challenge. A tap dancing number was easy. The acrobatic number, as I reflect on it, was truly remarkable.

Eventually I would quit doing acrobatic routines for many reasons. In the beginning I had worked many little clubs where the floors were not always clean. I still can't believe I ever did "chest rolls." From a standing position I would bend my body forward slightly and roll over. Face down, head turned to the side—and I'd land on my feet. Oh, the dirt on my face alone! I tried all kinds of shoes, even rubber swimming shoes. Then there were the highly waxed floors. Tap dancing became a hazard. I fell many times. There were fancy steps that were really too dangerous to attempt…but I did them anyway! I coined the phrase "Living is hazardous to your health."

My first year I kept a neat record of my jobs and the entertainers who appeared on the bill with me—like Bill Gillon, a sword swallower; Tony Ricco, a female impersonator/dancer; Mickey Reed, a harmonica player; and Stormy, a midget singer. Shakespeare wrote, "All the world's a stage." This became my world and I loved it!

FAITHFUL FORD

I was seventeen years old when I finally took my driver's test. Having my driver's license would come in handy, as the jobs I worked were so late in the evening. The average nightclub job was two shows, one at 11 p.m. and the other at 1 a.m. Mom would drive and accompany me to the shows, but she had to get up early in the morning for her job. When another act was able to give me a ride, I would take the trolley from home into downtown Pittsburgh to meet them and, after the show, take the trolley from downtown in the wee hours of the morning to get home. From the trolley stop, I had quite a walk, as our Cairo Street house was not near a trolley stop; I was at least a dozen blocks away.

One engagement my fellow entertainers talked about a long time afterwards was a job I did in Hazelwood, quite close to Pittsburgh. Pop was driving the police ambulance at the time. The other act on the bill was a great local tenor, Johnny (Gallus) Glade. I took the trolley to town, and after the show Johnny and I met Pop in one of the narrow alleys by what is now Heinz Hall. Pop had driven us there and was there to pick us up afterwards in the police ambulance! This only happened once. I'm sure he could have gotten into trouble for using the ambulance as a taxi!

The good part was that soon after that, I finally got to take my driver's test. I took the test in the family's 1934 Ford, "Old Faithful." When I took the test, something was clanging loudly near the bottom of the car. Maybe it was the tailpipe? The police officer who tested me seemed to ignore the banging sound. As I am very good under stress, I did everything perfectly. I don't believe I have parallel-parked that well since. I suppose the officer figured out that if I could drive under those noisy conditions with confidence, he would pass me, and he did!

Having my own transportation to the jobs was wonderfully convenient. Many entertainers did not own a car. It was a plus for getting gigs. Mom and Pop worked during the day, which made it possible for me to have the car at night.

However, the car had two distinct disadvantages for hauling entertainers. First, there was no trunk for carrying equipment. Most of the acts had suitcases with wardrobe bags, instruments, and props. Second, there was no heat in the back seat. Only a few complained; most were grateful to have a ride.

When our faithful Ford wore out, it deserved a medal for determination and bravery. Near the end of its days I drove it alone to nightclub jobs. The poor thing would stall whenever I came to a stop. I often crept through red lights rather than stop. If I absolutely had to stop, I would flag somebody down to give me a push to get going again. The ride home was a cinch. Way...back... then, in the wee hours of the morning, I had the road to myself. Imagine the nerve I had! No cell phone. Just me and the fickle Ford.

FRANTIC
PHONE CALL HOME

In the beginning, before TV, especially on a weekend job in a small town, I would get recognized in the street during the day. "There's the dancer!" For a while we entertainers felt like celebrities. People would ask for our autographs. The big letdown from this "star" ego trip occurred on my first out-of-town booking. It was a six-day job at the Blue Crystal Night Club in Girard, Ohio, near Youngstown. It paid $75 less 10 percent to the agent. Youngstown was a prelude to what Las Vegas would eventually become. It had the "Mob" element. Cabarets and nightclubs were the big deal at the time.

I took the Greyhound bus from Pittsburgh to Youngstown for this gig. The agent booked a hotel room. The Blue Crystal had three acts on the bill: Freddy Horne, comedic master of ceremonies; Gloria Coe, novelty dancer; and Patti Eberle, dancer. Also, there was Joe Veltree and his rumba band.

The rehearsal went fine. We were to do two nightly shows. That first evening, after all the customers had gone, I was waiting for my ride to the hotel when I heard an argument going on behind the bandstand. It was between the owner, a magazine critic, and the leader of the band. The owner and the critic were not happy with me, but the bandleader was adamant in my defense. "She is a cute kid, a good dancer!" I overheard almost all of the arguing and was devastated. However, the bandleader prevailed: I was to stay.

When I arrived at the hotel, I called home. There was no phone in the room, and I had to go outside to a phone booth. It was probably 3:30 a.m. Mom answered and I cried my heart out. I wanted to come home. I was so humiliated and unhappy. When I told her about the orchestra leader sticking up for me, she convinced me to stay. The write-up about me in the magazine was decent, especially in comparison to the other two acts: "Patti Eberle, tall, slender, and pretty dancer, comes out singing the introduction and swinging into a soft-shoe tap to the chorus of 'Tea for Two.' Patti has a pretty smile and her toes hit the wood as the orchestra hit the high notes. In her number Patti does a hip-swinging hula." I guess Mom was right that I should not come home.

Over the next couple of years I worked steadily not only on my routines but on orchestrations and wardrobe. The payoff for me was being booked for a return engagement in Youngstown a couple of years later.

This time I was booked into one of Youngstown's most exclusive nightclubs, the Pines. The same critic, who didn't seem to recognize me, wrote: "Tall and slender,

Patti Eberle swings into a fast tap routine for her first offering. For an encore she offers a mixture of acrobatic smoothness of Spanish dancing. Patti will win you and win you." I had improved and was appreciated.

I would return again for a week. There was a really good write-up for me this time, a full-page ad in a nightclub-advertising magazine called *The Youngstowner* (December 26, 1949): "The Pines Presents a Parade of Stars... Tony Capri, the ambassador of fun; Pat Eberle, gorgeous dance star; Marian Fields, novelty baton twirling; Carl Roberts, singing-comedy emcee; and the Pines Orchestra, directed by Jerry Alfonso." I almost got top billing...and the write-up! Wow! I felt vindicated. "Lovely of face and figure and with talent to match, vivacious Pat Eberle with her intricate and snappy routines...a real treat...any way you look at her." I had come a long way from that first week in 1947 when my heart was breaking ("Mom, I want to come home!") to this "happily-ever-after" moment!

I never enjoyed working on the road. I loved doing the shows at night, but the days were so lonely. So when there would be a job within an hour's drive from Pittsburgh— like in Johnstown, Butler, or New Castle—I would commute, even if it were a six-day gig. (Remember, gasoline was only about fifteen cents a gallon!)

MORE SUCCESS

When I began working, there must have been thirty to forty clubs in the North Side (North Shore) area of Pittsburgh: the Liberty Café, Churchill Tavern, Red's Café, the Black Moor (by the river); and many private clubs. Many ran shows six nights a week. Television was not in the entertaining competition yet. These clubs had full houses every night. Pittsburgh and the Tri-State area (Pennsylvania, Ohio, and West Virginia) were booming, with a demand for live entertainment.

How I love variety. As I look at the old newspaper ads for the many places I have played, it reminds me of the versatility I enjoy so much: Beverly Hills Hotel in Pittsburgh's North Hills ("Pat Eberle—Comedy, Novelty Star); Ravetta's Hotel in Connellsville, PA ("Patty Eberle—Beautiful Acrobatic and Specialty Dancer"). I was always trying something different, like a tap routine holding a tambourine to an arrangement of "Hungarian

Dance #5," playing the castanets for a Spanish routine, or playing finger cymbals for an Arabian routine.

I started to get more and more publicity, and even though I didn't mind, I saw many variations on the spelling of my name: Senate Inn in Washington, D. C. ("Patti Eberle—Tops in Taps"); VFW club in Greensburg, PA ("Patty Eberly—from Copa Cabana in Cleveland, Sensational Acrobat"); Balconades in Pittsburgh ("Pat Eberle—Lovely Lady of Song, singing your favorite requests").

While I was working in Youngstown, I saw another future star. After doing our show, a group of us entertainers caught a show at another club. There was this really crazy, funny guy running all over the club, insulting people who were bent over with laughter. It was Don Rickles.

I always preferred working with a "good" act. It made the show better, whereas a "poor" act could pull a show down. I was enamored of every "good" entertainer with whom I would be billed. While I was entertaining, I was being delightfully entertained! Such an array of talent: solo artists, dancing teams, novelty acts. Among

my favorites I remember: a husband-and-wife team, Peyton and Raye, billed as "Puttin' on the Dogs." Their act featured lots of dogs doing tricks. Their entrance was clever: The wife would enter with a "stole" around her neck and then suddenly the stole would turn into a dog that leapt off her shoulder. There was Joe Allen, "The

Human Corkscrew." He would very slowly maneuver his body into a very small container. The audience would sit in amazement, clapping enthusiastically. For a finale Joe would tear a telephone book in half with his bare hands. What a way to make a living—and he succeeded...for a while. I realize that if some of these novelty acts were on TV's *America's Got Talent* today, they would be "buzzed" off very quickly.

WILL LACEY
AND VAUDEVILLE

Will Lacey performed in the world's biggest cities as "The World's Greatest Unicyclist." A native of England, he was an acknowledged European champion for twenty years.

I was mesmerized the first time I was on a bill with him. He would perform a variety of feats on that unicycle. While performing, he would also play a banjo or toot a trumpet and balance a top hat on his head. His appearances included performing for British royalty in London, and at such venues as the Coliseum in Paris, the Apollo in Berlin, the Wintergarden in Dublin, the Theatre Royal in Glasgow, the Empire in Barcelona, the Olympia Circus in Havana, the Majestic Casino in Monte Carlo, and more! That was in his heyday. When these types of places dwindled, he needed to continue his career—it was all he knew.

I believe he was close to sixty years old when I worked with him. It wasn't surprising that he would come to Pittsburgh. With World War II and the booming steel mills, nightclubs were popping up all over the place. Pittsburgh became a destination for many vaudeville acts.

I only worked with Will Lacey a few times. For him to perform his act required a stage show as he needed space. Mom came to one of these shows. We both admired the man's talent. As an older man, Lacey still did an excellent job. To both of us, though, he appeared to be lonely. As Mom had done a couple of times for lonely entertainers, she invited him to our house for dinner. We enjoyed his English accent. After dinner, however, we did *not* enjoy his poetry. He would stand in our living room and recite one poem after another. Just picture it: Pop; Mom; eighteen-year-old me; my sister Corinne, age fifteen; and my brother, Harry Jr., age thirteen. We all had a hard time keeping a straight face. "Strange" is a word that comes to mind. I'm proud to say how polite we were.

Soon afterwards he wanted Mom and me to visit him in his hotel room. It was a modest hotel. When we entered his room, we gazed upwards. The ceiling was covered in a blue silk material that was draped in puffs, resembling clouds we supposed. My mom and I later guessed it might have been parachute material.

Lacey requested a professional picture of me and had it enlarged. I mean, ENLARGED! Beneath it he wrote a poem/song titled "I Don't Want to Get Hurt." The song went, "I don't want to get hurt, 'cause I'm fickle. So let me fly to each flower. Don't tell me how long I must stay. I don't like the same kind of honey. That's why I change flowers every day." Not bad! They say we write from our experiences. Looking at a photo of him as a younger man, he seemed to be a handsome fellow. With his constant traveling, the words to the song suggest he was a "love 'em and leave 'em" kind of guy. The fact that he was getting romantic ideas about me put an end to our dinners, which had been meant in goodwill.

Another vaudeville man-and-wife team made an extremely successful transition. They became the Evans Family, with a daughter, Marietta, and a son, Lester. From the first time I saw this act it remained my favorite. They were well seasoned. The Evans Family traveled the world in USO shows during World War II. They worked with many famous movie stars and made several appearances on TV's *Ed Sullivan, Toast of the Town* show. Their act would open with the very handsome son doing a neat tap dance. He would then introduce his lovely sister, who would do a stylish acrobatic routine. Next, the pair would introduce Mom and Dad, Mom in a lovely gown and Dad in a tuxedo. These two would perform a smooth soft-shoe routine. They'd finish, all four together, dancing to the music "Beyond the Blue Horizon." Eventually the family settled in Pittsburgh and had a successful dance studio.

Now, about "THE BODY BEAUTIFUL"... I don't even remember her name. But that's what she called herself, and indeed it was! Her figure was great. I'm sure she was a real beauty in her youth. She was possibly in her sixties when I met her, but of course, to an eighteen-year-old she seemed really old! She was a dancer. I only worked with her one weekend. The first night we worked in Erie, PA. After the show we stayed overnight and drove to Meadville (Sharon Stone's hometown) the next day. She did the driving in a classy red convertible. She gave me an 8x10 glossy of her that was gorgeous! She had a beautiful wardrobe. What was so fascinating about her was her rather awkward attempt at a facelift. She would stick pieces of adhesive tape around her face to lift her skin back and up. It worked, except that she was constantly fussing and stroking and encouraging her hair (or at least I think it was her own hair) to cover the tape. I felt sorry for her. *The sweet bird of youth is only granted in its time*—another one of the sayings I coined. I felt the lady was very sad and lonely. On the ride from Erie to Meadville she picked up a male hitchhiker. I was glad it was daytime.

The Body Beautiful

MORE EXPERIENCES

My stubborn nature—I was always saying, "Yes, I can!"—contributed to many falls.

In one acrobatic number, on one of those slippery floors, I was doing nip-ups, a maneuver much like a somersault. I would start with my head and hands on the floor and flip over and over in a layout position, each time landing on my feet. In a nip-up the body is arched to be able to land on one's feet. I would do one nip-up after another all the way down a big dance floor. One night the floor had too much wax on it. On about my fourth flip one of my legs bent under me. Even though it was very painful, I was able somehow to finish my routine. I found a chiropractor who said the cartilage in my left knee was out of place. He adjusted my knee over a period of several weeks during which time I did the least stressful routines and no acrobatics.

There was a geographical string of jobs from Franklin to Oil City and then to Titusville. In Titusville there is a place called Pit Hole. I have no idea what the reputation for this place was, but all an entertainer had to do was mention Pit Hole and it got a long, hootin' laugh from the audience. Naughty places, I'm sure. In Johnstown, it was Rachel's Place; in McKeesport, it was Brick Alley; and in Altoona, it was Hannah's Place. (If any reader is from any of these areas, ask your father, uncle, or grandfather if he remembers any of these places!)

I worked a lot of club dates in Altoona. I always smile when I recall the hotel where all the acts would stay. This hotel had a very large lobby and an upper mezzanine balcony. The entertainers loved performing at night, but the days were long. With many acts staying for a weekend or a week in the same hotel, the boredom was reduced by our shenanigans. We would do an impromptu show daily, utilizing the lobby and balcony—everything from a hammy *Romeo and Juliet* to singing operatic ad-lib renditions. There was always an audience of surprised and amused guests, which made us get really carried away.

Show business is always offering obstacles to overcome—and I found it fun! A big show at Renzie Park in McKeesport presented an unusual challenge for the piano player who was to play for the show. The only keys on the piano that worked were the top twenty high-pitched notes. These notes would only play when the piano was tilted halfway up in the air. It took three men from the audience to keep the piano tilted throughout the show. The show must go on, though! We were all troopers.

An incident occurred involving me and the "tilted" piano player. Frank, in addition to playing piano, was a very good musical arranger. He had done some fine arrangements for me…with one exception. At the time I was doing a weekly nightclub date with another band led by Dick Smith. Dick was a trumpet player and a punster who liked to kid around. We had worked together before and were friendly.

This particular night, in between shows, I had to use the restroom. To get to this room I had to walk past a long bar. Dick was standing at the bar and when he saw me, he said, "Hey, Patti, I got a great arranger for you! Frank _____. At this point he had no idea that he was putting his foot into his mouth…nor did I. I struck a dramatic pose and I said to Dick, "Are you kidding me? I wouldn't have him do a score for me EVER!" I was going on and on, with Dick looking very uncomfortable and embarrassed. You got it: Frank was standing right beside him. So I explained to them both: The last arrangement Frank had done for me was for a twelve-piece orchestra. It was very expensive. There was a serious mistake in the arrangement, as the second trumpet part was missing. When I showed the mistake to Frank, he fixed it and actually had *me* pay for his mistake. Young, dumb, and naïve as I was at that time, I went along with it. Later, when it dawned on me what he had pulled on me, I was really mad. At the bar that night he said to me, "I'll make it up to you, Patti!" I would never trust him again.

During my career I would work with many man-and-wife teams. Often they would be quarreling loudly one instant and making an entrance with big smiles in the next! It was all an act!

I also worked with many ballroom dancing teams. Many of these teams traveled constantly. For years they would perform the same routine with few variations. How mind-boggling it would be for them today to see the intricate and constant variations on today's *Dancing with the Stars*. I watched a transition that took place over a couple of years. In the beginning the audience appreciated the beauty of the skillful dance steps. As this interest waned, most of the dance teams found a way to be entertaining: comedy.

Much later in my career, at the Royal York Hotel in Canada, I worked with one of the most successful comedy dancing teams. The female wore a long gown and after the serious dancing, she would start to trip and slide, with hilarious results. The male dancer would roll up his pant legs and get the girl to stand on his shoulders. She would drop her long gown down over his face. If you can imagine it, it resembled a fifteen-foot figure towering over the audience: pretty lady on top, holding her long skirt gracefully; hairy-legged man on the bottom, cavorting with bizarre dance steps. There was always uproarious laughter. This act would appear on *The Ed Sullivan Show* regularly... for a while!

EVA HERBERT

Eva Herbert was a singer I worked with on many of my early shows. She was a big woman with a big smile. We were working the Palace Nightclub in a little Pennyslvania town called Monongahela. It was actually a type of roadhouse club. One had to cross a bridge over the river to reach the main town. For the first part of the week the audience was mostly men and always a full house. The men would have a couple of drinks, see the show and leave, driving back over the bridge. Shortly before the second show the same men would return. On Fridays and Saturdays mostly couples would fill the audience.

A very animated and lively couple owned this club. One time the husband became so enamored of a beautiful dancer that he began chasing her around the club. He had a long sausage in his hand, and as the story went, his wife chased him with a skillet in her hand!

There was a nice dressing room for the acts. Wide-eyed, I would watch Eva Herbert apply a concoction to her eyelashes. Holding a large tablespoon with black wax on it, she would light a match and hold it under the spoon to melt the wax. With a little eyelash brush, she would apply this wax to her eyelashes. It made her eyelashes longer and made her eyes look bigger. She explained all of this while applying the wax. One time she asked me, "Do you want this? I have more at home." Her generosity was unexpected and gratefully accepted. Later I would discover that false eyelashes worked best. The white adhesive glue is easy to apply. The white glue fades and the effect is effective. Plus, the fake eyelashes are easy to remove, and one doesn't have thick mascara to remove from lashes.

Eva sang a novelty song that was always a big hit with audiences. It became her signature song. The lyrics reflect the era of the clubs run by the Mob in the 1920s. The song is about a time when women had absolutely no opportunities in the workforce. A wife, a mother, a homemaker… those were the norms for women. This song is about other choices. It's titled "It's Better Than Taking in Washing!" I've talked to some women who have no idea what that means. I explain that one way a woman could make some extra money at that time was by washing clothes for wealthy folks. Although the song is a bit risqué, it pales in comparison to lyrics that are accepted today. Eva's delivery of the song was perfect. With a twinkle and a wink she really sold this song:

It's Better Than Taking in Washing
Although there are people who live by their wits,
It's better than taking in washing.

The heck with your morals…a suite at the Ritz,
It's better than taking in washing
Although you're supported by gambling and dice…
Though you do things not regarded as nice…
Fun isn't bad and if you get your price,
It's better than taking in washing.

I know a gal who's kept in a flat.
It's better than taking in washing
Each night her hat rack holds a new hat.
It's better than taking in washing
Who gives a darn if she's giddy or gay?
Virtue is nice, but virtue don't pay.
We gals have to get along some other way.
It's better than taking in washing.

Madame duBarry wrote home to her kin:
"It's better than taking in washing,"
And even the wives of King Henry gave in.
It's better than taking in washing.
Adam and Eve had a permanent break;
Adam told Eve to go jump in the lake.
Eve bit the apple and said to the snake,
"It's better than washing."

I make my living this silly old way.
It's better than taking in washing.
Singing all night and sleeping all day.
It's better than taking in washing.
I may sing songs that are naughty, it's true,
And you may blush at a line or two.

Kindly remember from my point of view:
It's better than taking in washing.

Eva Herbert was about twenty-five years older than me. I assume she worked in some of the speakeasies during the Prohibition era. I don't believe she was in vaudeville. She was an inspiration to me because I thought when I got older, I, too, would still be able to do floorshows. Little did I realize that in twenty-five years, the nightclubs as I knew them would be gone. When Eva retired, she moved to Florida. We kept in touch until her death, when she was well into her nineties. She could have told me so much more.

Eva Herbert

DRESSING ROOMS AND STAGES

There were some good dressing rooms, some bad dressing rooms… and then some *really* good and *really* bad dressing rooms! Sometimes they were just like in the movies: lovely, clean, and spacious. However, many times it was obvious that the dressing room was an afterthought. I experienced everything from one the size of a broom closet to one occupying an entire basement where I could hear empty beer cans tumbling noisily down a chute. Many were in the office of the club. The ladies room often was my dressing room, and once I had to change in the car! The dressing room in the Liberty Café that I worked many times was very small—and very hot in the summer and very cold in the winter. In the winter I would bring a little portable electric heater.

Often all the acts on a show—male and female alike—had to change in the same room. In the winter it was a cinch for me. I would hang my long coat over my shoulders, turn my back to the other acts, and easily change into my wardrobe. A couple of times there would be a male act who would say, "You don't have to cover up for me; I've seen everything!" I would say to him, "You haven't seen *me*!"

The floorshows would be performed on the dance floors in the clubs. In other places there were wonderful stages to perform on...and in other clubs not-so-wonderful stages! There is one I will never forget. The stage was out in the country, outdoors, on the flat bed of a truck, which sat right on the edge of a cornfield. The show took place in the daytime, and the sun and the sky were my spotlights. The scenery looked like a movie set from the musical *Oklahoma.* My opening tap routine seemed totally relevant: I wore a short-skirted cowgirl outfit complete with cowgirl hat and white boots and danced to a snappy arrangement of... "Oklahoma!" It was a wonderful musical arrangement by one of Pittsburgh's finest arrangers, Klomen Schmidt, and this was the perfect setting for it. I'm not so sure I could say the same about my next number. It was a cancan dance, characterized by lifting up and flirting with my skirt in combination with high kicking. The Cornfield Cancan!

At the time I had an entire score of "Begin the Beguine" for a tap routine in my repertoire. This number had some very intricate steps. It would have been very difficult on that flatbed truck!

THE ANIMAL CLUBS

I once shared the bill with a lovely ballerina from England, a war bride. In between shows she and I would chat. We all got a good laugh one time when she told us about what she wrote in her letters to England: "I'm working all these animal clubs!" She was talking about the Moose, Elks, Eagles, and Lions clubs. Each and every little town in the United States had these clubs. At most of the "animal" clubs, the acts would use the office as a dressing room. I've done many costume changes under the watchful eye of a stuffed elk or moose head.

B. P. O. E (Benevolent and Protective Order of Elks), an order founded in 1868, is an American fraternal social club. The group calls its members the "Jolly Corks." The Elks was originally established as a private club to elude New York City laws governing the operating hours of public taverns. Early members were mostly from the theatrical performing troupes in New York City. The Elks' charitable arm was established in 1928. It produced millions to benefit charity projects. Members would jokingly refer to themselves as "B. P. O. E.—The Best People on Earth"! As of 2006, lodges were located in about two thousand cities and towns across the United States. Some former members include U. S. Presidents Franklin Delano Roosevelt, Harry S. Truman, and John F. Kennedy. Entertainers who were members included Lawrence Welk, Will Rogers, and Clint Eastwood. For many years B. P. O. E. provided live shows benefiting three local veterans' hospitals in the Pittsburgh area.

The Loyal Order of the Moose was established in 1888. It supports the operation of Mooseheart Child City and School for children in need and a Moosehaven retirement community for its members. I watched as one of Pittsburgh's Moose clubs (Bloomfield #46) grew into a club that would match some of the elaborate nightclubs of the day—a beautiful stage and dressing room, and a great orchestra. The Moose club in Bloomfield often booked name acts and would have a full house.

Before this club was remodeled I appeared with a future "name" act. Before the remodeling, the shows were put on in the large basement. A young fellow pleaded with the bandleader, asking if he could sing a song with the band. He was slightly built with a complexion problem. I'm glad they let him sing on the show because in the not-too-distant future I could tell people I worked with the great Frank Gorshin. He became a regular on *The Ed Sullivan Show*, doing marvelous impressions of stars like Burt Lancaster and Kirk Douglas and, later, played the Riddler character in the first *Batman* movie and television series.

Fast forward to a "back by popular demand." My comedy partner, Cindy, and I were to headline the show. Before the show Cindy was rushed to the hospital for an emergency operation. Up until we teamed, I had been regularly doing solo singing and comedy shows. I felt I was ready, willing, and most importantly, able to do the show on my own. When the manager came back to the dressing room and wanted to know if I could do a solo act, I said I could! He said, "We have a full house. Are you sure?" After he left my dressing room, for the first and only time in my career, I started having palpitations. It felt like my heart was beating out of my chest! I did the show, and it went over very, very well. The circumstances of my solo act were explained to the audience, and I was given all the attention, laughter, and response that I had hoped for!

In the much distant future, life would come full circle...in a funny way. This Moose club would move to the outskirts of the city, and the entire original building would be converted into offices. Unbelievable as it may seem, my gynecologist had retired and my new doctor's office would be in this building! I would wonder what spot I was in: Was I in that "palpitating" dressing room? Was I in the middle of the stage? I have many great memories of that Moose club.

Some of the other private clubs were the Knights of Columbus, which profits many Catholic charities; the Shriners, which raises money for charities with its famous Shrine Circus; and the Knights of Pythias, which was a partner of the Boy Scouts of America. I did many shows for this group in Canonsburg, home of my favorite singer, Perry Como.

In Pittsburgh there was the Musicians' Union Club. I arrived on the scene a little late for its heyday. It was considered the "swingingest" place to go. While most of the nightclubs closed at 2 a.m., this club came alive at 2:30 a.m. Many famous musicians would make sure they stopped after their performances to "jam" with their fellow music lovers. All over the country, the fame of the Musicians' Union Club was known. Many acts would finagle a visit.

The Musicians' Union Club, like other after-hours spots, could serve alcoholic beverages. Usually the entertainers had different late-hour restaurants in which they could hang out. After a performance it felt good to unwind.

At one time there was something called "blue laws." In the 1700s a law was designed to regulate commercial business on Sundays, particularly to prohibit specific forms of entertainment or recreation on Sundays. This was supposedly made to accommodate the Christian Sabbath. Fortunately for me this had changed by the time I got into the business. At least the private clubs could sell alcohol on Sundays. An interesting item I read in the paper (*News 1927*): "After a Sunday concert, which drew an audience of 4,000, nine members of the executive board of the Pittsburgh Symphony are arrested on charges of violating blue laws. All are found guilty and fined $25.00 each." Most blue laws have been repealed, declared unconstitutional, or are now simply unenforced.

STRIPTEASE SHOWS

My "job" has been entertaining couples out for the evening, wanting to have fun: bowling league parties, company picnics, corporate galas, birthday parties, many annual celebrations…and more! I could go on and on. I've had great audiences and not-so-great audiences. I've experienced almost every conceivable situation. I have loved it. I have enjoyed the challenge and the adventure. I'm like an emergency medic or fireman: *What am I about to face? What am I getting into? Will I be successful?* It's never been monotonous and most certainly never dull.

For example, in the first couple of years of singing and dancing, I would occasionally be put into a show with striptease dancers. Their shows were called "stag" shows because the audience was entirely men. They were very private affairs. The venue would always be on the outskirts of town, never in the heart of the town itself. I wish these private types of entertainment had continued to operate this way.

Eventually I figured out that I was the legitimately hired entertainer in case an event got raided. However, none of them ever were! It was soooooo interesting. The strippers were always older than me. They treated me with sincere concern; they were very protective, as if I were their baby sister. Many of them had clever routines, and some were really good dancers. All of them had shapely bodies, of course.

At the end of one of these shows a stripper beckoned to me. "Come and look through this curtain, and we can see some dirty movies!" I just shook my head and said, "I don't want to." I don't know why; I've always been curious about a lot of things. However, somehow this didn't seem right. Rev. Sattler would have been proud of me.

The personalities of the strippers would surprise many people. There were very few gals who were tough; most of them were sweet! I would ride to these shows with a car full of strippers. I was usually quiet and amazed at some of the wild stories they would tell. Often in the dressing room I was the caring "kid" listening to their sad stories.

On the way back from the job one night they were "howling" about an incident that had happened on an earlier show. The men were being fresh and not treating them nicely. They were really nasty and insulting the girls. What the guys didn't know was that the strippers looked out for each other—and sometimes engaged in devilment. After the show, the girls packed their bags. On their way out, as they passed through the kitchen, they swiped a huge ham. The ham was intended to be the treat for the men. However, the insulting treatment the women received was being repaid. The strippers got into their car and sped away, ripping off pieces of ham to eat and laughing at the same time. "We showed them!" they crowed. I think that's called justice.

I would tell my mother about these shows and say to her, "I got a bigger applause than the strippers." She never told me that it sure wasn't me who drew the crowd for that kind of show. What trust Mom had in me! If she had been stricter, I would never have experienced the full spectrum of show business.

Being a stripper on these kinds of shows would be scary to me. There was never a stage, and the stag audience was very close.

I only did about five of these types of shows. Eventually, in the clubs, a different type of act became popular: exotic dancers. They didn't take their clothes off, but their scantily clad costumes and routines contained many sexy movements.

ADVENTURES IN CLEVELAND

The first time I drove to Cleveland was to have professional 8 x 10 glossy, black-and-white pictures taken. Conner/Geddes had a proven reputation for professional theatrical photographs. I was told they were the best in the Tri-State area.

I always felt that investing in the best was wise: in wardrobe, arrangements, and pictures. The pictures turned out so well that Mom and I had a hard time choosing which ones to use for publicity.

The second Cleveland trip was an eye-opening experience. In Pittsburgh I had become friendly with another dancer. We even considered teaming up. Her name was Leslie. She went to Cleveland to do some nightclub jobs and came back raving about the many, many nightclub jobs. Looking back, the downtown section of Cleveland at that time, probably around 1948-49, was like a mini Las Vegas, even more so than Youngstown. Clubs lined the streets. Leslie gave my name to one of the agents. To work there an act had to sign up for two weeks, so I did. The club where I worked was called the Gay Nineties. The bartender would stroll in the middle of this big round bar, play his guitar, and sing. The club's policy was live, continuous entertainment. The show consisted of all-girl dancers. We would do four or five shows a night. There was a stage and a live trio to accompany the performers.

As I said previously, I did a few of those "stag" shows back in Pittsburgh. Surprise #1: At least half the dancers danced topless. Surprise #2: After the second show, the bartender came back to the dressing room and told me I was supposed to come out and sit at the bar. He said, "Customers will buy you drinks!" I said to him, "But I don't drink!" He said, "That's okay. Instead of whiskey, you can drink tea!" This was another way for the club to make money. Whiskey money for tea! I wasn't interested in this setup at all. Leslie hadn't told me about this part. The bartender insisted it was part of the job! The next day I went straight to the agent's office and told him how I felt. "I'm a dancer," I said. We argued for a while, and he begged me to stay and promised that the second-week commitment would be to an uptown job where I would not have to mix with the clientele. Surprise #3: An uptown job!

Back at the Gay Nineties, my guardian angel—albeit a very tired guardian angel—was certainly watching out for me. At this club I learned what a "B" girl was. Besides wanting the entertainers to mix with the clientele, there were also girls hired to sit and have men buy them drinks. The funny part about this is that I think the men knew the girls were hired to do this, but they didn't seem to care because apparently they wanted the company of an attractive female. One of those pretty, young girls happened to be the sister of a fella's friend. I think this fella really loved the girl and was worried about her. So, with this situation, the fates were kind to me that week. My guardian angel turned out to be this fella. The entire week I sat with him. I think he felt I was in the wrong place too. He bought me tea. He also kept an eye on his friend's sister.

The following week I did go uptown and stay in the dressing room between shows. Yes, the money was good, but I was glad to get back to Pittsburgh. This "square" town suited me fine! In a few years there would be an exposé in all the papers about the "B" girls. I suppose the "B" could stand for a number of things. Bar girls? Bad girls? At the time of the exposé I was singing and doing more comedy. I wrote a parody about "B" girls to the tune of "A, You're Adorable."

Not too long after I came back from Cleveland I was offered a job on the radio. Looking back, I wonder if it was supposed to be a form of repentance. It was a regular running radio show, a religious program. The lady in charge was the piano player and she wanted me to be the singer. I declined. I now regret it. I missed a unique opportunity.

About this time there was an audition for dancers for the Civic Light Opera. Ah! Now here was something different and challenging. Mom, with all her wisdom, had me wear a blouse and the bottom of one of my costumes. It was a short, wide-pleated, white satin skirt. It was a sharp outfit. I was doing great in all the types of dances required...until they told me to put on my toe shoes. I had a beautiful pair, but had never taken to ballet in that form. The choreographer liked me and was visibly disappointed when I was disqualified for not being able to toe dance well. What I did get out of the tryout was a nice photo in the newspaper of me and a couple of other dancers. A few years later toe dancing was not a requirement for CLO shows.

I briefly taught tap and ballet. It was all too slow for me. One of my students was a very good little dancer, and I was giving her extra steps. She caught on so well. The head of the dancing school bawled me out for doing this, but he was nice about it because he wanted me to stay. But, repeating the same step over and over for half an hour was boring for me. Those who can do it, I congratulate!

PITTSBURGH ENTERTAINERS

I would like to write about a few of my Pittsburgh colleagues. Where do I begin? This array of talented (and some not-so-talented) entertainers were all fascinating to me. Just like in the early days of one's life, when one's parents are so important, there were some people in my "infant" days of show business who left a lasting impression.

In the first years of my career, one of the most common combinations of acts on a show was a singer, a comedian, a dancer, and a master of ceremonies, also known as an MC. The MC's job was mainly to introduce, with enthusiasm, the many different acts. (Today, for example, this is still an important job on *The Tonight Show with Jay Leno* and *The Late Show with David Letterman*. It is also a titled occupation for a really big show, like the circus.)

As the nightclub scene unfolded, the MC also had to have an act—often the MC would sing or tell jokes. In the heyday of nightclubs there were three to five performers on a show. Many clubs also had a line of girl dancers. The many different acts included: singer, dancer, magician, juggler, contortionist, roller skater, acrobatic tumbling team, ballroom dance team, or character dancer. Character dance could be Spanish, gypsy, belly, Hawaiian (or hula), Arabic, and yes, even striptease. The character dances I did were the hula, Arabic (using cymbals), and Spanish, with castanets.

I worked with so many comedians, mostly male, who often told the same jokes to different audiences year after year. Eventually audiences would begin giving the punch line. To this day, in conversation with ordinary people, someone will deliver a popular "straight line," the line setting up a punch line, and I sometimes can't resist saying the punch line that follows. Sometimes it'll be a risqué punch line. I suppose some of these lines are just embedded in my mind. A few of the many, many gags—and they did get laughs:

"He took her in the fog...and mist!"

"First time a fella went on a safari he parted the large bush, and there lay a beautiful, naked girl. He asks her, 'Are you game?' She says, 'Yes.' So he shot her."

"I ask my kid, 'What do you want for Christmas?' He said, 'I wanna watch!' So we let him!

"Wife tells her husband to stop drinking or I will leave you! 'How does that make you feel?' Husband says, 'Thirsty!'"

At the end of the last show of the night: *"Be careful on your way home tonight because most people are caused by accidents!"*

Comedian **Bobby Fife** was friendly, upbeat, and well liked by everyone. He worked all the little clubs with great success. What he didn't learn was how to do a "clean" act. He would close his show with an imitation of a very inebriated man and get tremendous laughter throughout, with one gag after another. For his grand finale he would become a confused, stumbling, cigarette-dangling-from-the-lips DRUNK! He would mess up his lines. By the time he delivered his last line, the audience would practically be rolling on the floor. Barely standing, he would stand there swaying, with both hands in his pockets. He would try to steady himself while staggering. He would begin moving his hands very obviously in his pockets. Then he'd mumble, "Plums...when did I buy plums?"

Comedian **Tony Garland** had much success with his "Texas Tony" routine. A Pittsburgh guy, he would wear a big Stetson cowboy hat. He had a good delivery with his gags, slowly and skillfully getting great laughs. He would talk about an old man visiting the doctor, complaining about urinating too much. The doctor asks him, "How old are you?" The man says, "I'm ninety-five!" The doctor says, "You've peed enough!" And then the man tells the doctor, "It's also my bowels; they move every morning at 7 a.m." The doctor tells him, "That's wonderful!" The man says, "But I don't get up until 8 a.m.!" At one time Tony was the voice for Donald Duck on a Pittsburgh radio station. For a few years he opened the show for singer Bobby Vinton, the pride of Canonsburg, PA.

Dancer **Carol Greer**, a very pretty girl, was once married to Tony Garland. I can be generous in saying she was a very good tap dancer, because I had moved on with the comedy team and was not tap dancing when she came onto the scene. I was older and doing great! I felt complimented to hear that she was being called a young Patti Eberle.

I worked some of my earliest shows with **Jack Blasi**, the "Wizard of the Banjo." He would play many standard popular songs of the day. "The World Is Waiting for the Sunrise" was one of his specialty numbers. He would do three choruses and each time he would speed up the tempo. On the third chorus he would tell the audience that he was going to "play like heck"! Quaint and corny, yes, but he was very good at what he did and he kept very busy working.

Then there was the team of **Saxie Williams & Penny**. Saxie was a terrific tap dancer, and Penny was a great singer. They were black. In my younger showbiz days, being a black act put one at an unfair disadvantage. For example, Lena Horne,

a beautiful woman, a good actress, and a good singer, wasn't able to ascend to the best jobs. The highest she could climb in blockbuster movies was a featured spot in a splashy musical. She later did great on TV appearances. I got to see her live on a Pittsburgh stage. In my opinion, she was a superstar.

Blizz & Burke was a local team that mimed popular recordings. I absolutely loved these two guys, whose first names were Paul and Eddie. One of their numbers was a popular novelty song called "Martha! John!" Those were the only lyrics throughout the recording. There were many variations in their intonations, however. The rubber-face contortions of Blizz & Burke could match those of comedian Jim Carrey. They were hilarious. They did a number in which Eddie would pretend to be a girl. He'd wear a sweater and use two oranges for boobs. He'd pretend he was trying to keep those oranges in place, but in an exaggerated, out-of-control manner. Hysterical! When I was booked on a show with them, I knew I was in for a fun evening.

The **Silver Cyclones**, Ethel and Arden, were a roller-skating husband-and-wife team. They had a large, circular, wooden mat rolled up for their spot in the show. It was very exciting, fast, and furious. In the finale Ethel would wear an apparatus that swiveled around her neck. Arden would have a cord around his neck that connected to the apparatus on Ethel. Arden would spin swiftly in the center of the circle, and as he spun, Ethel would spin horizontally in the air!

After touring the country, they decided to stay in Pittsburgh. The two of them operated a theatrical costume business for many years. Arden was a very talented man. He was able to make leather spats that looked like boots and could be zipped over my tap shoes for a cowgirl routine.

Shirley Bell was a fine singer who worked steadily in club lounges. She was married to a pharmacist, Edgar Markowitz. We became dear friends. Shirley longed to do floorshows. We worked on a few shows together. We both loved to sing and knew hundreds of songs. One time we worked the Butler veterans' hospital and had a grand time. Coming out of Butler on Route 8, we found the highway to be in terrible shape, possibly the result of a bad winter. We were singing our hearts out, laughing and having a glorious time as I swerved around the many potholes in the road. A policeman must have thought we were drinking because he stopped our vehicle. In all circumstances like this, I have had "good fortune" in just telling the truth. I pointed out to him the bad condition of the highway—though it was quite obvious. I told him we were entertainers and had just performed at the veterans' hospital. He listened intently, then smiled and said, "Okay! Be careful!"

Shirley would have constant problems with her heart. I believe the years of singing in the smoke-filled lounges may have contributed to her condition. I don't remember ever seeing her smoke. I often did one or two shows a night in polluted rooms. When she was hospitalized, I would visit her. On one visit, when she was getting discouraged, I was able to get her to laugh. It made us both feel good.

 **Billy Sloane** began his career in vaudeville as an acrobat. His finale was stacking chairs up to ten feet high and then standing on his hands on the top chair. When the demand for live entertainment spawned the nightclubs, banquets, and special events, Billy put together a wonderfully entertaining act called, not "Name That Tune," but "Name That Dance." He had a stack of music with every style of dance: Irish jig, tap, Russian (all that squatting and kicking), soft-shoe, rumba, polka, and so on. The last dance was always a "striptease"! He must have worked with many strippers because he had the moves down to perfection (in a comedic way). Accompanied by drums beating slow and sexy, he would first take off his tie

teasingly and twirl it. Next he would unbutton his shirt in the same fashion. This is all he would take off. His finish with the live band and drumbeats was to stand on his head while doing bumps and grinds. It always "brought the house down," as the saying goes.

Billy would close with some clever patter describing the differences between males and females. He would say, "WOMAN...W-Winsome, O-Obedient, M-Mischievous, A-Ample, and N-Nosy!" Of course, there would be mock moans and groans from the women in the audience. And then, with perfect timing, he would describe "MAN...M-Marvelous, "A-Adorable, and finally, N-Necessary!" The audience would cheer and laugh!

I would often drive Billy home from a job, I'd park at his house, and we would sit and talk and laugh all about show business. We both loved performing.

Dottie Dell did an entire juggling act while walking on a huge ball as it rolled around the floor. It was an unusual and sensational feat. We were all stunned when a terrible accident took her life. I believe she was only forty years old. She was drying her hair while in the bathtub and dropped the hairdryer in the tub.

Gaby Delcy—I kept hearing about this "dancer." She would be held over for weeks at a time at many little local clubs. I thought she had to be a great dancer. I finally got a date to take me to a club to see her perform. I was astounded! The act consisted only of walking and posing. Nothing

offensive, of course, but no dancing! I doubted that she had any training in dance, but it didn't matter to the guys. . She was a German beauty, a lovely, blue-eyed blonde with porcelain skin. For her time she definitely was the "Body Beautiful"! The very clever, strategic designs of her costumes would hold the audience's attention; the outfits barely covered what needed to be covered. She could whistle very well and did this at the mike, standing in a skimpy outfit and wearing a feathered Indian headpiece that trailed down her back. Later in her career she started singing songs in a soft, sweet voice.

I eventually was on a bill with her. The agent booking the show came that night. When the agent saw the outfit Gaby was going to wear, she freaked out! As I recall, the top consisted only of a narrow piece of cloth that wrapped around the back of her neck, draped over each of her ample breasts, and tucked into her waist. It did not fit too snugly. That was it! It was quite revealing for this era, unless one was a stripper. The agent made her secure it more tightly to her body. Today Gaby, as far as wardrobe goes, would give Cher, Madonna, and Lady GaGa a run for their money. Around Pittsburgh there were none like her at the time.

I heard a funny story from a mutual friend about Gaby. The two of them had joined a health club. On one occasion they were both nude in a steam room. Gaby had been practicing muscle control with her breasts. Without touching them she could make them move one at a time or two at a time; she could get them to twitch and jump. There were other women in the room with them. As the story goes, their eyes were popping out of their heads!

I don't recall Gaby ever doing this on a show, but I do remember working with a couple of female strippers who displayed a definite talent for muscle control. They would put flourescent tassels on their pasties. The tassels would "perform" identical motions with extraordinary precision (like synchronized swimmers). Some strippers would even put tassels on their bums. Then they would have the lights turned off. A strobe light would be focused on the strippers. Show business has surely provided the most eye-opening and delightfully zany experiences for me!

Pauline Wray was an incredible acrobat who also worked many shows. She wasn't a very attractive lady nor was she a "Body Beautiful," but she was an enormously talented act compared to Gaby. In the beginning of my career, good talent was genuinely appreciated, regardless of good looks or bad. With the advent of TV, the close-up meant that each and every feature of a performer could be examined critically. The sad truth for TV performers was that the "pretty face" (male or female) got the job.

I've forgotten the names of some of the more memorable acts of my early gigs. There was a spinning plate act. The plates would be kept spinning, perfectly balanced on a stick and would, as planned, start falling and crashing to the mock astonishment of the performer. Watching the slow reaction of the audience was really fun. At first the audience didn't know "the accidents" were on purpose and felt sorry for the performer. When it became apparent to them that they were on purpose, they howled. Replacing those plates after each show had to be no small expense.

Ted Blake was another funny and clever comic I worked with. The Second World War had been over for a couple of years, and Ted did a hilarious routine about army life. He would have the band vamp between jokes as he marched around. Instead of carrying a rifle, he wielded a plunger. For years he wrote a funny column in the *Pittsburgh Musicians* monthly magazine called "It's All in Fun by the Village Square."

I first worked with **Janie Allen** when the agent booked three of us young girls at the veterans' hospital in Altoona. We each had our solo act. What fun the three of us had on that long trip! The fellas loved the show: a blonde, a brunette, and a redhead. The redhead was Janie. The three of us got on famously, chatting, singing, and laughing. I always thought that Janie could have had great success. Her singing was good, but it was her exuberant personality that set her apart from the rest. She put her heart and soul into everything she did. The sad part was a troubled marriage. Her husband, who had a very rich father, promised her the moon and stardom. What he gave her was five kids and very erratic behavior on his part. It turned out her husband wasn't rich. She eventually divorced him, and her life afterwards was a struggle. We remained friends. She even joined my church, and everyone loved her. Sadly, she was diagnosed with lupus and died way too young. I admired her talent and personality, and I loved her.

Rummy Bishop was once teamed with Joey Bishop and another pal in a zany comedy act. They called themselves the Bishop Brothers even though they were cousins. I worked with Rummy often. He did a good comedy act. When Joey Bishop got famous, he tried to help his old buddy, Rummy. Joey would host TV's *Tonight Show* and have Rummy appear. Rummy, though, was never very successful. As relaxed as Joey was, Rummy was the opposite. Unlike the nightclub success he experienced, Rummy was never comfortable or funny on TV. He would star for eleven years in a swinging club called Allen's Nut House in East Liberty in Pittsburgh.

Zorran was in great demand as a magician and a pickpocket. He would amaze and delight when he walked into the audience, shake hands with many of the patrons, and return to the stage with his pockets full of wallets, watches, and bracelets that he had slyly picked from the group. Zorran's real name was Vladimir Trifkovic. He was a Yugoslav. After making a hit with European audiences, he decided to try his luck in the United States. He came to Pittsburgh in the mid 1950s and immediately began playing the big clubs and banquets. He continued through the era of nightclubs. He won over his audiences with his pickpocketing skills. That was the "comedy" of his life. The tragedy was his death: he was murdered… shot. I believe it was a love-triangle situation. The tragedy, sadder still, is that no one came forward to claim his body. Entertainers from all over the country pitched in to pay for his funeral.

Francisco Soriano had an excellent tap dancing team with his first wife. When they divorced, he performed solo. He would do some novelty songs. One of them was singer Cab Calloway's "He-de-hi-dee-ho!" Fran had retired and not danced for quite a while  when he accepted a tap dancing date. It was a big show out of town at a large hotel in Beckley, West Virginia. I'll never forget it. After finishing his tap dancing spot, he "crashed" as soon as he made it to the dressing room. He was limp and gasping for air. He scared everyone. This was his last tap dance. He retired for good. Singing in the church choir in Tennessee filled the void for entertaining. We were lifelong friends; he lived into his eighties.

Mignon and Wally Parker were a couple who played on most shows together. Wally was an acrobat and Mignon was a belly dancer. When the nightclub scene began to dry up in Pittsburgh, like gypsies they moved to Phoenix, Arizona, where Mignon acted in little theatre groups. Mignon and I had something in common: we never wanted to stop entertaining. Find a way to entertain, and Mignon and Wally did it! We kept in touch for years.

The story about **Nino Repeppi** is a poignant one. It was near the end of the heyday of the nightclub scene. My husband Marty's trio was backing up a show at the once-crowded Elks club, which was now not even a quarter full with people. Nino, who always wore a tuxedo, was an excellent tenor. Early in my career I worked with Nino many times. He would go over fabulously and get standing ovations. Many clubs would hold him over for weeks. There was a classy operatic touch to his singing. For his first number this particular night, he sang what was once a show-stopping song. His voice was still in top form. The sparse audience hardly paid any attention to him. There was very little applause. With his Italian accent, Nino addressed the audience and said, dramatically and slowly, "My…name…is…Nino…Repeppi, and I can see nobody gives a sh@★!" Marty said the band broke up laughing. I found it sad.

A lot of musicians were in the same boat. As the variety-acts business slumped, so did work for the musicians. By this time audiences could see and hear the best tenors in the world on shows like *Ed Sullivan*. Seasoned musicians had to adjust to the arrival of rock and roll. When the disc jockeys came on the scene, it was another nail in the coffin for the live musician.

In the beginning some of the musicians resented the entertainers. The difference in what we got paid for our short time performing compared to the hours they would play was significant. There were some who figured out, "Can't beat 'em, join 'em." One of these was **Carl Gerald**. The first time I worked with him was at the Victory Club in Wampum, PA. Carl was a versatile musician. He was an excellent xylophone player. He also played several brass instruments: trumpet, sax, and oh that trombone! For his finale he would play a lively marching song—"The Lassus Trombone"—and march around the room with the ever-so-effective slide trombone. The response was fantastic!

Bob Long, a steelworker during the day, sang and did comedy in his act. There was a top singing star, Johnny Ray, who had a big hit record at that time called "Cry." Johnny Ray would get very emotional singing this song during his performances, and so did Bob. He took it a step further too, producing a very wet hanky and wringing it out. He would then take his jacket off, slowly begin tearing a perfectly nice white shirt apart, and wind up on the floor as he sang, "So let your hair down, and go right on, baby, and CRY!" The audience loved it. I'm not sure if his wife did, as she was the one who had to keep sewing that shirt back together.

Harry Albacker was a magician. Most of Harry's life was devoted to show business. He was a genius in advertising hype, especially about himself, because most of it was true. When he was sixteen years old, he was hit by a car in downtown Pittsburgh and taken to the morgue. Suddenly he was discovered moving... yes, breathing! He recovered. He would then advertise: "Harry Albacker, the only dead magician alive!" He lived most of his life in Aspinwall, a small town adjacent on the

Allegheny River. When he was a little boy, he attended a birthday party for a member of the Heinz family (of Heinz ketchup fame) from neighboring Fox Chapel.

Harry did a fine, fast-talking magic act. He traveled extensively, too. He once told an interviewer that "the whole world is my address," and to an extent that was true. He had performed at the White House several times for teas and birthday parties. He used to give away rabbits as souvenirs that he pulled from a hat. Rabbit recipients included First Lady Eleanor Roosevelt, President Dwight D. Eisenhower, and Caroline Kennedy, the daughter of John F. Kennedy. (Caroline received one of his favorite rabbits, Zsa Zsa.)

When nightclubs were still in full swing, Harry discovered he was not getting calls from agents. I do believe TV overexposed certain acts like magicians, jugglers, and some spectacular novelty types. People wanted something different. Harry became a little bitter about this, and he began promoting himself. For the rest of his life he would travel the country in a big box van with his little mutt, Troubles, named for a character in the "Mr. Bojangles" song. Before that, his companion was a beer-drinking rooster who could play the piano. It was one of those little toy pianos, and Harry would put corn seeds on the keys. Before that, he had a guinea pig named Gertrude who gained national attention when she was kidnapped during a show. She was returned.

Harry was very proud that he made his income every year as a magician. It is believed that Harry opened for about seven hundred malls. Each summer he toured the South, doing fair dates. For years he wrote a column about the thriving carnival circuit for a magazine called *American Showman*. He once made a big poster exclaiming "Harry Albacker, the 'no headache' magician"! He took a picture of me standing with my hand to my head beside the poster. It was printed in the magazine. In 1993, at the age of sixty-eight, Harry had just finished a magic show for a senior citizens' group when he had a heart attack. I miss him. We had become close friends. We often talked on the phone. He had the sharpest, driest humor.

I could write a book about specific songs, specific entertainers, or an association of a song with an entertainer. For example, I could write about singer Tony Bennett and his "I Left My Heart in San Francisco." In my not-so-big-time world of entertainers, this could be a plus or a minus. The plus was having an eternal association of that tune with one particular artist, and the minus is becoming stale and not trying new and different songs. In my case, it warms my heart when I hear a certain tune. I close my eyes and I visualize that entertainer (most have passed on) singing or dancing to that tune. I read once, "Remembrance is a form of meeting." I always enjoy that visit!

MORE PITTSBURGH ENTERTAINERS

Addison and Thayer

Norma Milazza

The Hollanders
"A Dutch Treat"

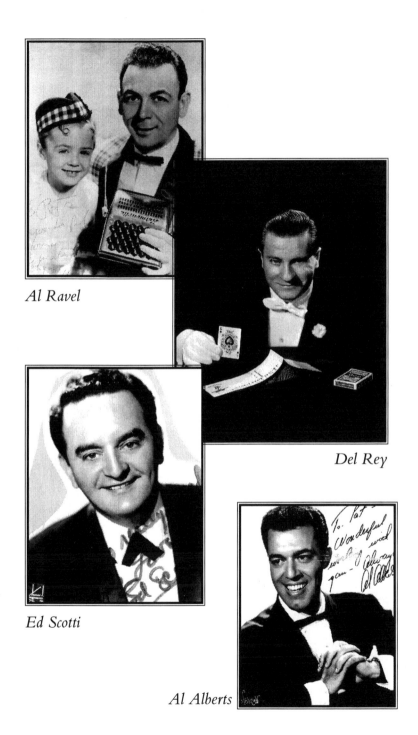

Al Ravel

Del Rey

Ed Scotti

Al Alberts

By the mid 1950s Elvis was changing music, and TV was stealing audiences. Booking agents dwindled in number, and entertainers began booking themselves. More women were in the work force. At one time a housewife looked forward to a weekend of nightclubbing. Now, working women wanted to rest or catch up on housework. Now there was "free" entertainment on television. One no longer needed to leave the house to be entertained.

The legendary stars of my era at least had a longer staying power. Many young people have no knowledge of some of the legends in show business. The public has become saturated with overnight sensations. Fame comes so quickly, and fades just as quickly. The popular *American Idol* is a good case in point.

It took a few years for television to become "king of the hill." Commercial television arrived in Pittsburgh in 1949. Most of the sets had about a ten-inch picture tube and were expensive—about 350 dollars. That price is equal to about $3,150 today. A quote from the editorial page of the *Post-Gazette*: "We have seen radio, which began with such promise for spurring the mind and heart, sink too often to a moronic level of bebop narcosis and giveaway shows.... Experience has taught us to be skeptical of new wonders." I believe we have all witnessed the same thing happening to TV. And now the Internet.

Many of the nightclub comedians went on to successful careers in TV. Other acts that didn't make the transition to TV became bitter. They believed that TV just "ate 'em up and spit 'em out!" Many very good entertainers simply refused to go on television, assuming it would be a one-shot deal. After a dueling struggle that lasted several years, television was declared the winner. Those wonderful hundreds of clubs that I enjoyed working in so much gave up and closed.

The setup of the intimate nightclub is still my favorite venue. Working at many senior citizen centers and residences, as well as at AARP shows, I prefer the nightclub setting, though my audiences these days all know the same "hit" songs of our era. These songs would linger for a couple of years; some would become classics. The best part was that all ages could sing or hum the melody. Today it seems that so much of the music is fragmented. Each generation has its own music. I call it the musical Tower of Babel.

PITTSBURGH THEATRICAL AGENTS

Every Monday I would get all dolled up in my best clothes, which included the mandatory hat and white gloves, and make the rounds of the agents. Some of them had spacious offices. Some offices were so small that the entertainers would be lined up in the hallway. Most of the time there was friendly chatter among the acts.

The variety of personalities in show business created a vast, flourishing panorama. There were cool, calm, and wacky personalities. There were puzzling personalities. The same thing applied to the uniqueness of each Pittsburgh agent. Over the years I was able to be friends with most of them.

The agent **Eddie Hileman** was down to earth and somewhat gruff. He wasn't a very classy man, but he took his job very seriously. He was always respectful to me. I will always be grateful to him for giving me my first job at Ziggy's. Eddie had lots of little clubs, joints, and fraternal clubs. There was an Eagles club in McKeesport that ran shows every Saturday and Sunday with a full house. There would be different acts for each night. One time I got my dates mixed up and went to this club on the wrong night. I did the show. When Eddie found out, he was furious—the competition between agents was fierce. I felt terrible. I agreed to meet with him and the club's manager. Turns out the club manager liked my act and wasn't a bit angry. He said to Eddie, "It's a good thing she was on the show that night because the other act was a bummer, and Patti saved the night!" I was relieved, and so was Eddie.

Larry Kennith had the opposite demeanor of Eddie Hileman. He was always in a suit and tie, and always a gentleman. He was neat and meticulous. I once did a picnic show for him. The group of entertainers were treated after the show to a fried chicken dinner. Larry was the first person I ever saw who ate fried chicken with a knife and fork!

Jimmy Finnerty was an earthy, uneducated but smart fella. I don't believe Jimmy passed grade school. Once he gave me this introduction on a show: "Yuns are really gonna like this act!" He was the stereotypical round-faced Irish drinker—and drink he did! He acquired the booking business when his wife retired, though it would remain the Jean Carr Agency. Jimmy's wife had been a stripper. I remember seeing some pictures of her in her outfits; it seems she was very inventive with her wardrobe and routines. Jimmy was much younger than Jean, but said Jean, "He kept following me and hounding me! Finally he persuaded me to marry him!" They both had tough personalities. Jean would tell a story about Jimmy fooling around with a dancer in a car in the parking lot of a club. She said, "I found them in the back seat of the car and I reached in and pulled him right off of her!" The Jean Carr Agency was loaded with work for lots of steady clients. Although Jimmy was somewhat uncouth, he was smart and evidently in the right business.

Don D'Carlo had a huge ledger with pages and pages of club dates. I always enjoyed him because he was so colorful. Although he was not very tall, he had a confident demeanor and would strut around with his chest out and a cigar in his mouth. Covering the walls of his office was a vast collage of 8 x 10 glossy pictures of every act imaginable. The wall seemed to "move" with all the active talent displayed: singers, dancers, jugglers, magicians, comedians, comedy teams, female impersonators, and of course, strippers. One of his top strippers was Chesty Morgan whose name suited her perfectly. (And this was in the days before silicone implants.)

Many traveling acts would make their first stop at D'Carlo's office. A lot of them stayed at the Edison Hotel. It was reasonably priced and centrally located. It was probably used by many a vaudevillian. The train and bus stations were nearby.

D'Carlo certainly enjoyed the pretty young talent who were anxious to get booked on a job. He probably had his way with some of them. I had established a reputation as a "good girl." I believe I was able to stay that way because of the self-confidence my mother instilled in me. With my mom as a role model, I could see that respecting oneself demands respect from others. Only once did D'Carlo look at me amorously, and I simply burst out laughing! That was a sure turn-off for him. He never did it again, and we became really good friends. I would work his entire book again and again. I was one of the few who would call his residence. I often talked to his wife. I would say, "This is Patti Eberle" and she would shout to Don, "It's Beverly calling!"

Don loved to brag about a booking he did for an Italian club in Ellwood City, PA. The club wanted three acts and he booked three different jugglers. Even though the clubs always expected a variety of entertainment, the three juggling acts went over well with the audience. Don had a soft spot for many of the vaudeville acts that were finding the demand for their kind of talent waning. These three jugglers needed a job and Don arranged it. And pulled it off!

Don D'Carlo died in 1989. His obituary summed up his career: "An agent for fifty-five years remembered better days before TV killed off nightclubs. A former actor, carnival promoter, and theatrical agent. After serving in the army in World War I, he began his showbiz career doing small parts in silent movies starring Pearl White and Frances X Bushman. He started his booking agency in Pittsburgh in 1932. During his heyday he was booking talent for almost one hundred clubs in Pennsylvania, West Virginia, and Ohio, with acts ranging from dogs, ventriloquists, and mind readers to acrobats, comedians, and magicians. In later years, after most local clubs closed, he booked acts for conventions, private parties, and dances."

Anne King had been a Charleston dancer and one of those marathon dancers of the late 1920s. She was petite and ladylike. As an agent, she booked many of the choice banquet-type shows. I was fortunate she took a liking to me. It was important to her how an entertainer dressed and behaved on and off the show. In this case, clean living served me well. She did have an irritating habit in her booking procedures. She would call an act and have them "hold" on certain dates. When the acts got together, they would discover they were all holding the same dates. It was to her benefit. But it meant that many acts were holding a date that only a few would actually get. I remember going to a funeral parlor to pay my respects to an entertainer who had died. Many entertainers were there. Just for the fun of it, one comic started circulating and whispering to the acts, "How many dates are you holding for Anne King?" It got quite a chuckle from everyone. I was one of the lucky ones; I got most of the dates she had me hold.

Marge Nelson was loud and brassy but still a lady. She came to all of her shows with a spotlight and a good piano player for smaller groups. Marge didn't book clubs; she specialized in big banquets for big companies. She had been a novelty singer in vaudeville. Her husband was Nat Nazzaro, who was the president of our local AGVA (American Guild of Variety Artists) union. Some of the other agents resented this, and I can understand why: There probably was a conflict of interest, with her getting in on some of the better contacts. She had the top accounts on her books. However, one couldn't help but like her. "Hi, hon, how ya doin'?"

Sid Marke—what an eccentric man he was! I think he was in vaudeville also. He always wore an old worn hat and had a big cigar dangling from his mouth. He had connections with the "big time" in New York. He got interested in my comedy team, which I will talk about later. Our comedy team worked some fantastic shows for him. He always wanted us to tell the corniest jokes (which we would do IF he came to the show). For example: "Why do they cut the heads off of sardines?" Answer: "So they don't bite each other in the can!" Moan...

Ed Schaughnecy was a top-notch agent with many irons in the fire. He was also an extremely popular radio personality in Pittsburgh—"Uncle Ed." His booking agency had the best jobs in the best places. On the first job I did for him, he emceed the show. I did a couple of tap dance numbers. He complimented me and told his brother-in-law, "She's a good dancer—book her!" That was another one of those happily-ever-after moments.

On one of Ed's Shriner picnic shows, a funny incident occurred involving a straw hat that had colorful fabric on the sides attached to strings that tied under my chin. (This hat enabled me to keep my hair in tight pin curls that I would comb out right before the show.) Some men were sitting on the grassy field as we performers approached. One man looked up at me and said sarcastically, "What kind of hat is *that*? I'll give you twenty bucks for it!" I called his bluff: I took the hat off and handed it to him. Blustering in front of his friends, he had to go through with the proposition. (I must have looked goofy with my pinned head.) I think I paid two dollars for the hat. It was like being thrown a straight line, and I couldn't resist responding with the comeback. Today, that twenty bucks would be more like fifty bucks!

George Claire was my favorite Pittsburgh agent. This man had class. He was smooth and handsome. He had been a great tap dancer, dancing in shows and clubs in New York and around the world. One time when George was doing a show as a tap dancer, two visitors came backstage. They were Gene Kelly and his brother Frank. They wanted to correct some of the dance steps George was doing. The brothers had a dance studio in Pittsburgh. Later, when Gene Kelly got his break on Broadway as the lead in the musical *Pal Joey*, George took over the dance studio.

As a theatrical agent, George once worked for the famous William Morris Agency in New York. Returning to Pittsburgh, he became a very successful booking agent in 1945. He would book seventy to seventy-five acts into local clubs and theatres. His former clients would say he was the busiest and best agent in the city. I was quoted in our local newspaper as saying, "George is a great dancer and could have been another Gene Kelly." George quipped in response, "Maybe, if I'd been taller!" George shared many interesting stories in a newspaper interview. One, in particular, was about the late, great Jackie Gleason. When Gleason had flopped in New York, he called George. Gleason told George, "Get me out of this town!" George booked him in all the top spots in Pittsburgh, including the Carousel and the Italian Gardens. It's such a human story of how someone can be so down in his career, then rise to super stardom, like the phoenix rising from the ashes! Remember my devastation on that job where only the orchestra leader liked me and I wanted "out of there"? We performers have such sensitive egos!

Even though I was now a professional, I was always looking for ways to improve and grow. George agreed to teach me a tap routine. I was delighted to have another angle on tapping. After teaching me one step, he suddenly got busy with his show bookings. He asked me if I minded if a member of the male, black, tap-dancing team of Billy and Eddy finished teaching me the routine. I don't remember which one taught me, but I was thrilled. I would learn a unique style that was not taught in dancing school. Thanks, George!

Eventually most of the booking agents worked out of their homes. There were no more Monday trips to town. This was a gradual change, like the Internet replacing the Yellow Pages. Finally, there were no booking agents as I had known them. Career entertainers like myself would begin booking themselves. Negotiating a price was a foreign experience for me, and just keeping the books straight was a bummer.

CARNEGIE TECH

Although I was having much success with my singing and dancing, I still had the itch to be a stage actress. Whatever dreams or aspirations I had, my dear mom always encouraged me. I signed up for a course at Carnegie Tech (now Carnegie-Mellon University). It was September 1949 and I was almost twenty years old. I took a five-month class. Carnegie Tech/CMU is well recognized across the country for its acting courses. There have been many famous alumni from this university: Jack Klugman (*The Odd Couple*), Ted Danson (*Cheers*), Barbara Feldon (*Get Smart*), Jill Eikenberry (*L.A. Law*), Rene Auberjonois, Holly Hunter (*The Piano*), George Peppard (*The A Team*), and Sally Jesse Raphael (talk show host), and many more.

I loved the classes. I still have a large book on pronunciation. We were not supposed to pronounce the "r" sound in words, so we would say "whoads" for "words." I drove my family crazy practicing this technique: "That is Co(rr) ect!!" "It's You(r) fault!" What co(r)ne(r) of the room?"

"A(r)e you su(r)e?" One barely made any "r" sound at all. This was considered P(R)OPE(R). I have watched some old movies (black-and-white) and because I'm aware of it, I get a kick out of the silent "r." After all of this, along came the great Marlon Brando and method acting. No more silent "r." Lots of mumbling and bad English. Look at Robert DiNiro in *Taxi Driver*: Instead of "Are you talking to me?", it was "Ya talkin' to me?".

One of the lessons at Carnegie Tech/CMU required us to stand in an enclosed booth and record our voices using a scripted piece. There would be a critique as the entire class listened to the recording. I received the biggest laugh when I mispronounced a girl's name from the script. I had never known a girl with this name. So, for "Phoebe" I said, "Phooooobe!" Why isn't it spelled "Pheebee"?

With about a month to go in the school year, my plans would decidedly change. I was still doing shows while going to school, and then I saw an ad in the newspaper: "Vocalist to join musical act; under 25, write fully, listing experience, enclose snapshot. Write E452, *Press*." Forever looking for new challenges, I answered this ad. I would say singing takes top priority for what I love to do. I auditioned and got the job. A news item reported, "Blonde Patti Ebeling is currently singing as "Sue Scott" with the Bobbie Harper Quintet. She has also danced in many nightspots in and around the city. Patti is well known in the Tri-State area as a specialty dancer."

BOYFRIENDS

I was quite fickle and silly with boys. I had many boy-friends. I was having lots of fun, but clean fun! There was a popular boy in high school who was a senior; I was a junior. He truly had it all: he was blond and handsome, and had a perfect build. He was on the football team, and he was nice. Never in high school could I have imagined a date with this Adonis. But later, after I had graduated and was doing one of my high-diving exhibitions at South Park swimming pool. I'm guessing I caught the eye of this gorgeous guy who was working at the pool as a life-guard. He asked me for a date. He came to my house and we went to a local movie theatre. Wasn't I the puffed-up one as we walked past the local guys—not to mention the girls—hanging out on the corner! After the movie he walked me home. Wasn't it generous how my parents would see that the parlor would be available for this date? We sat on the sofa. It was our very first kiss, and he pinned me down, our feet still on the floor. I pushed him upright.

A few words and seconds later, there was a repeat performance. I'm sure he probably got his way with lots of girls,
but not with me! This would be our one and only date. (I
believe that if I had given in, it would still have been our
one and only date!) A few years later I read that he married a sister of movie actress Grace Kelly.

I did get serious with one of my boyfriends. We actually spoke of marriage. However, suddenly he became
jealous and possessive. He would accuse me of smiling at
some man in the audience when I was performing. He
said to me, "When we get married, you have to quit show
business." That was the final straw. Me quit show business? I thank God I never married him; I would have been
so stifled and unhappy. This episode in my romantic life
kept me from getting serious about any other boy for a
couple of years.

I'll never forget coming home from some event with
Mom and Pop. I was sitting in the back seat and talking about my love life at the time. I said, "Every boy I
date wants to marry me or sleep with me!" I was twenty
years old. I nonchalantly concluded, "I don't think I'll get
married. I'll just sleep with them!" Pop's car came to a
screeching stop. I love getting reaction...and I did! Back
in 1950 most of my girlfriends were married before they
were my age. The proposals of marriage I was getting
were not from men I wanted to marry.

MARTY FALOON: THE MAN I WOULD MARRY

The want-ad band job that I landed started rehearsals that summer of 1950. We met several times a week. It was a quintet: piano, marimba, drums, guitar, and singer. We rehearsed at the drummer's house in the Squirrel Hill neighborhood of Pittsburgh. It was going very well. However, as the summer came to an end, the guitar player wanted to go back to college. So, in finding another guitar man, the leader located one who was to be my future husband.

I met Marty as we were exiting a photo shoot for publicity pictures. Here was this handsome fella coming toward me with the most pleasant smile. As we practiced that late summer, we decided we liked each other and would date. I was dating other fellas at the time. My mom had had an operation and was in the hospital. I would visit her and tell her about these three fellas who wanted to marry me, and I couldn't decide which one! My wonderful, wise mother told me it was my decision to make. I'm glad I chose Marty—for many reasons.

Marty loved music, especially the guitar. He could also play the banjo, electric bass, harmonica, trombone, and piano. He had perfect pitch—he could hear a whistle or siren blow or a bird chirp and tell you what note it was. "That's a 'B'," he would say, and he'd be right. He could tell which string was flat or sharp on the guitar or any other instrument.

A fortuneteller at Murphy's Five and Ten told us our marriage would be like mixing fire and water. I'm guessing it had something to do with the horoscope. We were both Libras. Maybe it's not supposed to be good if you are the same sun sign. We proved her wrong. Whenever we went to a movie, Marty would be looking at me instead of the screen!

Marty's childhood was unlike mine. His father died of a brain hemorrhage when Marty was two years old. His mother operated a little diner. She had three children, Marty being the youngest, and needed help with their care. When Marty was five years old, he became a foster child. The Henrys, a loving family, raised him for about six years after which he moved back with his mother. Marty was treated with kindness and love by the Henrys. They tenderly pulled Marty through some severe illness. We would always keep in touch with this wonderful family.

The Henrys must have been aware of Marty's natural talent for music. The first instrument he ever owned was a harmonica they bought for him. I forget how he got his first guitar, but it became a lifelong love affair. At fifteen years of age, he was playing in a band at a club that had live entertainment. I guess back then there weren't the state laws for minors in drinking establishments—or laws for working late hours.

Marty would remember playing for some of the acts I worked. He graduated from Westinghouse High in 1939. (I was ten years old that year.) He made the honor roll with his good grades, but music was his true love. Mr. McVickers, the school's bandmaster, taught some of Pittsburgh's finest musicians. Marty remembered after-school jam sessions with pianist Erroll Garner and DoDo Marmarsa.

One of his music friends was Larry Tamburri (Larry would go on to become president of the Pittsburgh Symphony). Larry and his talented brother had a band at the Beverly Hills Hotel nightclub. I did shows in this club many times before I met Marty. The two brothers were always pleasant gentlemen. I've said it before and I'll say it again: Pittsburgh has produced many marvelous, talented musicians. Henry Mancini and the late great Oscar Levant were both born here.

Years later I discovered a handwritten poem by Marty. He was only nineteen years old at the time he wrote it. Here is an excerpt:

Music
If there were no more music
to soothe this aching world
Sin would be multiplied a thousand fold
and a devil's flag unfurled.

"Bow down," this devil would command.
"Close ears to all but me.
Stop all this chord and rhythm
and dwell in misery.
Give all your thoughts to sadness.
Give up your soul to gloom."
Nature would rebel
and cause the flowers not to bloom.
But this can never happen.
This can never be.
Music must be in the world
to chase out misery.

MARTY'S LIFE BEFORE PATTI

After high school Marty toured the country with the Don Bestor Orchestra. (This was a famous orchestra that had provided the studio music for *The Jack Benny Show* on radio.) The orchestra would back up such stars as Martha Raye and the Three Stooges. They played a stage show for a week with the Three Stooges. Marty said all three of them were the nicest fellas. They were nothing like their act. The week of backing up Hollywood's comic, Martha Raye, was memorable for Marty. He raved about her singing. He would go into her dressing room, and they would play good jazz recordings. Martha Raye's mother always traveled with her.

After about a year Marty was drafted into the Army–Air Force band. The band was stationed in Miami. Because he could play the trombone, he was accepted. When it was discovered how well he fit in with a small jazz group, he was treated to some real perks. The "Brass" would have the group play for different social occasions.

There would be regularly scheduled marching times. In the band Marty often played the cymbals.

As the war wound down, more soldiers were needed. Marty would brag at how good he was with a rifle. This was probably not the wisest skill to admit to at this time in history. He was then assigned to a B Company 253rd Infantry regiment, where he served as a sergeant and rifleman in the 63rd division "Blood and Fire." Near the end of the war, it was the snipers he and his comrades worried about. He saw young men die. When he returned home, he didn't talk too much about the war. He did say that Germany was a beautiful country, with forests like those in Pennsylvania. Marty would eventually be awarded a Combat Infantry badge, a Bronze Star, and a European Battle Star. The personal tragedy was that his older brother, Bill, was killed in Italy during a battle.

Still in Europe after the war ended, Marty became the leader of an orchestra. The men of his 253rd Infantry, to stifle their boredom, decided to put on a show for the troops. A complete cast, musicians, and stagehands were recruited from the large pool of men for the burlesque theatrical production. The orchestra orchestrated a full-scale musical stage production of the opera *Carmen*. It was a comedy farce, with more than forty in the cast. The female parts were played by the men. It was quite bawdy, and the GIs loved it. The timing was perfect. The production would play in all the marvelous theatres and opera houses, plus hospitals in Europe. The show played to more than 300,000 GIs waiting for their discharges to get back home and it received rave reviews. Here is a sample: "Following its hilarious run at the Victory, *Carmen* will move to Bremmerhaven, playing the 17th Port Battalion from October 13 to 16. Now a corporal (Marty had to take a demotion if he wanted to stay), Marty Faloon is the terrific rhythm man of the ensemble. He makes his electric guitar sing out the trickiest choruses without effort. He comes from Don Bestor's band...which is a pretty good recommendation for this likeable hepcat."

The famous Hollywood star Marlene Dietrich appeared on some of these shows. She played the electric saw! Marty said she was beautiful.

It was on this show that Marty and Charlie Byrd met and became lifelong friends. The two of them also had a lifelong love affair with the guitar. Charlie got his big break playing with Stan Getz on the hit record "The Bossa Nova." He went on to great success with his classical jazz guitar. On one of his many albums he credited Marty Faloon as being one of the great influences on his music. Both Marty and Charlie were inspired when they got to see and hear the great jazz guitarist Django Rheinhardt. I have a picture of the three of them smiling for a photo at the Hot Club of France, located in Paris.

Charlie, Django, Marty

Marty described the club in eloquent terms: "I wish I could convey clearly the atmosphere of these French cafés. There is a certain, very romantic cloud over the room, and one can see the way of life in its every form. There are the gypsies, the prostitutes, and the people who would defy anyone to classify them. The music is given to moods, and you can hear frantic jazz, beautiful waltzes, stirring gypsy tunes, and rumbas. The only drink is champagne, and the occasional popping of corks as the bottles are opened brings one back to earth and lets one know that one is mortal and should not try to delve too far into reasons for things like these."

When Marty came home to Pittsburgh, he played in various bands. He was with a band at the Bachelors Club in Pittsburgh when he backed up a rising comedy team. It was Dean Martin and Jerry Lewis as they were beginning their meteoric rise to success.

PRELUDE TO MARRIAGE

Fast forward to the autumn of 1950. Marty and I continued rehearsing with the band and began courting.

Marty and I had been dating for three months when we decided to get married. The quintet we had been rehearsing with arranged to be part of a big audition at the William Penn Hotel ballroom. The audition was for small combo groups. I sang two songs: "Everything I Have Is Yours" and "Love Me or Leave Me." The first tune went fine, but the second... Perhaps it was nerves, because the leader set the tempo twice as fast as we had rehearsed it. However, I did it! I kept pace with the tempo, though I wanted to laugh during the song because it seemed so funny to me. Even so, they liked the group and wanted to hire us. We were to tour all over the South. Neither Marty nor I wanted to travel. If only there were local gigs, we would have done it. I know we disappointed the group. Marty had experienced cramped bus scheduling with the Bestor band. Musicians really didn't have to travel that often. They could stay in one club for weeks, months, and even years.

With all my exposure to married couples in show business, I always said, "No way do I want to marry an entertainer!" Not only did married entertainers quarrel or even ignore one another, they were constantly on the road, on the move. I had enough of that nomadic style and I didn't like it. Someone once called me a "nester." When I found out what it meant, I realized it was the truth. I loved the adventure of entertaining, but I loved my home, my bed, my kitchen...even my toilet. I indeed was a nester. Marty and I were both in accord with that way of living. At this time Marty had a steady weekend job in a little club. I was still dancing. The total income was not enough to sustain a household. We would live with Mom and Pop for a couple of months. Suddenly Marty got a great opportunity with the Bill Bickel Trio. The trio had a steady week job at Johnny Laughlin's Shamrock Room on the North Side. Many a celebrity would come to this busy, thriving dinner club. TV personalities who frequented the club included newscaster Bill Burns, and Hollywood's film actors Jack Palance and Pat O'Brien. Marty would talk about the laughter and the enjoyment they had from the many Irish jokes Pat O'Brien would spontaneously share. Many sports figures from the Pittsburgh Pirates and the Pittsburgh Steelers went to the Shamrock Room. The owner, Johnny Laughlin, was married to a member of the Rooney family, owners of the Steelers.

I was almost twenty-one years old and ready for marriage. Marty was twenty-nine years old. (We would be married for fifty-two years.) We shared a total love for music. Money? We didn't have any! Savings? We didn't have any of that either!

Right before my wedding day, I worked a full week at the Greystone Inn in Mansfield, Ohio. I had to take a train, and my agent, Don D'Carlo, goofed on the time. As I walked into the club, the first show was already in progress. The owner was behind the bar, and I approached him and put down my suitcase. He said to me, "You missed the first show. I'm gonna deduct it from your pay!" I looked at him and said nothing, then picked up my suitcase to leave. He quickly said, "Never mind, it's okay!" This place had three shows a night. I figured it wasn't my fault that I was late. Still, what nerve I had!

THE WEDDING

· ·

The night before the wedding I worked a country club with two of my favorite people, Blizz & Burke—two fellow performers, two married family men who were never out of line. When we worked together, there was pure laughter. They had a lot of material this night, teasing me about getting married the next day.

We tried to keep the wedding as simple as possible. Remember, we were broke! We got married on a Sunday at the Lutheran church where I was baptized. Because it was a Sunday, Marty would only miss the Monday and Tuesday portion of his week at his music job.

Marty reluctantly borrowed some money from Johnny Laughlin, the owner of the Shamrock Inn where he played, for our weekend honeymoon in Niagara Falls. We flew to Buffalo, New York. I had never been on an airplane. Marty thought I was nervous about flying, when actually I was nervous about about so much I didn t know about.

In 1950 many girls and boys were naïve about matters relating to the birds and the bees.

The prices at the hotel seem archaic compared to today. Hotel Statler was a "big deal" hotel at the time. A three-night stay: $9.50 per night, including a meal and valet. Total with taxes: $31.75. Wow!

SNOWFALLS
AND RAINBOWS

Within ten days of our marriage there was an historic event. In Pittsburgh, the news reported on November 24, 1950: "Auto, bus, and trolley traffic is brought to a standstill by a 30-inch snowfall—the heaviest in the city's history. Snow banks are piled as high as automobile tops."

The good news was that it was Thanksgiving. There was plenty of food to weather the storm. Three days later, tbe news reported: "The city and its environs are snow-bound. Newspapers fail to publish; most stores are closed. Deaths from the storm total 15."

They say there is a rainbow after a storm, and we got several rainbows. Marty was contracted to play on the radio every evening at 6 p.m. with one of Pittsburgh's finest orchestras, Baron Elliot. Almost simultaneously, he was asked to play with the Bobby Cardillo Trio on one of Pittsburgh's first live shows on television. The first MC was Orson Bean. His humor did not catch on with the audience. However, backstage he kept everybody in stitches. Orson did go on to much bigger things. He was replaced by Pittsburgh's own popular radio personality, Bill Brant.

To think that only a year earlier, Pittsburgh's first television station—DuMont's WDTV, Channel 2—went on the air. It originated on the stage of the Syria Mosque, an excellent choice as the Syria Mosque was one of the most magnificent auditoriums in which I would ever perform. The acoustics were perfect. (On February 28, 1920, the great Italian tenor Enrico Caruso sang at the Syria Mosque.)

The schedule for Marty's music playing was unbelievably hectic: daytime "live" TV, early evening radio, and 9 p.m. to 1 a.m. at the nightclub.

A couple of clippings in the newspaper verified how good-looking Marty was. "The Drama Desk" by Harold Cohen (*Pittsburgh Post-Gazette*): "Any time Errol Flynn needs a double, he can page Marty Faloon, the guitarist with the Bill Bickel's Starliters at Johnny Laughlin's Shamrock Room." Another clipping: "Look fast at Bobby Cardillo's guitar player...he's a dead ringer for Errol Flynn." (Errol Flynn was one of the first dashing Robin Hoods of movie fame.)

Because I was doing shows all during this time, we were able to save a lot of money so we could be on our own. It was especially nice that we could give my family back their living room.

GAY PERFORMERS

As television began to lure customers away from the night-clubs, clubs struggled to find forms of entertainment that weren't being shown on TV.

There was the female impersonator. Early in my career I worked with a few memorable solo impersonators. I always felt sorry for them; they couldn't use the ladies' or the men's restrooms. They would carry a jar to pee in! In those days it was against the law to travel dressed as a woman.

One of the female impersonators I worked with was **Tony Ricco**, a bitter, sad man. He did a "Carmen Miranda" number wearing a huge hat decorated with all the fruit on top, as part of a colorful rumba outfit. Once I drove Tony to a show on which we were both appearing, and on the way back to Pittsburgh I had to pick Marty up as he finished his own gig. Tony got all giddy like a young girl when Marty got in the car. I thought it was funny, but the frustration for Tony must have been awful.

The **Jewel Box Revue** was a popular group of female impersonators who toured and often would be held over for months in a club. The performers were extremely talented singers and dancers, and had beautiful faces, bodies, and wardrobes. I was never on a bill with this troupe, but I loved to catch their show in the local clubs.

Back in the late 1940s and '50s the word "gay" had a very different connotation. Then it meant light-hearted and merry, or brightly colored. I worked with several entertainers who were gay in the current sense but who never dressed as women. I loved to be on the shows with most of them. They were "gay"—sparkling, clever, and amusing.

Raphael! I first worked with Raphael in a private club in Franklin, PA. He wore a tuxedo-type costume for his act. Young, maybe eighteen years old, he was a good dancer. He was so desperate to be a sensation, and he was, but not in a good way. This was the early 1950s and he was so far out! He would be performing a really good dance routine and then, halfway through it, he would start bumping and grinding like a striptease dancer. The audience would be stunned. There were always a few in the audience who would encourage him, and Raphael took that as success! I worked with him several times, and off the stage he and I had a great time. We would both act giddy and really silly. One time we met at an Eat'n Park restaurant. He parked his car and then I drove us both to West Virginia for a show. After the show we came back to get his car, and then he drove, following my car for a short distance. I couldn't resist a foolish old trick I had done before. (Remember, there was not the traffic we have today, plus it was very late at night, in the wee hours of the morning.) I moved my body onto the passenger side of the car and stretched my leg to the gas pedal and my arm to the steering wheel. From behind the car it appeared as if nobody was driving the car. My love of action/reaction! Raphael started beeping his horn, then drove around me, waving his arm, laughing and beeping! I lost touch with Raphael and often wondered what became of him. He was so much fun.

Gene Darling was not very feminine looking. He wasn't a bad dancer, though, and he had a beautiful, fantastic wardrobe. He made his own costumes. After working with him, I asked if he would make a costume for me. He made an outstanding outfit of the best pink satin. It was a Gay (no pun intended) Nineties creation for my "Hello, My Baby" number. The top was strapless; Gene knew all the tricks in getting it to stay up. It had a bustle, with soft netting to cover my bum. Under the bustle he made a "breakaway," an opening in the front of the long skirt. I would sing the song and then snatch the skirt off for the tap dance portion of my routine. In making this wonderful creation Gene needed me to go for a couple of fittings. Marty came along to one of these fittings because I had sparked his interest when I told him about all these interesting entertainers I was meeting. Out of wardrobe Gene Darling dressed like a man. The day I told him I was bringing Marty, he greeted us wearing blue jeans, looking male all over except that he had on a gray sweater with falsies underneath. As Gene was checking my hemline on the skirt, he would actually pose in different suggestive positions on the floor. I always thought Marty was good-looking, and apparently so did Gene! I don't know if Marty was flattered, but he would grin when we acted out the story. It was good I married a man in show business because he understood the many different people and personalities. Yes, marrying Marty was definitely a plus.

OUR FIRST APARTMENT

With all the work coming in, we were able to make a move to our own little nest. Once again I would be living on the other side of Mount Washington. The Duquesne Incline was about a block away. The apartment was a couple of rooms in the owner's house. It consisted of one large living room with our sofa bed, a nice-sized kitchen, and a shared bathroom. Rent: $30 per month.

We purchased a tape recorder with two reels. Being something new at the time, it became a big attraction for visiting friends and relatives. We would sing, talk, and laugh, although we didn't think our voices sounded like THAT! It came in handy when Marty practiced his guitar. I became interested in playing guitar chords, so we bought a Martin D-18, an acoustic guitar with a big sound. I found it to be very difficult learning to play. The ends of my fingers really hurt. Marty told me, "You have to build up calluses." He was patient in teaching me.

Charlie Danver, the local showbiz critic, wrote this at the time: "Marty Faloon, guitar player with the Bill Bickel's Starliters, presented his bride, the former Pat Eberle the dancer, with a red convertible for Valentine's Day." Former dancer? In those days it was commonly expected that once a girl got married, any career she had STOPPED.

We were settled in nicely, we thought, when our lives changed. The radio orchestra Marty played with every evening at six made a recording that went like hot cakes! The tune was called "Shenandoah Waltz." This recording landed us in Washington, D. C., at the Carlton Hotel for the summer of 1951. We kept our apartment in Pittsburgh. While in Washington I was able to book many dates for myself in and around the area. I even did a television spot. One of the clubs I worked featured "Diane De Lys, Vivacious Exotic Dance Star in her dance of 'The Devil and the Virgin.'" What a unique act this was! One side of her was a beautiful dancer. Attached to her was a life-like male dummy.]During the dance the male part would "seduce" the girl part. Also on the bill was "a singer, a novelty act, and Patti Eberle, tap stylist."

While living in Washington we rented a lovely apartment on the outskirts of town. In the daytime we often went to the zoo. We both loved watching the monkeys for long periods of time. We vowed we would buy a chimp some day and raise it! That never happened.

Besides music, there was something else that Marty and I loved: dogs. All of my life we had a dog in our family. When Marty and I went to a pet store in downtown Pittsburgh, we were both drawn to one puppy.

Remember how we loved monkeys? We felt that this dog, like the monkeys, had eyes that were very human. We paid twenty-five dollars for this dog. As we drove home, Marty tried to calm our new addition. He kept saying to him, "That's okay, little fella!" So we called him "Fella." He was a mixed breed with a prominent terrier personality and appearance. We loved him and treated him like a firstborn child.

Fella was definitely the smartest dog we would ever own. Slowly and steadily I trained Fella to do all kinds of tricks. He could sit up on a chair, dance, play dead, and more. Actually, he could do almost anything I thought he could do.

Bill Bickel was good about public relations and sent mailings out to his fans. Whenever the trio would start working a new spot, Bill would notify everyone on the list. "BILL BICKEL and his STARLITERS—opening October 8, 1951—Sylvan room at the Roosevelt Hotel." … "Bill Bickel's Starliters have recorded a new tune called 'I Pray for You,' by Matt Furrin and Michael Elias of Greensburg and dedicated to Pennsylvania's Twenty-Eighth Division overseas." …"…The trio played background for London Record sides which Al Morgan cut here during his recent Copa engagement." … "The Bill Bickel Trio, a two-year fixture in Johnny Laughlin's Shamrock Room, where the outfit has played on and off for five years, is leaving there and will invade the Vogue Terrace for the first time next Thursday."

The Vogue Terrace was a fine, upscale supper club. I loved working the room. There was tiered, half-circle seating for the audience. Many stars were booked at this club. When Duke Ellington did a weeklong engagement there, he invited Marty and me to a private Sunday night performance. We were both impressed with Duke's graciousness. So many stars were snobbish, but Duke was extremely polite and kind.

The entertainment business has many offshoots. Bickel utilized one of these in making records. He placed an ad: "Special plan for songwriters. Your song professionally recorded. $1 per record on a commercial label. Featuring Bill Bickel Trio with Jimmy Confer, Vocal (or equivalent artist). Minimum order 200 records. At the Steel City Studios, 634 Penn Avenue, Pittsburgh." Marty learned how to cut the records. I would enjoy watching the process as the needle recorded and the fine black spiral substance curled away.

News from *The Drama Desk*, Harold Cohen: "The Marty Faloons…are trying to work out a schedule whereby they can see each other occasionally. What with his Vogue job, playing for banquets and weddings, and studying engineering at the Steel City Studios, Marty barely manages to see his tap-dancing wife, Pat Eberle, coming and going these days."

I was very busy with many club dates. Erie, PA, had a unique setup that proved very profitable for acts and the agents alike. The agent figured out a system whereby an entertainer could do up to five shows a night in five different clubs. The synchronized scheduling was a remarkable feat. Chauffeurs were employed to handle the transportation. I would do two dance numbers on a show; whatever costume I had on for my second routine at one club would be the costume I wore for the first number at the next club, and so on.

For one of those special multi-bookings I drove my 98 red convertible Oldsmobile. (The 98 didn't mean 1998; the 98 meant the BIG model.) Fortunately, it was big and heavy; it hugged the road. I took three other entertainers, all male, along with me: a ventriloquist, a sketch artist, and a singing MC. Instead of heading north toward Erie, I drove south for about forty-five minutes before I discovered my mistake. I turned around and hit the road, going eighty-plus miles per hour. I was hoping to make it in time. The guys were white with fright, knuckles groping whatever they could. None of them complained, as there was a lot of money at stake. This trip would be one of the quietest in my career, with only me muttering now and then, "I promise, guys, we will have a peaceful, legal-limit drive on the way back." We just made it! As we approached the hotel meeting place the agent was pacing. The relief on his face was obvious; he said, "Gee whiz, guys...."

WEST VIRGINIA GIRLIE SHOW

An agent booked me and a ventriloquist, Ralph De Genes, for a job in Clarksburg, West Virginia. It was to be at a big nightclub starring the famous stripper Gypsy Rose Lee. It sounded interesting and exciting. Well, it turned out to be VERY interesting and exciting. The first surprise was there was no club. The job was at a spawling outdoor fairground. The next surprise was that the ventriloquist and I were to be part of a "girlie show" (strippers). The only connection to Gypsy Rose Lee was that the MC was once married to her. He was also in charge of this "extravaganza."

As soon as I was aware of this deceptive booking, I put a call into the agent in Pittsburgh. I considered this to be a catastrophe. I was very angry, and I wanted to cancel. The agent claimed she had no idea. "Please stay the week!" she pleaded. I balked, but I stayed. I was glad I was persuaded to stay. It was a slice of show business I didn't know existed. The main features, of course, were the female strippers. There were five of them, each young and pretty.

Once again, Ralph and I were the "legitimate" acts just in case the law got tough. They had to keep things "legal."

To draw the people (mostly men) to the show all the girls, including me, had to dress in different outfits. The outfits were packed in a cardboard box. The five strippers and I would put on these wrinkled, green, short-skirted outfits that once had some shiny sequins on them. There were no dressing rooms. I would change behind a big row of hanging costumes. There was a long platform in front of the huge tent. Before the shows, all we girls had to do was

stand and pose on this high platform. The MC (a "barker") was a cute dwarf who would shout, "Come! Come see the beautiful dancing girls!" He would walk back and forth in front of us. He would extol the wondrous talent of these lovely ladies. He would go on and on until all the tickets were sold and the tent full.

Inside was a large stage with curtains. The audiences sat on folding chairs. There were three shows a night. Ralph, the ventriloquist, and I, the tap dancer, did only the first two shows. The third show was billed as the "RED HOT" show. It was so hot I thought I saw Ralph's dummy come alive!

Back in Pittsburgh I had worked with seasoned, older girls. Some were good dancers with clever routines. Here in Clarksburg some of these girls looked younger than me. I don't know where they found them. I surmised they were recruited from little towns along the way. Some of these pretty, well-endowed girls believed this to be a glamorous, showbiz career, but a couple of them—young ones too—looked tired, bored, used, and worn out. As far as being dancers, no, they weren't that. They would strut around the stage, tease, and take it all off! The stagehands and the other male workers didn't even notice them. Not Ralph, the ventriloquist, however. I wonder if his eyes ever got back in their sockets. The same was probably true for me as I looked on in astonishment.

The first two shows the girls ended up with pasties and G-strings, with very little covering on the top and bottom. However, the "RED HOT" show was something else. The girls would do their striptease number and then came the GRAND FINALE. The curtains would close. There would be another long intro about the fantastic and glorious scene that was about to be revealed. As the MC talked in front of the curtain, the girls had time to stand on pedestals: one in the middle and two on lower pedestals on either side of her. As young as these girls were, I found it amusing to watch them get ready. Just before the curtain would open, a couple of them would suck in their tummies and pose totally nude!

I wrote home about all this, and two carloads of relatives and friends wanted to come and see it with their own eyes. I don't believe Pittsburgh had anything like it. I don't believe it would have been legal.

I've decided the Clarksburg experience was just like another course of study for me. Who knows when I might use some of what I had seen! I would remember Tony Orlando's big hit, "Say, Has Anybody Seen My Sweet Gypsy Rose?". It's a song about a wife who left her family to become a stripper. I had firsthand knowledge of what became of such a wife and how she might have "danced."

ANOTHER MOVE

With our dog, Fella, our family was growing. We decided to look for a bigger place. We found a perfect first-floor apartment in a big house in Sheraden, still in the city.

One of the reasons for choosing this place was that the Henrys lived across the street. This was the wonderful family who raised Marty for a few of his young years.

I was quite satisfied to have Fella as my devoted buddy. However, on a visit from Bill Machiko (Bill was the new accordion player with the trio) and his wife Jan, a great change was about to occur in my life. The Machikos brought their beautiful, blond, blue-eyed baby boy with them to our house. He was about one and a half years old. I was in awe of this tiny creature. The baby did the usual walking and exploring, pulling all the pots and pans from under the sink and playing with them. As soon as they left and our front door closed, I turned to Marty and said, "I want one of those!"

BINGO! A BABY!

Right away I was pregnant. I began saving money for our own house. I often visited a cousin with a baby and witnessed apartment living with a family: noisy, hectic, and no peace. I was determined to have a house for my family.

I kept entertaining. I wished I hadn't given up so many times while learning to play the guitar. Marty taught me the chords so I could accompany myself in doing what I loved, which was singing! During this time, 1953-54, there was a popular, local, "live" country western group on TV: *The EasyZ Ranch Girls*. It was on in the late afternoon five nights a week. I watched it every day. Around this time the producers wanted to replace one of the girls. I tried out, but my guitar playing was weak. I sang the commercial song with gusto, backed up by the girls: "Easy credit, easy credit. Wilkins is the place where you can get it. Where credit won't cost you an extra cent. You get quality and value for what you spent. So, here's a little tip for every lady and gent: It's easy credit! You said it! That's the Wilkins Easy Credit song!" (Back in the 1950s one could buy jewelry with a monthly payment of just fifty cents. Easy credit!)

The accordion player was the leader, and she liked me. I was actually a couple of months pregnant at the time. (I guess I figured the guitar would hide my condition for a while!) After my audition there was some discussion down a hallway in a back room. I didn't get the job.

After this episode I got serious and began practicing faithfully. I became good with the rhythm for backing up my singing. I will always be grateful for Marty's patience in teaching me, even though he would get mad at me for not going further with the guitar. I didn't love the guitar like he did; my favorite instrument has always been the piano. I would take piano lessons for a little bit, then quit. I did this my entire grownup life. At one point I decided, "I'm really going to master this!" This time I studied the piano for a few months…seriously. However, what I really loved best was singing and interacting with the audience. It dawned on me that playing the piano made it impossible for me to have the eye-to-eye contact that I so enjoyed. On the other hand, the guitar was perfect for this because I could be looking at the audience and getting all of the reactions that I love.

I was beginning to have a lot of fun singing, joking, and ad-libbing with the audience. One number I did was "Love and Marriage." Throughout the song I would tell husband-and-wife jokes. For example: "A husband and wife were celebrating their fifty-fifth anniversary. The wife looks at her husband and says, "I'm so proud of you!" The husband says, "What? What did you say?"

Louder, she says, "I'M SO PROUD OF YOU!" The husband says, "Speak up! I can't hear you!" She says, **"I'm so proud of you**! Then the husband says, "I'm so tired of you, too!"

The last line of the song "Love and Marriage" contains two very difficult chords. Marty would show them to me and I would say, "It's too hard!" He would say, "You can do it!" The position on the frets and strings had my fingers twisted in unbelievable stretches. What I like about the guitar is that I rarely look at my fingers when I play. With these two chords, not only did I have to look, I also had to concentrate. The two chords were used in the song where I sing, "So I tell you BRO (one chord)...THER (another chord), you can't have one, you can't have none, you can't have one without the other." I worked on these chords for a couple of weeks. When I decided I was ready to try them on a show, Marty said he couldn't wait until I got home to see how it worked out. On the show that night, when I came to that part— "Bro...ther"—instead of attempting the chords, with a big smile I took my right hand and swung it out in a gesture and sang, "Brother," totally skipping the chords. With a wink and my index finger wagging, I finished, "No! No! You can't have one without the other." Needless to say, Marty was disgusted with me. I was happy that the song, jokes, and gestures went over very well, though, with the audience.

A few times Marty and I played the guitars together. I could strum out a beat of chords as he did his marvelous jazz renditions to the tune of "Sweet Georgia Brown." He was pleased with my rhythm, but was always annoyed that I wouldn't try more difficult chords.

In time, many shows no longer had live music. By backing myself up on the guitar, I was able to continue in show business for a long, long time.

I had fun secretly saving money from my jobs for a house. It was a good thing because there was a surprise in store for us: Marty's long run with the Bickel trio ended. The Bickels were having marital problems and thought a drastic change would help. And so they moved. I mean MOVED. The *Pittsburgh Sun-Telegraph* reported on May 5, 1954: "Bickel California bound, Marty takes over the Starliters. MARTY FALLON AND THE STARLITERS." Yes, he started using "Fallon" instead of "Falloon" as it was easier to pronounce.

When we were ready to look at houses, Marty was delighted that I had saved a sizeable down payment. I was about five-months pregnant when we started looking.

Finally, we saw a small, four-room ranch in Beechview (stlll in Pittsburgh) with a big backyard. Nothing—and I mean nothing—had been done as far as upkeep of this house. Under other circumstances we would have said no immediately. But about a half hour after seeing the house, I called the agents and said, "I'm getting really big. The baby is due in a couple of months. We'll take the house!" Just a couple of weeks before we moved, we rescued an unwanted dog, Carney, and so our family was really growing.

OUR OWN HOUSE

Drama critic Harold Cohen reported in the *Pittsburgh Post-Gazette*: "Marty Faloon, who heads the Starliters, and his wife, dancer Patty Eberle, have their first date with the stork in November."

The couple of years living in Sheraden was the only time I did not live on a mountain. Standing on a part of Mount Washington, one can look over a deep valley and see the other mountain, where my home would be for more than fifty years. This four-room ranch house on Gladys Avenue needed much cleaning and painting. Oh, the work I did as a pregnant woman! With my mother's help we painted all the rooms. Seven months pregnant, I would actually mow the big yard with a handmower. Meanwhile, I was still working. I tried to work as much as possible because we really needed the income.

From the time we moved into our new house Marty was struggling from job to job. He tried selling Niagara massage machines. A month before Christmas, the post office was hiring temporary letter carriers. Marty left early one blustery October morning to stand in a long line to apply for the job. I received an urgent, frantic phone call from Marty: "I forgot my discharge papers!" These papers would give him a fair advantage for the time he served in the army. I was now about eight months pregnant. I had to call a cab, walk past a long line of men, and reach Marty in time. We were so thankful that he got the job.

I'M A MOMMY!

On Sunday morning, November 7, 1954, Marty drove me to the hospital. It was not a quick delivery. Marty had a gig that evening and missed our baby's entrance into this world. We really needed the money.

Eventually Marty became a regular mailman. Although at the time it did not pay much, it was a steady job. With Marty's sideline gigs, we would do fine. In the years ahead, he would perform his mailman duties faithfully. "Neither snow nor rain nor heat nor gloom of night stays these couriers from the swift completion of their appointed rounds." I must say this was the same creed as that of show business: "The show must go on!"

I had no idea how much I would fall in love with motherhood. William John Faloon was named after Marty's brother, who was awarded the Purple Heart after losing his life in Italy in World War II.

When the nurse finally brought my baby to me, I was hooked. I was totally enthralled with this tiny wonder. I would reflect upon all the extreme physical activity I had been doing while pregnant: tap dancing too long, falling too often, painting walls, mowing grass, and just doing all the work it takes to move into a house. Now I was holding this miracle! In that instant I became a willing, loving, and devoted mother. All self-absorption was gone. The importance of "me" disintegrated. I would continue in the show business that I loved, but it would never compare to being a mother.

I loved my husband, and when Billy was born, I fell in love all over again. To have the privilege and the power to mold a human life is to me the most interesting, rewarding, and important role I would every play.

Within a couple of months after Billy's birth, I was back in shape and booking shows. How fortunate this career has been for me, for the nightclub jobs were in the evening. I often had Billy tucked in bed before I had to leave for a show. Sometimes I enlisted the help of Grandma, who lived nearby. I'd drop him off at 10 p.m. and pick him up at 2:30 a.m. (The year Billy was born was the year that the first mass inoculation of children against polio with Dr. Jonas Salk's vaccine began in Pittsburgh.)

MORE SHOW-BIZ ADVENTURES

The Chez Dee was a lovely, weekly nightclub that I worked many times. A very popular singing and guitar-playing duo, the Kentuckians, often played the room also. One of the fellas was adorable and reminded me of the young Bee Gee, Andy Gibb. He drove the females in the audience crazy. I recall the younger Kentuckian's amazing energy and stamina onstage—and in the parking lot between shows!

When I heard that a former movie and TV star, Marie Wilson, was going to do a show at this club, I knew I wanted to see her act. She had enjoyed success in the movies and on her own TV show, *My Friend Irma*. She played an adorable "dumb blonde." Later she performed in Las Vegas. (She has three stars on Hollywood's Walk of Fame.)

Marie did some really clever specialty songs. I enjoyed her show at the Chez Dee. Most of the audience was not warmly receptive. She was on the other side of her heyday, and for some reason the people seemed to resent that. After the show I requested to meet her in her dressing room. I talked with her and told her I was an entertainer. I told her how much I enjoyed her show that night and her TV show. She was very friendly, but I could tell she was not happy. The problem of not remaining on top: People can be so unkind. They begin to compare you to your younger self. Some people actually expect those in show business, especially women, to never grow old. The reality is, we all do…if we're lucky. It wasn't easy for her to be working in this little club, yet she wanted to keep entertaining. She told me about a part she was offered in a movie. She said she told them to give it to Jayne Mansfield because Jayne needed the work. This wonderfully talented pro, who someone called a "has-been," had a loneliness for which I felt great empathy. Once a fellow mailman told Marty, "You're nothin' but a has-been!" Marty said to him, "Better a has-been than a never-was!"

A new hot spot opened in downtown Pittsburgh at 122 Sixth Street. It was called the Hollywood Show Bar. It featured a very long, curved bar with the stage in the middle. A small combo backed up all the female entertainers, all of them pretty and talented. An article in the *Pittsburgh Sun-Telegraph* attested to "Pat Eberle's ballet-tap wizardry and the Four (Alright Already) Buddies vocalizing at the Hollywood Show Bar, downtown."

In the early 1950s I did a show in a little club in Braddock, a mill town. There were still many little clubs on the outskirts of Pittsburgh. This club was a three-night booking. There were two shows a night, one at 11 p.m. and the second at 1 a.m. The clubs legally had to close at 2 a.m.

The final evening I got into my car, which was parked across the street from the club. A young fella coming out of the club began flirting with me, but I ignored him and we both got into our vehicles. He had a pick-up truck ("pick-up"…how appropriate!) parked in front of the club. I pulled out in my car, and then he screeched a U-turn and followed me. This had never happened before. There was not the traffic back then that we have today, especially at that hour. I ran through stop signs and stoplights. I was scared and shaking. As we came to the crest of a four-way intersection, the light turned red and I stopped my car. He stopped right behind me and started to get out of the truck. At that moment a police car came from the opposite direction, and the fella jumped back into his truck and took off. Although I was shaking all over, I was also really mad. The policeman came over to my vehicle and told me he had been after this fella for a long time. He asked me if I would appear in court and testify against this fella. I determinedly said, "Yes, I will!" Mom didn't want me to testify. The brazen fella called our house a couple of times. Marty got on the phone, and this fella alleged that he was "just having a little fun." He also claimed he knew some people—political friends—in Harrisburg. He obviously had found out that I agreed to testify against him. Marty told him that my father was a policeman and two of my uncles did police work.

In a couple of weeks we appeared before a constable. The "bad boy" was accompanied by his lawyer and two friends. The two friends said he was driving to their place to play cards at 2:30 in the morning. Hah! I was glad he had to pay a lawyer and implicate two lying friends. The lawyer stood up and started by saying that this "broad"—ME!—was coming out of this club. Marty stood up, strongly objecting to him calling me a broad. The lawyer apologized and then continued, stating that I was sitting at the bar in this club. This time I stood up and said, "I don't drink and I don't sit at bars!" (I wasn't counting the B-girl bit in Cleveland!) Talk about character assassination! The saddest part of this case was seeing the policeman who had asked me to appear to testify. He stood in the background, meek as a lamb, trying to "melt" into the wall. I guessed the bad fella did know some people in Harrisburg who probably put the officer's job on the line. We were told the guilty guy would be reprimanded. Some might say he got away with a slap on the wrist. I prefer to believe I caused him enough grief that he might give second thoughts to frightening other female victims.

The showbiz lifestyle is often misunderstood by people outside the business. One time, another entertainer, who just happened to be a male, was driving us both to a job. He was worried about having trouble finding my house.

To make it easier for him, I parked my car near the main road a few blocks from my house. It was late. It was dark. When he picked me up, I got my little wardrobe bag and suitcase out of my car, put them into his car, and away we went. Later, in the wee hours of the morning after our gig, we reversed the routine: He drove up to my car, and I took my bag and suitcase out of the car and put them into mine. And then I drove the few blocks to my house. I've often thought how this transaction might have appeared to anyone observing us.

I would continue my singing and dancing while Billy was a toddler. It had taken me seven years to reach many of my goals as a singer and dancer, working the best dates and being recognized for my talent. I constantly practiced and polished my act. I worked with everyone from the small-time agents to the top booking agents in Pittsburgh. From the nightclubs I would progress to the coveted show dates that included country club affairs, top company events—all the high-budgeted affairs which were considered the "Big Deal" shows.

Here is a publicity highlight from the *WINGFOOT CLAN News Magazine* about the Goodyear Theatre in Akron, Ohio, January 16, 1954: "Pat Eberly and her original 'Rhythm in Motion' dance and singing routine will headline the bill at the Goodyear 25-year Club's first show of the 1954 season. A big show with an array of talent. George Kendall will hold the audience in suspense with his exciting escape act. Dolly Delane will portray character parts from musical shows. Jack Blasi, king-of-the-banjo artist. Harris and Rochelle, a comedy act, 'Varieties in Nonsense.' Jerry Harris, MC, and the Harold Riehl Trio."

To end the show was the full-length feature film *Desert Song*, in Technicolor, starring Kathryn Grayson and—are you ready for this?—Gordon MacRae, the wonderful singer I saw live in New York when I was seventeen years old. This was one time I would be on a bill with Gordon MacRae!

Everything I've ever accomplished pales in comparison to motherhood. I love being in and seeing live shows, but, for me, my kids were the "Greatest Show on Earth"! The real Greatest Show on Earth was in Pittsburgh on July 16, 1954, at the Heidelberg Raceways, ending an era of entertainment. It was the last tent performance of the Ringling Brothers and Barnum & Bailey combined shows.

THE GUITAR

Thankfully, I renewed my partnership with my guitar. The big Martin D-18 had a loud acoustic sound. I would eventually have it electrified for a fuller sound for larger audiences. I began to practice in earnest. I started with mostly country tunes. I liked the songs, and the chords were few and easy. I would accompany myself as I sang. One of the great things about a guitar is how easy it is to change the key of a song. One can keep the fingers in the same positions while moving up or down the strings and frets.

At the age of twenty-six, I added the guitar to my act. The first show I did with the guitar was at a local Moose club. I sang "Sue City Sue" and the classic song by Hank Williams, "Your Cheatin' Heart." Later I would sing a country tune wearing my short-skirted cowgirl outfit and do a tap dance to "Oklahoma." Eventually I would close this number with a tap routine to "The William Tell Overture," which would allow for great, clear tap steps.

Can't you just hear it? Da-de-ump, Da-de-ump, Da-de-ump, ump, ump! Hi ho, Silver, away!

I'm so glad I decided to play the guitar because soon there would be no live band to back me up. It was sad, but it was a reality. I would become "self-contained." I didn't need a band; I supplied my own musical accompaniment.

The guitar helped me in pursuing other paths leading away from dancing. I enjoyed the dancing part of my career, but singing remained my favorite. I bought a couple of knee-length dresses. Each one had a showy jacket with lace, a boa, or sequin trim. While there were still bands, I would open the show with a song or two. Then I would have the band play "stripper"-type music, like "St. Louis Woman," with lots of heavy drums. I would strut around, wiggling my hips…never bumps or grinds, though. Watching those strippers on those earlier shows helped me with the moves. Then I would take the jacket off, swing it around, and wiggle my shoulders. Next, I would bend down and take the guitar out of my case. I would put it on and say into the microphone, "Now, wasn't that more interesting than me just picking the guitar out of the case?" It worked very well, judging by the laughter and applause I received.

DANCER, SINGER...
COMEDIENNE!

During this time I also began throwing in a joke or two. It always got a good response, so I began doing more and more comedy. Here is the lineup for one of the shows in which I was adding comedy to my repertoire:

"Bill Bailey": First, I would sing the original chorus of the song. Then I would impersonate different styles, especially the body movements that singers used. For the second chorus I would imitate the singer who "sings" with her eyes. I did everything from a wide-eyed look to lowered, sexy eyelids to arching eyebrows. The third chorus I'd focus on the lips, doing Marilyn Monroe's pucker or Judy Garland's quiver. The fourth chorus I would swivel my entire body à la Charo with her trademark "Koochy! Koochy."

"I'm a Woman": a hit recording by Peggy Lee.

"Hey, Good Lookin'": I'd ask, "Who's the good lookin' fella in the audience?" I'd sing the song to him.

"Back in the Old Routine": I had a neat musical arrangement where I would sing the song and then do a soft-shoe dance with a hat and cane. When the cha-cha became popular, I would do another chorus to that rhythm. When the cha-cha recording became a big hit, I was anxious to incorporate the new beat, but the tune was unfamiliar to musicians. However, I wanted to be "with it," so I suggested to Marty, "Why can't I do the dance to the tune of 'Tea for Two'?" This was a tune all of the musicians knew at the time. Marty did not think it was a good idea. Soon afterwards some musicians recorded a tune called "The 'Tea for Two' Cha-Cha" and it became an instant hit. Someone else thought of the idea and made a heap of money.

"In the Shadows Let Me Come and Sing to You": A very old song that was still known at the time. This was possibly one of my first audience participation numbers. I would ask a man in the audience to come up on the stage and I'd ask him to finish each of my lines with "To you!" So I would sing, "In the shadows let me come and sing…" and he would finish it with, "To you!" "Take me in your arms and let me cling…" "To you!" You get the idea.…

"I Can't Stop Loving You": A big hit song first recorded by Ray Charles.

Here are some of the gags that really got laughs. I still use a few today:

> *A young starlet took an ocean voyage. She kept a diary of everyday events. Monday, she wrote:," The captain asked to take pictures of me on the top deck." Tuesday: "He invited me to dine at his table."*

Wednesday: "*He made proposals to me not befitting an officer and a gentleman.*" *Thursday:* "*I refused the captain and he threatened to sink the ship.*" (I would then put my right hand over my heart and say, "*I saved eight hundred lives today!*")

A young married couple is sitting in a restaurant and suddenly the wife reaches across the table and smacks her husband on the face. She says, "That's for being such lousy lover!" A few seconds later the husband smacks the wife across the face and says, "That's for knowing the difference!" (This gag seems quite outdated today.)

Women are talking in a restroom. One lady says, "My husband has been doing housework for an entire week! He did the laundry, scrubbed the floors, and even washed windows!" The other ladies say, "How in the world did you get him to do that?" She says, "He read in a magazine if a wife wasn't too tired she made a much better love partner." Ladies ask, "Did it work?" Wife says, "No, he was too tired!"

A BROTHER FOR BILLY

I had a dancing job in April 1957 with a singer named Sandy Doren. She would become very special a couple of years later as our relationship spawned a very successful comedy team.

I didn't want Billy to be an only child, so I was working on growing my family. At the time I was still being booked primarily as a dancer, but I didn't feel I had established my singing and comedy act. When I found out I was pregnant again, I decided to discontinue dancing. I had taken many spills and chances carrying Billy, unaware of the precious passenger growing in my belly.

Harold Cohen, *Drama Desk*, July 12, 1957: "Patti Eberle has hung up her dancing shoes. She and her husband, Marty Faloon, the guitarist with the Marty Irwin Trio at the Chateau Club, have another date with the stork (their second) in January."

It was my turn to name the baby. I was torn between Steven and Sean. Sean is certainly an Irish name as is Faloon. Steven prevailed: Steven Martin Faloon.

Lucky me! Lucky Steven! I was in top physical and mental condition. When I left the hospital, Billy seemed like a small boy. In ten days—back then, most hospital stays for new mothers were a week long—when I returned home with the baby, Billy seemed so big. The contrast was striking.

There was none of that "nervous wreck" period that most new mothers endure. When I brought Steven home, I made sure I spent special times with Billy.

Steven was a delight; he was so pleasant. Very early on, Steven loved to sing. All their lives my children would hear their mommy singing around the house, and I always encouraged them to sing, too.

FELLA'S TASTE OF SHOWBIZ

On July 26, 1958, Fella, now six and a half, did a show on WQED-TV in Pittsburgh. Through the years I was constantly teaching him to do tricks. On the TV show he performed his stunts perfectly. I'd set up a little net, and he and I would play volleyball with a balloon. He would let me put all kinds of hats and costumes on him. As a "cowboy" he would walk upright, I'd "shoot" him with a toy cap gun, and he would "drop dead"! Wearing a miniature sombrero on his head and a colorful, layered skirt on his waist (does a dog have a waist???), he would place his front paws on my backside and we would dance one-two-three "La Conga"! In our grand finale Fella would wear a fireman's hat and climb up a five-foot ladder, then walk over a wood plank. At the end of the plank was a house "on fire" in which a baby doll was "trapped." Fella would rescue the baby doll, then drop the baby to me. Ta da!

I was so pleased with Fella's performance, I figured he was ready for some live shows with me.

Marty devised a car seat for Fella. The first show Fella ever did was at a private Elks club. I did my act first while my friend Mae watched Fella. Then I introduced Fella onstage. He jumped up into a chair, and sat up beautifully. Unfortunately, the band played a long, LOUD chord. At the sound Fella leapt off the seat, ran into the barroom, and hid under a pinball machine. My poor friend Mae was on her hands and knees trying to retrieve him. When he finally came out, he reluctantly performed most of his tricks. "Play Dead" got a lot of laughs because he kept lifting his head nervously, looking at the crowd. The problem was that when I'd rehearse with him there was never loud music and never a crowd; up until that time, the only crowd Fella experienced was the people he met when Marty took him to one of his (Marty's!) favorite bars.

We did a few more shows together. With all the extra props and preparation required, Fella would have a short career in show business. For his final show, which by the way was on a stage *away* from the band and the crowd, Fella delivered a perfect performance. I didn't know this was going to be his last show until after the show when the club's cook came hustling down the hallway with a treat for the dog act she had heard about but hadn't seen. "Oh, I love dogs," she proclaimed. When she entered our dressing room and looked at Fella, she said, "Uhhhh, what kind of dog is *that?*" The look on her face registered "ugh" as she looked at my beloved Fella. I was crushed. Oh, how much looks matter in showbiz…even for dogs! By most standards, Fella was not a pretty dog, but I thought he was because I loved him. Someone said he looked like a hyena…I wouldn't have gone that far! After that incident, though, I decided to "retire" Fella.

Fella on the scale getting weighed

PAPPY

. . . .

With all the relatives in the vicinity there were constant parties: Stanley Sweeper, Tupperware, and Avon. There were also many birthdays, graduations, weddings, and baby showers…in that order, in my day!

There was a popular tune by Theresa Brewer titled "I Gotta Go Find My Baby." For a baby shower I penned different lyrics to this song. I substituted the word "pappy" for the word "baby" in the lyrics, and then I changed the title to "I Gotta Go Find The Pappy!". My chum Mae would be my partner for this bit. She would sing the song and I would accompany her on the guitar. She dressed as a hillbilly: bare feet, corncob pipe, pregnant (she stuck a big balloon under her skirt).

And so she sang:

*When I woke up this fine bright morning, it didn't
    look right to me.* (She looks down at her
    belly.)
*It seems like somethin' was awful wrong, and I
    wondered what*
it could be. (She scratches her head.)
*I've been thinkin' about it all day long, tryin' to
    figure out what went wrong.* (She wears a
    dumb look
    on her face.)
The answer just now come to me! (Her eyes and
    mouth both open big.)
It was about six months ago out in the barn…

Chorus:
Oh, I gotta go find the pappy, wherever he may be.
*I gotta go find the pappy and bring him home to
    me.*
*If I have to swim the ocean, well, look out, Mr.
    Sea.*
(Mae would bend over and pretend she was
    swimming.)
*I gotta go find the pappy and bring him home with
    me!*

There was a second verse, but I don't remember it. The
parody went over great, and there was laughter throughout. At the time I had no idea that this number would
bring a new and exciting change in my showbiz career.

SANDY

In July of 1958 I was booked on a show with Bob Garber, an MC; his wife, Cathy, a marimba player; and a singer, Sandy Doren. Sandy would later change her name to Cindy. This fortuitous booking occurred at a nightclub engagement in Baden, PA. It wasn't a long drive from home, and each act commuted separately every night to and from the club.

This little troupe wound up having great camaraderie. For a week we laughed, we joked, and we clowned around. Sandy and I really clicked. We would easily, almost naturally, bounce comedic phrases back and forth. Eventually she and I would become partners...and best friends. We both had our own talents and truly applauded and appreciated each other. We laughed...a lot!

This particular club in Baden had all the signs of Mafia involvement. Two bosses would sit in a booth each night smoking cigars. They were not a bit forceful, but they did try to get friendly. A couple of times they would call

Sandy and me over to the booth. They would compliment us on our talent and then say, "Would you like a drink?" We would decline. There was no serious pressure, but we were both uneasy about it. At the end of the evening we would have lots of fun planning how we would exit, together, and vanish quickly into our cars. Actually we were both so naïve. We would laugh at the "funny little guys with the big fat cigars"!

MAFIA

· ·

When I began doing shows in 1947, there was definitely a lingering Mob element in many of the clubs. I remember my dad commenting on a very popular club where I often worked. Pop told me the owner had been a bootlegger, and that's how he made all of his money.

Nightclubs and booze have always been close partners. So, when the legal restriction on the sale or manufacture of alcoholic beverages began during Prohibition, it opened the door for the Mafia. They used the nightclubs as a way to launder their money. Money that they made illegally "off the books" was mingled with the money they made "on the books" so that "dirty" money was made "clean"!

Gangsters organized illegal private clubs. There were rackets, the payoffs, and eventually huge casinos, gambling, drugs, prostitution, and gang wars.

SINGING COMEDIENNE

As Sandy and I rehearsed to get the new team going, I kept busy with solo bookings. I was always trying new numbers. I was reaching my goal of being a singing comedienne. I had wardrobe made for these shows. One was a dark-green, satin, Mandarin-collar-style costume with a long slit down the side. My legs have always been one of my good points. One leg showing was better than none!

I did a show in a Moose club with a great magician named Tony Polito. I was always glad when there was a man in the audience named Tony. I would say, "Oh, I love the name Tony.... Spelled backward, it's Y-Not!" Tony Polito always wore a classy black tuxedo and tails. One of his great tricks was pulling a string of razor blades out of his mouth. There would be ooh's and aah's from the audience.

One night (a night that was to be monumental for me) there was a big crowd awaiting the show. I was in costume as the show was to begin. Suddenly in the dressing room there was mayhem. I overheard, "What do you mean, you can't go on? The show is ready to start! We have a full house!" Tony, with all of his props—and believe me, magicians have a lot of props—had forgotten a very important item: his pants! He had his tuxedo jacket—but no pants! Tony said, "I can't do my magic show!" The men in charge were livid. "You've got to be kidding! We've got a big crowd out there!"

I talked to Tony recently, and he remembers the night well. He confessed to me that without the rigged pants with the strings he couldn't attach the birds to his rear end in his grand finale. It's now hard to imagine the suave composure he possessed when he made his entrance. This snazzy tux...with live doves hanging from his posterior! Finesse indeed.

So the milestone for me was that I did the entire show by myself. An hour show. It was a first for me. The show had a band of excellent musicians, and thank goodness for that because I did not have all the music for what I ended up deciding to do.

This was the lineup:

1   "Walk Right In, Sit Right Down" (followed by a couple of gags)
2.   "You Gotta See Your Mama Every Night"
3.   "Bill Bailey" (with the impression styles)
4.   Some soft shoe, and then the "Tea for Two Cha-Cha"
5.   "Shadow Waltz" with a man from the audience
6.   Twist song and dance: "Come On, Everybody, Let's Do the Twist!"
7.   "Please Don't Talk About Me When I'm Gone" (I sang the song and then did the Charleston.)
8.   "You're Nobody Till Somebody Loves You"
9.   "Let Me Entertain You" (I sang this and told many jokes.)

Some of the gags:

A man goes to check into a hotel and he spots a pretty girl making eyes at him. Soooooooo...they check in as Mr. and Mrs. The next morning he comes down to pay the bill. The clerk says, "That'll be $750." The man says, "But I've been here only one night!" The clerk says, "I know, but your wife's been here a week!"

There was a big convention in the city, and hotel rooms were scarce. A man goes into a hotel and begs for a room. Finally, they tell him, "We do have one room upstairs, but there's a lady in the room. If we put up a screen between the beds and you promise to behave, we'll let you have the room." The man says, "Yes!" After just a short time the man comes dashing down to the clerk and says, "That woman in the room… She's dead!" The desk clerk says, "We knew that, but how did you find out?"

There's a husband bragging about how his wife treats him. "She fixes great meals for me, puts me in a warm tub, massages me, and then makes sweet love to me." He then says to the other man, "Why don't you try it?" The man says, "Okay… Where do you live?"

On the way home from work one day a husband stops at a bar to have a drink. At the bar he gets friendly with a woman. The next thing you know, they go to her apartment. Then they go into her bedroom. The next thing you know, it's 3 a.m. The man says, "My wife is going to kill me! So, you have any talcum powder?" She says, "Yes!" He says, "Put it on my hands." He dashes home and darned if his wife isn't waiting at the door with her arms crossed, and she's angry. "Where have you been?" He says, "Honey, I'll tell you what happened. I stopped to get a drink after work. A woman got friendly at the bar. The next thing you know we went to her apartment.

*The next thing you know we went to her bedroom,
and the next thing you know it was 3 a.m." The
wife says, "Let me see your hands!" He shows them
to her and she says, "You lying son-of-a-gun, you've
been out shooting pool all night!"*

Yes, I got big laughs with all of these jokes.

CINDY AND PATTI

Singer Sandy Doren and I managed to get booked on several shows together. We had had such a happy time on the Baden job with our silly camaraderie. Our personalities clicked; it was inevitable we would talk about teaming up.

In our team she would become "Cindy." She was blonde, blue-eyed, and pretty, with a dazzling smile and an amazing voice. She could sing in a beautiful soprano range and also in a deep bass. One of her specialty numbers was "My Hero." It was an opera-type duet but she would sing both parts, her high voice for the female and her low voice for the male.

Cindy was only six months younger than me, so we had much in common. We would spend many hours together, many of them just traveling to and from our shows. We could reminisce about our many childhood antics. We shared many values.. We were faithful to our husbands, we adored our children, and we loved show business.

We were physically quite a contrast. I was tall—5'7"—with fair skin, dark hair, and a bust line reminiscent of Audrey Hepburn's (not much on top). Cindy was short—5'2", fair, and Marilyn Monroe-busted. I was the straight man in our routines and she was the zany comic. Eventually I would write most of the original material, and she was always game for anything. We were doing *Laugh-In* before *Laugh-In* ever aired on TV in the late '60s. We offered variety and unexpected bits.

We began rehearsing the pregnant hillbilly bit that was so much fun at the baby shower—"Gotta Go Find the Pappy." This bit would be the catalyst for our immediate success as a team.

Our out-of-town (off-Broadway) tryout was in September 1959 at a beautiful Moose club in Erie, PA. We did our usual solo performances and closed with our "Pappy" number. I had kept some of the wardrobe from the baby shower: the loose, polka-dotted dress and straw hat with a daisy swaying on top. Cindy, with the corn-cob pipe, added a jug. The most important prop for this number was the inflated balloon she placed in the crucial spot under her dress. I introduced her as my cousin from West Virginia. As she sang, I accompanied her on the guitar. At the finish of the song, Cindy would take a pin out of her hat and burst the balloon, then say, "I was just funnin'!" before adding, "Did you see some of them fellers slidin' down in their chairs?" The reaction to the number was more than we ever dreamed it would be: laughter, applause, and almost a standing ovation. We were excited and thrilled at the enthusiastic response.

Years ago, on Broadway, vaudeville legend Fanny Brice was a "pregnant bride" in a Ziegfeld Follies show. Actress Barbra Streisand repeated this act in the biography made about Fanny Brice in *Funny Girl*, a hit movie from 1968. We just happened to do a similar number in the era between these two superstars.

We were booked in a private Elks club in Greenville, PA, and the hillbilly number was quite a sensation. Within a month they wanted us back. We had accumulated lots of material, so for the repeat performance we chose not to do the "Pappy" number. Not only was there a full house this night, but people were standing packed in the doorway.

Do you recall the line "It was about six months ago out in the barn" from the "Pappy" song? Well, halfway through our show someone from the audience yelled, "Behind the barn!" Others in the audience joined in. They wanted to see the number again. After about the third prompt, "Behind the Barn," I got a big laugh by saying, in the middle of our show, "What time?" However, Cindy topped me. After the laughter died down, she said, "Time? Hell, how much?" It was a five-minute showstopper of laughs.

THE FUN FILLYS

We would do more shows in Pittsburgh with the same fabulous success. We were so hyped up! We kept adding bits and songs. Because of the success of the hillbilly bit, we leaned toward country songs and humor. Our act probably resembled the TV show *Hee Haw*, which aired from 1969 to 1971. The country theme was the basis for the title we came up with for the act: "The Fun Fillys."

Some of our fellow entertainers made fun of our name. As the months went by, though, and we were in great demand, suddenly there was a reverence in their tone.

We were constantly changing and adding—glee-fully—to our act. In "Pappy," near the end of the song, Cindy would go out into the audience as if looking for the pappy! Some fellas would play along and slouch in their chairs. A couple of times a fella got up and rushed out the door to gales of laughter.

There are necessary elements in telling a joke. It's important to get the right intonation: the highs and lows, the soft and loud words that set a scene. The timing, especially, has to be right for the punch line.

Some of our gags:

Patti: *"Cindy, behave…Remember, a good girl deserves credit!"*

Cindy: *"Yeah, but a bad girl gets CASH!"*

Patti: *"Cindy's just full of fun and fancy-free!"*

Cindy: *"I may be fun and fancy, but I ain't free…and I give stamps too!"*

Cindy's toast to a newborn baby: *"Here's to you, little stranger. You've made your parents so glad. You've taken a load off your Mom, and made room again for dear old Dad!"*

When we first started doing comedy, we used a lot of joke material that we eventually found would not be appropriate in finer venues. Everyone was giving us stories to tell—friends, relatives, and people from our audiences. Some of the jokes would stun us! One lady had seen a show at her daughter's college. She thought this would be a good one for us: "To the woods!" he says. The girl says, "But my mother wouldn't like it!" He answers, "Your mother loved it!" (This was the beginning of the 1960s.) We never did use this joke.

After another show a lady said to me, "I've got a good joke for your Mae West impression." She said, "You look at a man and say, 'Is that a pistol in your pocket, or are you just glad to see me?'" Wow, we thought that was too much. I would never do it on a show. (A few years later a voluptuous redhead would say these same words to Roger Rabbitt in the cartoon movie of the same name.)

We had fun with the TV commercials. One of my aunts came up with a gem! It was a spoof of the Mr. Clean commercial ditty. We'd harmonize the song, "Mr. Clean will clean your dirt and grime and grease in just a minute...Mr. Clean will clean your 'whole' (long "significant" pause) house and everything that's in it...Mr. Clean!" At that pause the peals of laughter stopped the show. (The original Mr. Clean was a muscular man with a bald head. He had a hoop earring and a no-nonsense attitude toward dirt and grime. Eventually his part would be played by an animated figure. The electronic revolution had begun. The original Mr. Clean died in 2008.)

TV commercials were always fun to exaggerate. One of them was for the Toni Home Permanent for hair. We'd both put our arms up in the air and pretend we were combing the hair under our arms: "Which twin has the Toni?" Cindy would sniff a couple of times and say, "Somebody here is only half safe!" (A deodorant ad)

We would harmonize "Down in the valley, the valley so low... I met the Jolly Green Giant." Then Cindy, with a twinkle in her eye, would sing in her DEEP voice: "Ho, ho, ho!" imitating the Jolly Green Giant's ending to the commercial's song.

We would return to Erie, PA, many times. It was the home of our debut as a team. One time I had the flu. Cindy drove to our gig as I lay across the back seat. We rehearsed the music with the band in the office of this private club. I lay prone on the desk for the "talk-over" rehearsal. When I stood up to put my costume on, the room spun. Despite being ill, I still did the opening tap dance routine. I did it! Out of all the years in showbiz I canceled only one show due to a really bad sinus infection.

On the other hand, Cindy truly amazed me, performing despite her stomach problems. From the time she was a child she would get so excited she would throw up. She did this on several gigs. I would say to her, "Are you sure you want to do this show?" She would insist, "Yes!" She would leave the stage to "upset her cookies," as they say. Through the years we got to know all the hospitals in the area. Eventually she would be given some form of tranquilizer, I believe. (First they would check her arms to see if she was an addict. She wasn't.) Within days she'd be back, fit as a fiddle!

Louie Angelo, an agent in Kane, PA, probably began his career with musical groups, bands, and orchestras. Louie put out more advertisements than any agent I ever knew. In his brochures and pamphlets he would list hundreds of musical groups. "We have a selection of over a thousand rock & roll bands and singers." (He was exaggerating.) These ads would eventually refer to hundreds of variety entertainers. I worked many times for him as a single act. When the Fun Fillys became popular, he would feature us. One flyer described us as "one of the most versatile comedy teams in showbiz." Another flyer had our picture on the front: "Sensational Comedy Duo…" I corresponded with Louie when Cindy and I booked with him, and he and I had a great time bantering back and forth, especially about the fee for the performance. One example in a letter from Louie:

Dear Pat,

> *Your letter was received and noted. I'll be at the Kane Moose Club until 2:30 a.m. If the door is closed, just ring the bell and come in. I'd love talking to you both, but if it's about the money, you can save your breath, as for two entertainers you're getting top money and more money than I pay for "any entertainers." You can either take my dates and the money I have to offer or leave them, as I have plenty of acts that want the dates for "less" money. Of course, these small details do not spoil my "love" for the both of you.*

Kindest regards,
Louie

P.S. At your first show at Wellsville, please be "on time."

We both loved Louie. We always worked the best dates he had and really believed he got the best money he could for us.

Excerpts from some early Fun Fillys scripts:

Patti: *Cindy, that fella over there is really cute…he's really got something!*

Cindy: *Yeah, and I hope he don't give it to me!*

Patti: *Cindy, I think you oughta give that fella a nice hand!*

        (I do believe we had a fake hand and would give it to the man.)

        This next one was a gem. We got more mileage out of it than anything!

Cindy: *Granpa was havin' awful trouble with the mice in the barn.*

Patti: *So what did he do?*

Cindy: *Well, he figured out a way to catch 'em. He put a barrel of apples in one part of the barn, and then, in another part of the barn he put a barrel of nuts.*

Patti: *Did he catch 'em?*

Cindy: *Yep!*

Patti: *Did he catch 'em by the apples?*

Cindy: *Nope!*

        (We would stop right there and get a big, long laugh.)

Patti: *Cindy, let's clean up this act!*

Cindy: *Okay! How about I sing the "Italian Street Walker" song?*

Patti: *WHAT?!*

Cindy: *Oh, I mean the "Italian Street" song. Hey, did you hear about the Italian streetwalker in Venice? She darn near drowned!*

Cindy would then do the song in her beautifully trained soprano voice. She would milk the next-to-last note for laughs. The last note would be pure and lovely. At this time we'd often close with the Everly Brothers hit tune, "Bye Bye Love." Before the second chorus, I would pause and say to Cindy, "Did you say he caught 'em by the apples?" Cindy would shake her head and say, "Nope!" This would produce another big laugh.

Cindy's mother was a sweet and lovely lady. When she heard about some of our jokes, she would ask Cindy if we were doing those "risky" jokes. (I believe she meant "risqué.") This next joke certainly falls into that category.

(Cindy begins acting like a little girl, squirming and fidgeting. I would react accordingly throughout.)

Cindy: *I came home from school one day, really cryin' and cryin'. My momma asked me what I was cryin' about. I told her Jimmy Jones pulled his pants down and was wiggling something. And he said to me, "Yeah, you don't have one of these." My momma told me what to do the next time he did that. So when I saw him the next time, I pulled my pants down and I wiggled and told him what my momma said: "With one of these, I can get all of those I want!"*

(I don't recall where this came from, but at the little clubs we worked, it would get a lot of laughs.)

I understand why some comics have a hard time cleaning up their act when a joke goes over so great. Eventually we would drop this joke, though. It slowly became a running gag between Cindy and me. During a show she would look at me with a gesture... "Should I?" I would either shake my head "No" or nod "Okay"!

We had great fun with an old song, "Sweet Violets." We would take turns with each line:

There once was a farmer who took a young miss
In back of the barn and he gave her a...
Lecture *on horses and chickens and eggs,*
And told her she had such beautiful...
Manners *that suited a girl of her charms,*
A girl that he wanted to take in his...
Washing *and ironing and then if she could,*
Have lots of children and raise lots of...
SWEET VIOLETS, sweeter than all the roses,
Covered all over from head to toe,
Covered all over with sweet violets.

The chorus got so much laughter, but we never really found out why. We suspected the farmer had other substances that were covered up. But this was really a country song, and we were city girls after all.

We would tell country-type gags after each chorus:

Cindy: *There was this beautiful cow over in a fenced pasture. A sturdy bull on the other side was dyin' to get over there. Finally, one day, he took a running leap...and didn't quite clear the fence.* (Cindy would feign a pained expression and with a deep voice say, *"How now brown cow?"*)

Patti: *There were four bulls out in the meadow talking. One bull says, "I'm sick of this pasture. I'm gonna go out and be a bull in a china shop!" The second bull says, "I'm leaving too. I'm gonna be a strong bull in the arena!" The third bull says, "I'm gettin' out of here too. I'm gonna be a Wall Street bull!" The fourth bull says, "I don't care what you guys do, but I'm gonna stay right here in the pasture...for heifer and heifer and heifer!"*

Cindy came up with a great ad-lib one night. We had a male heckler in the audience. The lady with him said, "Pay no attention to him. He's drinking, and he's a yo-yo!" Cindy says, "Oh! A drunken Duncan!" (Duncan made yo-yos, and still does today.)

WILLIAM PENN HOTEL

In 2008 the William Penn Hotel became the Omni William Penn. Throughout my career the William Penn Hotel has been a favorite place to do a show. The Urban Ballroom on the 17th floor is beautiful, and it had a unique balcony encompassing the room. The stage was about five feet high, enabling everyone in that large room to see the show. And yet there was an intimacy—especially with the balcony surrounding the room. It was fun bantering with the audience on the balcony: "Do we look short from up there?" Looking up at an act, a person looks taller.

Many famous people have stayed in this splendid, historic hotel. To name a few: rock stars Bruce Springsteen and Mick Jagger, singers Billy Joel and Liza Minnelli, and the Dalai Lama. Jerome Kern wrote songs for the great musical *Showboat* there. Lunt and Fontanne, the great legendary Broadway actors, were stranded at the hotel during the 1936 Pittsburgh flood. Lawrence Welk's bubble machine was invented there, and it is still on display in an office.

*Marty Faloon, Regina Peterson, and Adam DiGaspari
performing at the William Penn Hotel in the 1960s.*

The spectacular entertainer Liberace was a guest at the hotel, and the story goes he ordered a birthday cake at two o'clock in the morning. Recently comedian Jerry Seinfeld, former President and First Lady Bill and Hillary Clinton, President Barack Obama and former 2008 Republican nominee for president, John McCain, were guests. In 1922 the legendary Lillian Russell was an opening-night guest. She now has a "private room" in Pittsburgh's Allegheny Cemetery.

In this cemetery, there is a prominent circular plot known today as Mount Barney, named after Revolutionary War Comander Joshua Barney. On my mother's side, I am a distant descendant of Comander Barney. When I researched some history, I read that he was friends with George Washington and Benjamin Franklin. How neat is that!?

FUN FILLYS/NEW YORK

We were having so much success as a team that we decided to have some 8" x 10" glossy pictures made. After checking around we were told the best studio in New York was Bruno of Hollywood. I suppose this was a coast-to-coast operation. New York and California: the entertainment capitals of America. The tip was true: we had great photos taken.

One of the perks of the trip was getting to see *The Jack Paar Show*. One of Pittsburgh's great tenors, Ed Scotti, sang at Jack Paar's wedding. He arranged for us to call the bandleader, Jose Mellis, who had tickets for us at the door. A young Hugh Downs warmed up the audience.

With the help of our magician friend, Harry Albacker, we had brochures made. Harry was a whiz at hype advertising, and he had a printing press. He printed brochures for us. The front of the brochure featured headshots of us both: "For a Fun Show... THE FUN FILLYS... One of the most versatile comedy duos in showbiz today!" On the back of the brochure we had full body shots. Our names were printed inside stars, too! The back read: "FUN! Refreshing new talent." Those two theatrical masks—depicting one laughing and one crying face—were both laughing. Large lettering read: **SINGING DANCING STARS OF STAGE RADIO AND TV... TOPICAL WIT... ORIGINAL MATERIAL...** *Their hillbilly satire is hilarious!"* With the help of Harry, we poured it on. However, we really were doing great.

MORE FILLY FUN

The year 1960 was a happy one for the Fillys and for Pittsburgh. The Pittsburgh Pirates won the World Series with Bill Mazeroski's memorable hit for a home-run in the ninth inning of the game, defeating the New York Yankees.

The Fun Fillys did the Kennywood Amusement Park employees' show for a couple of years. It was the "end of the season" show. I used the same opening gag each time, and it got a huge laugh. The line was: "I never saw so many happy people out of work!"

I realize I was the "leader" or "creator" of this duo. I got Cindy to dye her light brown hair to blonde. She had a beautiful, thick head of hair. She would often come to the shows in a casual housedress. I asked her to buy an up-to-date dress. Very often we didn't work stages that had a back entrance to a dressing room. I told her we were ON as soon as we entered a club. The neat thing was, we could wear the same dressy dress to almost every job. Most of our jobs were "gigs," also known as "one-nighters."

GREEN-EYED MONSTER

At an engagement in Jamestown, New York, my body was invaded by an ugly feeling: jealousy. The last part of that word is "lousy," and that is exactly the way this feeling makes its effects known. This engagement in New York was another "back by popular demand" show. The house was overflowing. The show went great. The dressing room we had was upstairs. Outside the room was a balcony-type landing. After the show Cindy and I lingered over the banister as the people exited the building (with their backs to us, so they didn't see us). At first it was fun. We were hearing 100 percent positive comments about the show. Did I say positive? I meant raves!

But then it occurred to me that most of the praise was for Cindy. "The blonde was so funny, wasn't she?" Looking back on my entire career and all the multi-talented acts I have worked with, I realized this was the first time I had experienced jealousy. At the moment I didn't give myself any credit for having created most of the material in our

202 • PITTSBURGH PIZZAZZ

act. As the "straight man," I would give all the punch lines to Cindy...the comic! Fortunately for me, as Cindy was lauded, one lady said, "Well, she doesn't give the other a chance!" That helped my feelings...for a little while.

A few weeks later we did a show for an elite Pittsburgh agent. He helped put it in perspective for me. He bawled Cindy out for upstaging me. For example, when I would be doing a "bit," Cindy would be behind me, still "on" with funny expressions and gestures. It is well known in showbiz that many comics have a hard time quieting down once they're on a roll. Cindy did listen to the agent.

That one time in Jamestown was the one and only time I would ever let jealousy interfere with my joy in performing.

BALLOON "BABY" FOR REAL

As a team we had this fantastic beginning due to "Pappy." Then Cindy discovered the balloon for the pregnant hillbilly bit would soon be the real thing. She was expecting. We were able to continue performing for a while as a team. Fortunately for me, even when we were performing our team jobs, I continued to do other shows solo. There were still many clubs operating floorshows.

Within a month of the baby's birth, we were doing jobs again in some of the finest clubs. Our reputation was sizzling. Johnny Guilfoyle, an agent, knew the agent for the great comic Red Skelton. Because Johnny was raving about our act, Skelton's agent wanted to book us right away. We were stunned when Johnny told us the percentage on the dates: 20/80. We said, "No way!" Johnny tried to tell us we'd be making tremendous money. We still said, "No!"

This is the script from a radio interview with a fella named Buzz. As the Fun Fillys we played up the hillbilly bit:

Buzz: *Have you had a lot of funny, interesting, amusing happenings happen to you during your partnership?*

Pat: *Many, Buzz. For instance, a new costume I was wearing one night had a lot of feathers on it. During the act I slipped a baggy dress over the top of the feathered costume, and in doing this I loosened up a lot of feathers.*

Cindy: *It looked like moltin' season. Feathers were flyin' everywhere. We really tickled the audience that night. Another time I needed a hat pin to break a balloon. Well, I couldn't find it anywhere. I'm saying to Pat, "The hat pin, the hat pin?!"*

Pat: *I remembered I had one holding up my baggy dress and gave it to Cindy. Then I had to finish the act holding the dress up with my teeth.*

Cindy: *Pat plays the guitar, you know. She needs both hands.*

Pat: *We had so many gimmicks and props. Cindy, remember the night we did the bit when I put a handful of beans in my mouth, and then, when you slapped me on the back, all the beans came out of my mouth...like losing all my teeth? And*

> *then one night I didn't load my pocket*
> *with the beans. I did find one bean.*
> *When you hit me on the back, the one*
> *bean came out…The look on your face*
> *was a riot!*

Cindy: *I thought she had swallowed the rest of*
them. I figured I'd be hearing from her as
soon as they digested!

We continued to have great success as a team. The creative juices flowed. The cutest and zaniest ideas flew. We were in our prime. At age thirty-one we had a lot of energy. Certainly our physical attributes gave us an added advantage. On our many road trips we talked and laughed constantly. In the wee hours of the morning, we would still be carrying on, entertaining each other. In later years we learned that a neighbor thought we were drinking all the time. Neither one of us drank.

The *Pittsburgh Post-Gazette* reported in an article entitled "Parkway Pickup Show Sleuth" (April 1961): "A fella wanted to engage the Fun Fillys to perform at a bowling banquet but couldn't locate them. So he got a friend, McKeesport detective Olin Bell, to track them down. He did, and the girls are all set for the banquet next month."

CAMELOT

· ·

During the Camelot days of the Kennedy Administration, our nation was feeling upbeat and energized. One of our zany bits included impressions of the leader of the Soviet Union during the Cold War—Nikita Khruschev—and the First Lady of the United States, Jackie Kennedy.

On October 12, 1960, Khrushchev disrupted a UN General Assembly session with an impromptu "gavel." He pounded his desk with his shoe when a speaker criticized his country.

I wrote a parody to the tune of "Tiptoe Through the Tulips" and called it "Tiptoe Through the White House." We had a musical arrangement made. I played Jackie Kennedy giving Khrushchev a tour of the White House. As I've written before, Cindy was game for anything. She actually donned a bald wig and wore combat boots. Cindy had a mother-in-law who only spoke Polish, so she learned the Polish accent quite well. She would take off one of the combat shoes and bang it on the floor, loudly complaining in that accent.

After Cindy's bit, I would speak in the soft, gentle voice of Jackie to calm Khruschev down as I interviewed him:

Jackie:	*How do you feel about the United States?*
Khruschev:	(Sputtering undecipherable Polish dialect; with hand gestures showing a vehement "thumbs down.")
Jackie:	*How is the Russian morale?*
Khruschev:	(Sputtering more Polish dialect; with hand gestures indicating a "thumbs up.")
Jackie:	*Actually, how do you feel about world peace?*
Khruschev:	(More dialect; Cindy would thumb her nose like a boxer getting ready for a fight. There were huge laughs at each line.)
Jackie:	*Do you think America can catch up to you in the space rocket field?*
Khruschev:	(Cindy puts her thumb out like a hitchhiker.)
Jackie:	*What is your opinion of the American man?*
Khruschev:	(Cindy sucks her thumb.)
Jackie:	*What do you think your comrades have lined up for you in the future?*

Khruschev: (Cindy draws her thumb across her neck, as in cutting with a knife.)

We would close this bit with the musical arrangement of "Tiptoe Through the White House...with me"! It went over great. It was hip and "right on" with the times. We were always updating our material to keep it current.

The *Pittsburgh Post-Gazette* reported, "Pat said 'if Khruschev ever returned to Pittsburgh and stopped there, he'd have to pay cash because it was the Conrad Hilton, not the Comrade Hilton.'"

We did a banquet show with a man who had a daily TV show in Pittsburgh. It was *The John Reed King Show*. He asked us to perform on his show. We did the show with our comedy bits. It was so awkward with the camera in our faces and the live audience way, way off to the side of the stage. We couldn't see or hear the reaction, which is crucial in comedy. It throws the timing off when the laugh doesn't follow the expected response. I thought we had bombed! I felt so embarrassed. We were offered the tape of our performance. I refused. To this day I regret that I refused it. We were able to see it later that day. I went to watch it with my mom and dad and was amazed to hear the laughs (not canned) we were getting. There were microphones for the TV audience, but we sure couldn't hear the laughs while we were performing. We did get a couple of jobs out of doing the show.

Before we did the show I heard that Phyllis Diller was going to be on the show the following day. I asked John Reed if he would give her my telephone number. I wanted to write some material for her. She did call me the next day and explained what she did and didn't like. She made it clear: "No puns!" Puns do get moans; I avoid them myself. For a couple of years she bought some of my ideas.

AMUSING, EMBARRASSING

We were booked for two shows in a beautiful nightclub in McKeesport, PA. Over the years it had several names. At one time it was known as the White Elephant. It had an expansive, elevated dance floor and a big orchestra. A wedding group had booked the entire room for the reception. After the first show the dance floor was lined with a long row of tables with every kind of delectable food one could imagine. There was a little table in front of the stage off to the side where the band and acts could sit between shows.

One of the musicians said to Cindy and me, "They invited you to get a plate and enjoy some of those goodies!" We said, "Yum! Yum!" Our first show had gone over very well and we were feeling confident and "hammy," so we weren't very quiet about filling our plates. "Oh, does that look good! Yummmmmmm, how about those goodies over there?" We were acting like a couple of clowns. We filled our plates and went back to our table.

After we had taken a couple of bites, a man came up to us and said, "Excuse me, but did we invite you to partake of our food?" Too bad for us that we had already swallowed, because the food stuck in the back of our throats. We apologized and mumbled that a musician had said we were invited. The smirk on the musician's face turned to remorse as he observed what he had put us through. The best thing to come out of this experience was that we would never do *that* again. We would always double-check!

On one of our out-of-town jobs, we arrived too early. There was this big stage with leftover hors-d'oeuvres. In the middle of the table was a huge punchbowl. It was almost empty, but there was lots of yummy, plump fruit—juicy pineapple, cherries, and more—on the bottom of the bowl. There was no one in the room. This would all be cleared away for the show. We both plucked some of the fruit out of the bowl and ate it. Cindy helped herself over and over again. Suddenly I looked at her, and she seemed a bit tipsy. Apparently the fruit had absorbed the booze in the punchbowl. I found a side door with a fire escape so we both could get some fresh air. We stood out there for quite a while. It was chilly, which helped. The circumstances of us arriving so early helped as there was time to recover, and we could do our show. That fruit punch definitely had a "punch"!

Showgirls aren't any different from other girls. Guys never asked if they could buy a girl something to eat. It was always, "Can I buy you a drink?" I would work with some performers who couldn't go on without a stiff drink. I always thought that if I needed a drink to perform, then I didn't love the business as much as I thought I did. Yes, there were times I was nervous, but as soon as I hit the floor the feeling disappeared.

We did many shows at the Churchill Country Club. One time the band was set up in an unusual arrangement across the dance floor; we did our show facing them from across the room. Usually we would say a band "backed" us up. This was the first time a band "fronted" us up! Ummm, that doesn't sound right, does it? On this particular job Marty was in the band. Near the end of the show I asked the audience to applaud the *great* band. Then I commented, "That guitar player is so cute. I haven't been able to take my eyes off him!" I strode across the floor, stepped up on the platform, and gave him a big kiss. It startled everyone, including Marty. Once we let the audience know we were married, there was a lot of laughter and applause. Another happily-ever-after moment.

The Horizon Room was built as an extension of the old Pittsburgh airport. One of the most memorable shows we did at the Horizon Room was a reception for a huge wedding. Everything was too, too much. For example, the cake was five feet tall. An ice sculpture was about the same height. There was continuous entertainment: three different style bands! Cindy and I were part of a list of entertainers. The bride was young and beautiful; the groom was not. (We thought the groom was her father!) The guests were dressed in fabulous finery. The wedding must have cost thousands of dollars. Today that would be a couple of million. There were happy faces everywhere except for the bride's (I believe it was one of those pre-arranged weddings).

Comediennes Phyllis Diller and Joan Rivers had worked this room. My sister, Corinne, and her husband, Charlie, once treated me to an evening in this lovely room. It was just the three of us. The star performer was Al Martino. What a wonderful singing voice he had! As singers often do, he circled the room, singing mainly to the ladies. He lingered quite a bit at our front table, singing mainly to me! After the show as we were leaving, he approached us. He was a perfect gentleman as he made his pass at me. Probably wanted to buy me a drink? I was getting a kick out of it because beyond his shoulder I could see the very large orchestra and most of the musicians were friends of Marty. They were watching intently. I told Martino how much we enjoyed his show, and we left.

FILLY FINISH

The Fun Fillys were enjoying working with annual conventions. The West Virginia "25" Club in Charleston, West Virginia, booked us at the Daniel Boone Hotel. It was considered a top hotel in that area. The hotel had 465 rooms, was fully air conditioned (this was a big plus in the 1960s), and had a large ballroom for entertainment. It was fun being on shows with a full orchestra and a variety of acts.

Cindy and I became keenly interested in the entourage that came in with two very pretty and very young female dancers. These girls were treated like divas. They were accompanied by their agent, hair-and-makeup girl, and more. Their costumes were fabulous. Their musicial arrangements were marvelous. With all this showy display we thought we were about to see a terrific dance team. We were so disappointed! The girls went over just okay. Cindy and I watched their amateurish routine for a few minutes and looked at each other in bewilderment. Here we had been thinking we had some competition from these young, pampered "chicks"! As the saying goes, "You can't judge a book by its cover."

Moose club members were very fond of Mooseheart, a safe haven for needy kids. The Fun Fillys did a super show for this group. After the show they begged us to do another show and said they would pay us a hundred dollars. We did the show and donated the money to Mooseheart. Wow, they really loved us now! It was a great feeling!

We were constantly improving as we were doing coveted shows in the Tri-State area. One of the biggest perks of all this was that the money we were making enabled us to get things for our children. We both truly adored our children. Possibly being so happy on the gigs made us happy mothers too.

And yet, in the very near future the Fun Fillys would be headed for the finish line!

FALLON & DUNN

The Fun Fillys did their first show for the agent Ed Schaughnecy at the veterans' hospital in Butler, PA. It was a lovely summer day, and the audience filled the outdoor area, even sitting on the hillside. The agency sent one of its top men, Lowell Smith, to review our act. After the show Lowell said to us, "I was rolling over with laughter! You two are a riot! Come into the office Monday, and we will have a lot of work for you!" Cindy and I were thrilled.

We went into the office on Monday. Once again Lowell praised our performance. He talked about the "great" money we would make with his agency. He said he would be in touch with us. We left the office walking on air.

About two weeks passed, though, without getting a phone call. We made an appointment to see Lowell again. It was at this meeting that our eyes were opened. He said our comedy was too broad and slapstick. He said even the name of the act—The Fun Fillys—was too corny. Even though Lowell saw how well we went over with the audience (including himself), there were too many reasons why we would not be suited to work his "sophisticated" spots (even though we had been booked in top places like the Ankara and the Hilton Hotel).

His criticism hurt at the time, but he ultimately did us a great favor. We began working earnestly toward changing our image, and we started with our title: we would now become known as Fallon & Dunn. The transition began in April 1966 in an ad for a show at the Redwood Ballroom: "Fallon & Dunn—the Fun Fillys." We had built a great following, and this ad would remind our fans who we were now. We slowly cleaned up our material. If anything was risqué, it had to be very clever. We got new wardrobe, discarding the hillbilly gear. Everything else was intact: our enthusiasm, our friendly rapport, and the fun we had with our audiences.

I often thought that if we had lived in the South, things might have been different. What comes to mind is the Grand Ole Opry. We could have been the Fun Fillys forever. Country fans are loyal for a lifetime.

The East and West Coast showbiz respect for country music has come a long way since the 1960s. I myself was a big fan of some of the country stars of the day: Eddie Arnold, Tammy Wynette, Chet Atkins, and Roger Miller. I loved Roger Miller with his wonderfully peppy and zany songs. I've sung "King of the Road" many times.

Both of us had appeared as solo acts at Pat McBride's nightclub many times. It always had an active and full house with a good band. One night after appearing as

Fallon & Dunn, a man wanted to give us a hundred dollars. We didn't want to accept it. The owner of the club and his family—some were waitresses and bartenders—told us that this was an eccentric, wealthy man. When he liked an act, he wanted to tip the performers. So we accepted the money. We thanked the man and told him the next time he saw us we each would have a new outfit. The money enabled us to buy two glamorous dresses adorned with sparkling solid-gold sequins and matching "shoestring" shoulder straps. We were really getting fancy!

A couple of times we were stalked by fans. Several times we would have a car tailing us for a while. It would be very late, meaning that it was very early in the morning, like 3 or 4 a.m. One time, as we were being followed into a small town, I desperately tried to find a police station... anything! The town was stone dead. At least the car following us gave up. We found an answer to our problem in a mail-order catalog: an inflatable man! We would place the fake man in between the two of us on the front seat and put a hat on his head. It worked. We were never bothered again. The two of us couldn't resist having fun with this new prop. Sometimes we'd be at a red light and do a Jerry Springer bit for the car behind us. One of us would whack the dummy with the back of our hand. It would wobble back and forth. We'd enjoy the reactions of the people in the car behind us seeing our behavior. The dummy would react with each movement.

One time as we pulled into the parking lot of a club where we were doing a show, we could see a parking lot attendant heading toward us. We both started beating up the dummy. The poor valet didn't know where to look or what to do. Casting his eyes downward, he continued walking toward us to do his job. I surely do love action-reaction! We were trying to keep from laughing as we unloaded the car. We could only imagine what he thought when he realized the guy was a dummy!

As Fallon & Dunn we had a devastating experience on a job for the agent Louis Angelo. Louie was a lovable hustler of an agent. He was husky, and his left arm was amputated from the elbow up. I never thought to ask him how it had happened. We would watch him in amazement at what he could do so effortlessly. He typed all of his own letters. He would take a wad of money, put it under his "half" armpit, then peel off one's pay. Here I'm about to talk about a devastating experience and Louie handled his disability with courage and gusto.

Louie booked us in a town called Kersey, PA. The booking was in a roadhouse club called the Towne House. Our dressing room was a bedroom. Past the dressing room was a small hallway leading to the bar and then the floorshow area and bandstand. Before the show we gathered our props and took the guitar off its stand and placed everything in front of the bandstand. We sat in costume in our bedroom/dressing room, talking and laughing. My guitar case was lying open on the floor. Cindy playfully tipped the guitar case lid with her foot, and it closed. At the end of the show we took our bows and left the stage. Back in the dressing room I lay the guitar on the bed instead of putting it away in the case. We both went back to gather the props. We did all of this very quickly. When we were packed and ready to leave, Cindy walked over to the guitar case, which was closed, and locked it, thinking I had put my guitar inside it. She carried it out to the car, not noticing how light it felt. When she dropped me off at my house, I carried the guitar and amplifier into my house, sensing that something was wrong—the guitar case was too light. Much to my dismay, when I opened the case, all I saw was the pink lining. I was heartsick.

The *Pittsburgh Post-Gazette* reported on September 6, 1963, in the "Pittsburghese" column: "That twister at St. Mary's reminds Entertainer Pat Fallon (formerly Pat Eberle) that she hasn't heard anything of her missing guitar, valued at three hundred dollars. It disappeared while she was performing in Kersey nearby, about a week before the big wind..."

I placed an ad in the local paper: "Pittsburgh entertainer, who lost her valuable guitar when playing a recent engagement in Kersey, is appealing to the person who stole same to examine his conscience and get in touch with her at Pittsburgh 16, Penna. She says no charges will be pressed." Cindy and I took a ride up to Kersey. We talked to the police and to a couple who had been at the club that night. The couple remembered seeing a young fella come from the wooded area behind the club with a guitar in his hand.

That guitar was my first Martin D 18, and I would never see it again. My homeowners insurance covered the loss so I was able to buy another used Martin D 18 in very fine condition. It's the same guitar I still play. I've been offered up to fifteen hundred dollars for this guitar, but I've not parted with it.

That guitar was very important in our act. To explain why, here is a short story: We were working a Moose club in Erie. It had a lovely little stage only about two to three feet high. The spotlight was so bright that there was total blackness in front of us. We never cared for this because we liked to see the audience. Somewhere in the routine I stepped forward—right off the stage. I landed on my back with the guitar safely above my head. I immediately got back up on the stage. This time I wasn't even dancing on a slippery floor. In fact, gradually in this act I eliminated my tap dancing. There would always be some form of dancing, though, in my long, long, long career as an entertainer.

In the 1960's these mini skirts (in hot pink) were "with it!"
(How about the boots!)

A TOUGH ACT TO FOLLOW

The transition of the Fun Fillys to Fallon & Dunn proved to be a smart move. We would return to New York and once again have the great photographer, Bruno of Hollywood, do our photos. As usual, he did an excellent job.

We kept our comedy fresh with new ideas flowing. There was a hit tune at the time by the rock band Blood, Sweat and Tears called "Spinning Wheel." We had a terrific arrangement made for our opening song. "What goes up…must come down. Talk about your troubles. It's a cryin' sin. Catch a painted pony, let that spinning wheel spin…" Unlike many performers who would use the same opening song for years, we always tried to open with the hit songs of the moment.

We'd ask for a male volunteer from the audience to come on stage. He would sit in a chair facing the audience. I would stand beside him and sing, "Oh, I think I'm goin' out of my head…" Cindy would stand behind the man. As I sang the song, she would mess up his hair, fondle his face, and even untie his tie. She would unbutton his shirt and pretend to pull a hair from his chest. At the bridge—the middle of the song—she would move around from the back, sit on his lap for a couple of seconds, and then let out a scream as she jumped up. The reaction from the audience was fantastic. We brought the house down!

We got a booking for a week at the famous Holiday House in Monroeville, PA. We were set to open the show. The closing act was Allen Drake, a fine comedian. When we opened the show the first night, we included the "Going Out of My Head" number, receiving the usual uproarious response from the audience. Allen Drake, the star, had the management cut the number from our act because the number was a hard act to follow, especially for this comedian who wanted to get the biggest laughs. We felt bad, but we were flattered at the same time.

Quite a few years ago a similar situation happened in Las Vegas. The Carpenters, a brother and sister duo, were the starring musical act, and singer Neil Sedaka was to open the show. Neil Sedaka is a super-duper showman. He wowed the audience, so he was a hard act to follow. The Carpenters had him cancelled from the show. I can't blame them. If an act is booked as the "star" and probably making a lot more money than the opening act, it would be uncomfortable to follow a sensation like Sedaka. I think the incident boosted Sedaka's popularity tremendously.

Our "Going Out of My Head" number was so successful that an excellent girl singer who was at the performance came up to us afterwards to ask questions about it. For instance, she wondered if we weren't afraid a man might get fresh with us. "Oh, no!" said Cindy. "I stand

behind him and am in complete control of the situation."
Not too long after this we caught a show at the Holiday
House and the same girl singer was doing *our* routine to
a different song. We were stunned. It went over well, but
she didn't get close to the response we would get.

At a different show later on, we ran into the same girl
singer. It was a big show with lots of acts in the William
Penn Hotel ballroom. I've written before how we loved
doing shows in this beautiful room with the wonderful
PA system. We had the coveted closing spot, and were to
follow this girl singer! Knowing she had been doing the
"man in the chair" bit, we refused to follow her. We didn't
say why. We didn't want to squeal on her for "lifting" (an
expression used when an act "steals" a part of someone
else's act) our material. Too bad she didn't say, "I won't
do the bit I stole from you!" Too bad we were so stubborn, for our act was strong enough without this number.
Cindy and I would never copy from another local act. It
just didn't make sense, since we were working the same
jobs in the same territory.

When Cindy and I were in our heyday, there were
several acts in the Pittsburgh area considered to be tops
in the field. One such comedian we worked many dates
with suddenly didn't want to follow our act. So we were
eliminated. He was used to being the closing act "star."
One night Cindy and I did an early banquet show. When
this would happen, we would try to find a late live show to
take in afterwards. There were still many clubs and private
clubs operating. This night we stopped at the Elks club
on the North Side. We caught the last half of the afore-
mentioned comedian. He did at least three or four of our

gags. He didn't see us during the performance. After the show we coolly went downstairs to wait for him. He must have been socializing. We waited…and waited… and then left, but not before leaving a note that said, "Great show… especially liked some of your gags!" We signed it Fallon & Dunn. Early the next morning Cindy got a phone call from him. He asked, "How much of the show did you see? When did you come in?" She just let him worry and wonder. It did prove one thing: we knew how to choose good material.

There was another show where a pretty, blonde, large-busted singer asked us if she could use one of our gags to open the show. We said no. Apparently she had been using it already…and continued to use it on her shows. This particular singer would bring a man up from the audience and sing to him. She would be wearing a long evening gown with a very, very low-cut front. Cleavage? Yes! Lots! During the song she would put her hands gently around the fella's neck and pull his face into…you got it…her bosom! It got her some good laughs, but this bit alone crossed the line. Like The Fun Fillys' pregnant hillbilly bit, it would prevent her from working the better spots.

PERFECT PARTNERS

The year 1963 saw the birth of Beatlemania and the death our president, John F. Kennedy. It would also be The Year for Fallon & Dunn.

A good partnership is much like a good marriage. "In sickness and in health" I used to think that "The show must go on" cliché was presumptuous, but then I realized that even for big fish in a little pond like Pittsburgh, it presented a responsibility. For many dates that Fallon & Dunn were booked on, we were the main attraction.

People who booked entertainment for their special events—whether a once-a-year festivity or a once-in-a-lifetime event—would plan it well in advance. They would choose the entertainment they wanted and they would count on the entertainment to fulfill the obligation. Cindy's and my reputation for being counted on was important to us. I believe that having this ethic has allowed me to endure so long. And certainly, through the grace of God, my good health has permitted this as well.

Cindy certainly lived up to our commitment. On the way to a job in the Somerset area ski resort at Seven Springs, we got lost. (We got lost frequently!) It was a cold and wintry night. I pulled into a restaurant parking lot. Cindy got out of the car and walked briskly across a wooden entry. It was very slippery, and she lost her footing. She thought she had turned her ankle. Even so, she got the directions we needed, and we arrived at our destination and did our show. With so much pain in her ankle, she didn't get much sleep that night. In the morning she went to the hospital. She had a broken foot. This was the holiday season and we had many dates booked. Yet we fulfilled all of our engagements. I would open the show with a couple of tunes. Then I would introduce Cindy, saying, "I'm so mad at Cindy! Not only did she go horseback riding, but she insisted on attempting a stunt!" Cindy would come out with a cast up to her knee that allowed her to limp onto the stage. We carried a stool she could rest on. Our shows went over as well as ever. Maybe you've heard the expression "Break a leg!" that performers use, meaning "Have a great show!" Cindy's version was "Break a foot!"

Ad-libs were the perks on any show. We were booked into a huge Shriners auditorium in Philadelphia. Fortunately the PA system was super. On one of our bits I had a man from the audience at the microphone. Cindy would stand behind him, rolling up his pant legs and dressing him in a hula skirt. The man muttered into the microphone, "Oh, I'm gonna get it!" Right back to him I said, "No, you're not!" It stopped the show! The banter was not planned but was soooooo much fun.

Then there was the eccentric and influential Pittsburgh agent who really got interested in our act. His name was Syd Marke and he had been in vaudeville. He had great connections in the showbiz world. I don't remember him ever having an office. Syd wanted to be our "personal" agent. He insisted the act be totally clean. This criterion was not a good idea when he booked us for a show on March 29, 1963. It was a tremendously big show at the Royal York Hotel in Toronto. The ballroom was huge, and we had an all-male audience. There were lots of acts on the bill. Most of these acts used such risqué material that they made any of our own risqué material seem pure. By keeping the show clean, we went over well, but not great.

BOOTS

In 1957 I was fortunate to be able to attend one of the first banquets with a group of Pittsburgh female entertainers who called themselves "BOOTS: BEST OF THE OLD-TIMERS." Many of these women were my role models. I was at least ten years younger than most of them. The rule was, you were supposed to be in show business for at least twenty years to be a member; I had only ten years under my belt.

The group was started by Eva Herbert, singer and mistress of ceremonies, and Mable Harold, a very good tap dancer. I got a free pass into this club because of the close friendship I had with Eva. BOOTS was comprised of a wonderful variety of entertainers: singers, dancers of all types, comediennes, and novelty acts.

In the beginning the annual banquet was held at a local nightclub spot that featured a live show with a very appreciative audience. Eventually, when the nightclub scene faded, the BOOTS would "be" the show. Several singers would sing the same song every year—their signature song. Yes, there were some acts that would arouse some pity, but the BOOTS group was always kind and polite to anyone who wanted to perform on our special night.

Eva Herbert's signature song, "It's Better Than Taking in Washing," was always expected and appreciated. She got lots of laughter with this number. One of the most beautiful sounds is laughter with applause. It's almost like food—nourishment for the soul. Eva was more than twenty-five years older than me. She eventually retired to Florida and lived to be a hundred years old. So you see, the nourishment was good for her.

The old-timers would say that rock and roll and the labor unions were the reasons the variety shows died. According to agent George Claire, "The requirements of the unions drove costs beyond the reach of show places that hired the big names and their orchestras. The headliners priced themselves out of the club market." He booked the Stanley Theater (now the Benedum). "When I booked a big-name band at the theater, they had to pay the same number of local musicians as standbys," he added.

Lenny Litman, who owned the Copa Club, had all the top stars of the day working his club. (I once sat in this wonderful, intimate club just ten feet away from legendary entertainer Frankie Laine and a very young American pop singer, Andy Williams.) Lenny said, "The good local acts always got work, and many were good enough to make it big. These acts—what they call 'fillers'—were very important to the local clubs. If it hadn't been for them, we would have had to bring in acts from New York."

After a few years male entertainers found a way to be part of the BOOTS. It was good: more variety! We now had magicians, more comics, and more fun! "Once you got it, you got it!" It's an old expression, but definitely true with many of these entertainers. Many had been retired for years, but when they got up to do their "thing," it was still there—that charisma, that sparkle!

Always for the finale of these shows was the "Shim Sham" dance. I would stand in the back line following the swingin' old pros in spontaneous rhythm. The energetic kicking and the shoulder shaking in this snappy routine was always the hit of the show. The once-young beauties never lost their flair in this sexy, swinging-style dance.

One year a lovely former dancer and dancing school owner came to a tragic end after the Shim Sham. Ruth Stevenson had a figure that was as perfect now as it was in her youth. She wore a stunning, knee-length, red dress and matching red patent-leather shoes. She had just finished the closing line-dance number triumphantly and was returning to her seat when she had a heart attack. The hospital was only blocks away, and the ambulance came quickly. However, her death was instantaneous. I've never been able to erase from my mind the picture of one of her shiny red shoes lying by the exit of this club. It reminded me of Dorothy's in *The Wizard of Oz*.

One year I wrote a parody to "These Boots Are Made for Walkin'"—a big hit for singer Nancy Sinatra.

> *Come and meet the BOOTS, we're all good lookin',*
> *Always keep in shape, that's our style.*
> *Others may give up, but they're all chicken,*

While we're kickin', we'll be livin' wow!

Chorus:

These BOOTS are made for movin' ...and that's just what we'll do!
Movin' here, movin' there, movin' everywhere!

We've worked all the joints and the high spots,
Any place they send us, we will go,
Moose, Elk, Dave and Jake's, the Blue Ridge,
Liberty Café on with the show!

Chorus:

These BOOTS are made for swingin' ...and that's just what we'll do!
Swingin' here, swingin' there, swingin' everywhere!

Just get on the phone, call up an agent:
Lanagan, King, Carr, or Finnerty.
Don D'Carlo for a dashing quickie.
Kury, Georgie, Marge, or Ann Harvey.
These BOOTS are made for livin'.
That's always been our style.
So all of you BOOTS you stand up
And BOOTS, you take a bow!"

In later years, Arden from the Silver Cyclones skating team and I kept BOOTS going. Eventually I was the only one left, the young one who got invited to the first BOOTS banquet and who got to see it to the end.

Over the years I had been able to get great newspaper and TV coverage for some of the banquets. So, as the BOOTS neared its finish, I sent a letter to a very popular TV show in Pittsburgh, *KDKA*, which often featured stories on newsworthy events. I was hoping they would do a story on the twenty-eighth annual banquet of the BOOTS, held at the North Side Elks Club. Most of the BOOTS members had worked this club, which was centrally located. At that time there was a weekly banjo club successfully performing there.

In my letter to KDKA-TV, I explained that there would be entertainers coming from all parts of the country who had played Pittsburgh on a regular basis. Some of them had worked on bills with stars such as Eddie Fisher, Edie Adams, the Andrew Sisters, Tennessee Ernie Ford, and Frankie Avalon. I wrote: "In the spotlight once again, many will do their 'thing' on this great nostalgic evening. It would be great if you could come and capture this sparkling evening!" They came and did a wonderful story about the banquet.

Columnist Joe Brown of the *Pittsburgh Post-Gazette* covered the event: "Menu magic. Invitations for the 28th annual banquet of the BOOTS club, an entertainer outfit, carried a dinner choice of stuffed chicken breast or roast beef. Harry Albacker, the magician, wrote in, 'Stuffed rabbit.' Served on a silver platter for him was a beat-up, stuffed toy rabbit, covered with gravy. Sandy Doren and Patty Eberle talked Shirley Bell into 'turning the tables' on Harry."

At one of our BOOTS affairs I asked the entertainers to relate some funny stories to me, and did they ever! During my performances that year, I would share their stories with the audience.

Anne Kelly talked about a fire-baton act that dropped oil all over the stage one night. Anne ended up doing her cancan dance on her "can"! Her treasured memory was meeting and talking with George M. Cohan, the famous American entertainer, playwright, composer, lyricist, actor, singer, dancer, and producer. He was considered the father of American musical comedy. His many popular songs included "Over There," "Give My Regards to Broadway," and "Yankee Doodle Boy."

Jerry Newman was a comic who later became a successful chiropractor. He once worked the Soldiers and Sailors Hall in the Oakland section of Pittsburgh, and got fired for using the word "pregnant" in his routine!

Marilyn Takos worked with Dick Powell and Ted Lewis. Powell was a singer, actor producer, director, and studio boss, while Ted was an entertainer, bandleader, singer, and musician. A beauty at the age of five, Takos was known as "Baby Cannon." At a New Year's Eve celebration at the Syria Mosque, she was placed on a pendulum that hung from a clock. She wore a white satin diaper. They swung her up to the rafters. She began to cry and was so frightened that she might well have needed the diaper! Marilyn was a professional by the age of six. When she was twelve, she traveled with a kiddy chorus.

Kitty O'Neill was another child act. Both Kitty and Marilyn remembered working with some really old-timers like zany comic Joe Penner, who was known for his catch-phrase, "Wanna buy a duck?"

Blizz & Burke were comics who mimicked musical records. The boys worked a pedal to start and stop a tape machine. On a show when the MC announced the first act, a dancer accidentally stepped on the pedal. That night she did her Hawaiian dance to "Cigarettes and Whiskey and Wild, Wild Women"!

The **Silver Cyclones**, Ethel and Arden, were a roller-skating team. One night, just before their act was introduced, Ethel reached down to straighten her short skirt and realized to her horror that she had forgotten to put on her panties! Her husband yelled to Dick Ware, the MC, to do another newsreel. (A movie reel typically alternated with a live act in vaudeville shows.) Ethel dashed to the dressing room and put her panties on, pulling them up over her roller skates. My reaction: "Ethel, take a bow!"

In 1983 the *Pittsburgh Press* gave the BOOTS a full write-up with big pictures. The heading: "FOR ONE NIGHT, THE OLD STARS ARE SHINING!" Because I started out so young with this group, I was one of the few still doing shows. At the time of this news piece, I was fifty-four years old. The average group member was in her seventies. Excerpts from the newspaper article follow:

> Show biz is in their blood. They know all about the ol' razzmatazz, about timing, and how to tell a joke, sell a song. There's a bond, a joy about being together.... Texas Tony Garland is still working. He opens for Bobby Vinton. Garland: 'I started out as a kid, ten years old,

impersonating Donald Duck. Then I worked as a standup comic with the strippers. Years ago there were 124 places you could work around Pittsburgh without repeating yourself. All the big clubs are gone. There's no showcase anymore.'

Francisco Soriano, MC for the evening, is up from Tennessee and dressed in nightclub-white tuxedo. A song-and-dance man for more than fifty years, Soriano worked with Sammy Davis Jr., Frank Sinatra, and Dean Martin. Says Soriano: 'I knew how to handle an audience. You have to sell yourself. I don't care how great you are, you've got to have personality. I learned early if you got class, you can work with class. There's nothing like it!'

Anne Kelly, a veritable youngster among the old-timers, said, "I danced on Broadway in the 1960s and retired in 1972. You're an artist. You use your body, your voice, your talent, you create. It's total satisfaction.'
And there are others besides performers. A crusty old agent in baggy pants is lamenting, 'I'm not good for much anymore. I had a thousand strippers working for me, and at least 250 of them...' 'Quit yer braggin,' cracks Peg Lanagan, another talent agent.

Tony Baldwin, singing in the midst of a Vegas-type act, is dedicating Sinatra's 'My Way' to all the BOOTS members who have passed away. More than a few eyes are misty and quite a few mouth the words. 'It's a shame,' says Peg Lanagan as Baldwin wraps up. 'Such a good voice, and no place to go.'

There's a little lady sitting near the back of the hall, working heart and soul with each and every act. 'I love it, I get carried away,' admits Helen Mangold. 'In every act, we see something of ourselves.' She was a dancer in her day: tap, gypsy, Indian. She studied to be a ballerina, starting lessons when she was eleven. When she started working in the old Flotilla Club—a floating nightclub on the river down at the end of the Sixth Street Bridge—she was just fifteen, but lied and said she was eighteen. 'The school authorities yanked me out, but I was having a ball.' She traveled all over the country as captain of the Rockettes, as in 'Olive and Amdur and the Rockettes,' a troupe that had its heyday in the 1930s. She quit dancing when she was twenty-eight. 'Wound up a hairdresser,' she says. She's seventy-two now. 'You miss it, but you have to be nice and young. Every year there are fewer and fewer at this affair.' No, she won't be performing solo tonight, but she'll be part of the finale, when the band starts playing 'Ain't She Sweet,' the signal for any old-timer who thinks he or she can cut it to fall into line on stage and do the old Shim Sham, a dance routine every hoofer knows. This year eight women and two men, including Helen Mangold, answered the call. When you got it, you got it...and nearly fifty years later, has Helen still got it? The moves, the oomph, the ooh-la-la! Can she still Shim Sham? Hold everything, boys, don't watch her feet! Watch her face. 'Ain't She Sweet'! Never sweeter than tonight.

The following year I was able to get publicity in the newspaper, plus a long segment on WTAE, part of the ABC network. (The latter would never happen that way today—segments are short. Important news gets a fast-talking minute or two.) The local program was called *Evening Magazine*. Doing the interview was a darling, vibrant reporter named Sally Wiggin. She got a kick out of our colorful agent, Don D'Carlo.

The last BOOTS banquet would be held in October 1990. One of the finest staff writers with the *Pittsburgh Post-Gazette*, Diana Nelson Jones, gave us a great article for our "finale finish." The article featured a group picture with some of the survivors. Attendance at our banquets had been dwindling. It had peaked one year at more than two hundred, counting friends and relatives. The title for the article: 'OLD-TIME PERFORMERS HANG UP THEIR BOOTS."

TRANSITION ACCOMPLISHED

Cindy and I worked hard on changing our image. We had a great feeling of accomplishment when we received a copy of the following letter sent to a potential client. The letter is dated April 19, 1964, and refers to a show we did at the Suburban Temple, east of Cleveland. The agent liked our original title and used it in advertising us:

> The Fun Fillys—winsome Pat Fallon and pert Cindy Dunn—are two very seasoned and sprightly mannered singing comediennes with the built-in advantage of a talent range that includes their ability to play their act unassisted (if necessary): a real rarity of these times, particularly in the category of comediennes (who in themselves are exceedingly scarce). Pat and Cindy are quite competent and dependable entertainers, and I unhesitatingly recommend them for your group, having brought them to

Cleveland previously for events that required careful selectivity on my part. The girls were accorded great enthusiasm, stemming largely from their individual personalities and the mutual enjoyment of their work..... THE COMEDY FUN OF FALLON & DUNN is not loaded with the spectacular—nor is it 'beat,' 'blue,' or 'smart'.... Instead it is refreshingly a sparkle, in impeccable taste, and wonderfully FUNNY!

You can imagine how happy we were to read this critique!

DICK JACKSON

Throughout our career as a team, Cindy had bouts of stomach problems. A news item I have is humorous due to the errors I found. "Towne Topic: Cindy Dunn, the dancer [nope] is in Magee Hospital for surgery, so her partner, Pat Falloon [nope] is doing a single now. The girls are booked for a General Motors convention in Cleveland August 1."

The show was booked for us by one of our agents, Dick Jackson. His agency was based in Cleveland. Dick Jackson will always be on the top of my list as the ideal agent. It was a privilege knowing and working for him. He was a gentleman and an excellent businessman. Dick's meticulous style in arranging the basics for a good show was infallible: he ensured we had everything from an excellent sound system, spotlights, and masterful musicians to back up our show.

Our heyday in the Cleveland area included appearances at Somerset Inn, Grotto Hilton, Pick Carter, Theatrical

Grill, Carter Hilton, Sahara, Engineers C.A.C., Cedar Point, Sheraton, and the Statler Hilton.

One engagement we had booked from Dick Jackson hit a snag. Once again Cindy had her stomach problems and had to be hospitalized. Characteristic of Dick's integrity and commitment to his clients, he arranged to fly me to Cleveland to do the show. He wanted his clients to retain the trust they had in him. I did a good job. It's possible that by my showing up, the committee was assured that the team of Fallon & Dunn hadn't simply accepted a better job offer. It was a smart move on Dick's part. I've known some entertainers who would grab a better offer and leave an agent stranded. I was glad I was always picking up solo jobs while I worked the team jobs with Cindy so that I had the experience and confidence to do a good show. We never reneged on a contract for a better offer.

Dick Jackson believed in us. He had a connection with *The Mike Douglas Show*, which was filmed in Cleveland at the time. Kaye Ballard, the comedienne whom Dick got on the show, went on to become a star. By the time Dick wanted us to be on the show Cindy was pregnant and beginning to show. This TV appearance wasn't to be, but it was nice to know it could have been.

TWENTY BUCKS A THROW

One of Dick Jackson's shows was at a huge ballroom in a hotel. There were a dozen acts on the bill. There seemed to be nearly five hundred men in the audience. The performers included an MC, a comic, a singer, a dancer, a line of dancers, a marimba player, acrobats, and yes, strippers. We dressed in a large meeting room in the hotel. After the show a lovely-looking, exceptionally tall, blonde lady came into the room and asked us, "Would you like to come out and sit with some of the men?" She said the men would buy us drinks. She talked for a few minutes, but when she got to "twenty bucks a throw," I started backing away, shaking my head no. I had not heard that expression before, but I certainly got the gist of it. Meanwhile, Cindy was still standing there, looking up at her, listening. I walked up to Cindy, firmly took her by the arm, and said, "We're not interested!"

Here was another face of entertaining that we had never heard of before. I think the word "proposition" or even "prostitution" comes to mind. Later we would laugh about the episode. Cindy was never able to share these stories with her husband, because he would get angry. On the other hand, I could always confide in Marty about these episodes. He would just grin. He was aware of the darker aspects of show business. The fact that we had total trust in one another helped.

Another example of Marty's worldliness: It was within the month that Cindy and I did a show for Louie Angelo in Kane, PA. It was a long, long drive to the show, which was a late one. There were no freeways; most of the trip was two-lane highways. We got paid in cash that night with many small bills, which made a big wad. I don't remember who came up with the idea, but as we started to divide the money, we decided to make one big roll with a twenty-dollar bill on the outside. The show being such a late one, we didn't get back to my house until almost day-break. When Marty came out to help me with my gear, Cindy showed him the big wad of money. She said, "Hey, Marty, look at this—twenty bucks a throw!" I'm so glad we could all get a big laugh out of that.

IMPRESSIONS

In the 1960s doing impersonations of famous celebrities was very popular. Some of the great impersonators were Rich Little, Sammy Davis Jr., and Pittsburgh's Frank Gorshin. Cindy and I had been having success with our impressions of famous people. We would keep them up to date, impersonating the likes of Jackie Kennedy and Nikita Kruschev.

When I first heard the theme song for TV's "All in the Family," I was positive that the song, sung by the main characters, Edith and Archie Bunker, would be perfect for our team. I sent away for the sheet music. We practiced and had perfected it to a tee. Cindy, with her low voice, would sing Archie's part. I was able to get Edith's ear-shattering, screeching voice down perfectly! We couldn't wait to try it out. The show at which we first sang it was a huge banquet. Our program was going over great until we did the song in the middle of our act. It died! We were doing it too soon; not enough people had seen the show yet. Most of the audience just sat there. Fortunately the rest of the show went over very well. We set the number aside for a couple of months. Then, when the show became a number-one hit, we used it again. This time it brought the house down, and we used it successfully for years.

We had a lot of fun doing impressions. "Hey, Look Me Over" became a hit tune, and we had a musical arrangement made. Throughout the song we would do impressions. Cindy did comedienne Phyllis Diller. She had the laugh down perfect. One of her lines as Diller was: "I decided to give up drinking. I take one drink before I go to bed. Last night I went to bed twenty-seven times!"

I did actress and sex symbol Mae West, and later actress and sex symbol Jayne Mansfield. I also did singer Dolly Parton, known for her "endowments." If I were to impersonate someone today, it would probably be actress Pamela Anderson. Actually, so many stars and starlets today have had "boob jobs" that there would be a huge selection of actresses from which to select.

One of the gags I would do as a buxom blonde star: "I worked a Shriner's Convention, and I heard three men talking. They had been out of town a week. The one man says, 'I'm looking for a big, tall blonde with long, gorgeous legs!' The second man says, 'I'm looking for a white, satin-skinned redhead with curves in all the right places!' The third man says, 'I'm looking for a flat-chested, wide-hipped, varicose-vein lady.' The other two men ask, 'Are you crazy?' He replies, 'No, I'm homesick.'"

Carol Channing was another impression I did. I would go around the house practicing her strange, deep, and scratchy voice. It drove Marty crazy. I had a great line that took me a couple of weeks to memorize. It was worth it! As Channing I would point to some guy in the audience and say, "That fella back there asked me to spend a nice quiet weekend with him at the Edison Hotel." (I would find out the name of the cheapest hotel in the town we were working, and that's the name I would use.) I would then say to the fella, "I'm afraid that my awareness of the proclivities in the esoteric aspect of sexual behavior preclude such an erotic confrontation!" He'd say to me, "I don't get it!" And I'd say to him, "EXACTLY!" Women liked Carol Channing. Most men didn't, including my husband! The last time I ever did Carol Channing for an all-male audience was at a banquet at the Roosevelt Hotel in Pittsburgh. I began with my back to the audience and then turned around, and with those big staring eyes and supersized smile, I said,,"It's soooooo....niiiiiiiiiice to be here!" A man in the front row muttered, "Jesus C_____!" And I said, "No...Carol Channing!"

ONGOING SHOWBIZ SCENES

One time I did a solo act at a lively spot called the May Club in Brentwood, PA. There was this handsome fella in the audience who was running for mayor of Pittsburgh. He was so pleasant and personable. I got him up to do the hula dance with me. His name was Richard Caliguiri. He eventually won the election and became one of Pittsburgh's finest and beloved mayors.

It was at the Civic Arena that I saw the first half of a Judy Garland performance. I was dancing in a local night-club and could only see a part of her show. If she hadn't been so habitually late, I could have seen more. I got to see part of her show but had to leave early. I also was able to see the fabulous Wayne Newton. What an entertainer! It's no surprise to me the staying power he had.

Cindy and I did a show at the Three Rivers Stadium, now gone and replaced by PNC Park for baseball and Heinz Field for football. We performed for an offshoot of the Shriners of America called the Ladies of the Eastern

Star. The VIPs were seated on an elevated dais. The audience of men and women numbered well over three hundred. The first part of our show went over well. Suddenly the man who had booked us got my attention during our performance. He told us, "The main lady on the dais is getting very upset with some of your material." Even though the audience was bubbling with laughter, we decided to tone things down. We continued with the audience participation number in which we would invite ladies from the audience to participate in our chorus line. As they came up to perform, we'd hand each of them a beautiful ostrich feather boa and let them swing it and wing it! One lady struggled to come onstage. She had a cane, yet she so wanted to be a part of the bit! I thought it was wonderful that despite her disability, she felt comfortable enough with us to participate. Later we found out that the lady on the dais thought we were trying to embarrass this participant. Despite this lady's negative response, I would go on to entertain the Eastern Star groups a few more times in my career and would have great fun and success with them.

At a previous show at the Three Rivers Stadium, the setup was impossible. We had to perform in a long and rather narrow room. To make it even more of a challenge, we faced the kitchen with its swinging doors in perpetual motion. We followed the late great sports announcer Bob Prince, who clearly had had a terrible time with the setup too. He introduced us, then muttered under his breath, "Good luck!"

Another once-in-a-lifetime memorable show was at a Veterans of Foreign Wars (VFW) club (now called the

Owls Club) in Homestead. There was a full house, and off to the side of the room where we would perform was a long bar that the seated audience could see in its entirety. As Cindy and I were singing "Sweet Gypsy Rose," an idea struck me! Cindy continued singing the song and I strutted with my long, pink, feathered boa. I climbed onto a stool and then onto the bar. In time to the loud beat of the drums I walked seductively down the long bar. I was stepping over glasses, cigarette ashtrays, and even fingers! The audience laughed, screamed, and applauded. Action-reaction. I truly love it!

By this time in my life, I was convinced that almost everyone would love to be in showbiz, whether singing, dancing, playing a musical instrument, or just being "on!" I saw the audience participation bits in my act as a way to help many people fulfill their moment of fun in the spotlight.

A BABY GIRL

I hesitated pursuing my dream of having a baby girl. With Steven's birth, the labor had been so intense, long, and traumatic that I was scared. The doctor convinced me that every pregnancy was different. From the moment I got pregnant with Lisa, it certainly was different. For a couple of months Cindy and I were both pregnant. We would kid our agents that instead of a duo, they were getting a quartet!

I began crossing off the days on my calendar. During the pregnancy, I was able to do shows. Holding the guitar in front of me covered up the pregnancy for a while. Thank goodness for the guitar! Throughout our team career, I practiced daily on the guitar. This could explain the future rhythmic talent of this baby.

Lisa Lynn Faloon was born on July 16, 1965. I got my baby girl! In both Marty's family and mine, Lisa was the first girl born in fifty years. So much JOY!

POSTPARTUM

By the time Lisa was born I had "lost" the routine of mothering responsibilities, as it had been eight years since Steven's birth. Wanting everything to be "just right" took its toll on me. I became overwhelmed with emotional issues.

Everyone was worried about me. I said I wanted to see a psychiatrist even though in 1965, there was still a stigma in seeing a psychiatrist. Thank goodness it has become known that some people are susceptible to depression, and that there are even hereditary tendencies. I remember my mother once speaking of "melancholia" blues. Doing shows with Cindy helped. Onstage, it's another world: carefree! Free from care and worry!

About six weeks after Lisa's birth, Fallon & Dunn did a show at Mayview. This was a hospital for emotionally troubled people. It seemed to be an appropriate place for me as my battle with depression had just begun.

I did get help. I did take the pills. I did get better. I got through the experience and now have a better understanding and compassion for the complicated ordeal. (Shame on you, Tom Cruise!)

SONG WRITING

Cindy and I did many shows at the beautiful Twin Coaches nightclub about a half-hour drive from Pittsburgh. At its peak, the club had two bars, a kitchen, a stage, dressing rooms, and 1,100 seats. Billed as the largest supper club between New York and Las Vegas, it attracted all the top stars in the country.

On one of singer Bobby Vinton's appearances, Cindy and I were able to meet him backstage after his show. Young and full of himself, he was a great entertainer. I wanted to meet him because I was always writing songs. I handed him a copy of a song. He folded it and put it in his *very* tight jeans. He then introduced me to one of his musicians. This fella told me to call on him at his hotel the next morning, and he'd listen to some of my songs. We decided on three o'clock in the afternoon. There was NO way I was going to make this visit alone. My dear little Aunt Edie agreed to accompany me. We arrived. The front desk called, and we were given his room number.

We knocked on the musician's door. When he saw me with my aunt, he must have thought, "Aw, Shoot!" (or something a little stronger!) He opened the door, and I don't believe he had a stitch of clothing on—only a towel wrapped around his lower half. The room was dark. As I looked beyond him, I could see a couple in bed. The musician mumbled something. I never did step into the room. My aunt and I simply left. I summed it up as "good 'ole band buddies providing 'company' for those lonely, traveling-on-the-road gigs"!

As far as my success in songwriting, Marty loved hearing me tell about another stab I made at getting someone interested in my songs. This time the setup was legit. The meeting place was more of an office setting. A man listened to my tapes and appeared **VERY** interested. I was thinking, "He really likes what he is hearing!" He did, but it wasn't my songs he was interested in. He said to me, "Wow! That's a great backup guitarist! What's his name? He's terrific!" Yes, it was Marty. I told you he was a great guitarist.

GLADYS AVENUE GANG

Just for the fun of it, I began doing some musical variety shows with the neighborhood children. My Lisa was about age two when the seed was planted for a neighborhood troupe. It all began with Susie who was five and Gracie who was six. They would come to play with Lisa, and I would teach them songs and routines. They were eager and well behaved. They would love to don the old dancing costumes I had stored away. This group would blossom into almost twenty kids. Janice was the oldest at twelve, and in the summer she would gather up the interested kids, and we would rehearse. I would play the guitar. There was much joy in teaching these little children the old songs although we would also teach the newest hits.

The sizable downstairs addition to my house served well in staging shows. The old basement became the dressing room. All of my props—top hat, canes, tambourines, wigs, feather boas, and many costumes—came in very handy. We had our own little theater studio. It was a joyful break for me from my household duties. The children were quick learners. All of their mothers were housewives. I, on the other hand, had my showbiz career in the evenings. (I had my "cake" and could eat it, too!)

MY BEST FRIEND

Because my mom was only sixteen years older than me, it was a given that we would share most of our lives with one another. If one is fortunate to have a loving mother, it is the greatest gift. I believe there is no truer or more complete love in a human being's life than the relationship one has with a loving mother. My mom was my best friend. She was a caring, confident mother who was always ready to listen to my innermost secrets. Mom was 54 when she was diagnosed with cancer. She endured a lengthy hospital stay.

At this time Steven was eleven years old when he came on a job with me and Cindy. The show was at a private German "Leidertoffel" club in Bloomfield, on the east side of Pittsburgh. Cindy and I had worked the club about a month earlier. The audience was one of the most reserved groups we had ever entertained. Our voices became higher and higher in pitch as we tried to get a reaction from them. But we persevered. When we learned that they wanted us back in a month, we decided to take Steven. He came on near the end of the show. At the closing of the show, all three of us took a bow, and—would you believe it?—we got a standing ovation! It felt good telling my mother something happy. She passed away a few weeks later.

The day after Mom died, Marty and I were sitting on our front patio in silent sadness when we noticed a group of the little ones from the Gladys Avenue Gang at the crest of our street. They were standing in silent homage, looking down at us. No words were needed. It was a reverent moment that I will never forget.

And, yes, we did our annual show that year. "The show must go on! Life must go on!" As we slowly recovered, I was thankful I had my family and my gigs to keep my mind occupied. A couple of months after Mom died I had a solo act booked at a private Elks club in Meadville, PA. Steven wanted to go with me. I hesitated in taking him. Oh, how he wanted to go! It was a Saturday, though, and he had no school the next day. So I said, "Okay!" At the age of eleven, he harmonized beautifully on the songs with me; his sweet, young voice hadn't changed yet. At the club, when it came time for the show, he was sound asleep. I shook him awake gently and said, "Do you really want to sing?" He did, and he did it magnificently!

During the summer of 1974 Lisa and I decided to take a long-weekend vacation at the nearby Marriott Hotel in Greentree. The Jackson Five were appearing in Pittsburgh and happened to be staying at this hotel. We had no clue until we saw their big bus parked outside. As we entered the gift shop, there was Michael and two of his brothers.

We were so excited. I grabbed the first card I could from the greeting-card rack and asked the future superstar to sign it. He did. It was a great finale to our little summer vacation.

A HOME
FILLED WITH MUSIC

Our home environment was all about music. Marty, being a great jazz guitarist, often practiced at home. We simply told the kids when they were tots that some day they would take piano lessons and that after a couple of years, they could choose another instrument to play.

Practicing the piano was a chore for Billy. He chose to play the electric bass. With rock and roll at its peak in the early '70s, Billy had made a good choice. He gathered a group, and they called themselves "Freeway." Because they rehearsed in our basement, I was able to learn the current songs of the era and use them in my shows. I actually liked some of them: the eternal "Proud Mary" and the Beatles' "Something." I also liked Neil Young's "Heart of Gold" and Three Dog Night's "Never Been to Spain."

Steven and Lisa would always play the piano. They had inherited Marty's natural musical talent. As they grew, they both became accomplished on their chosen musical instrument. For Steven it was the trumpet. As he grew older, he often used the tape recorder to tape a melody, and then he would play it back and tape some harmony with the original piece. Steven would jump at any opportunity to play his trumpet. He picked up several gigs at local churches, and was happy about getting paid for these performances. I always told my kids, "Show business is a great way to make extra money, but don't count on it for a steady career!"

Lisa chose the drums even before she began piano lessons. When I was pregnant with her, I would practice singing and playing chords on my guitar daily. That guitar on my swelling belly must have resonated into her soul. As a little tot, she would keep time with me by beating on a toy. We first bought her a snare drum. She instinctively could keep perfect rhythm. For her kindergarten class, she and I performed a couple of numbers together one day. I sang and played the guitar while Lisa played the snare drum. We soon bought Lisa a reasonably priced drum set. I also encouraged her to sing a lot of songs. When she was three years old, she could sing the entire lyrics to the hit tune at the time, "I Never Promised You a Rose Garden."

Soon I was also taking Lisa along to perform either in my solo act or with the team. Whenever I introduced Lisa, she, being a cute little girl, always received "oohs" and "aahs" from the audience. I told her that eventually would stop as she grew older. Of course, it did. Still, she was always much applauded for her skills on the drums, and for being a woman on the drums, at that! When she was in fifth grade, she did a drum performance for a talent show at school. She had been able to pay for a complete set of professional drums with money she had earned on the shows. It was a flashing, shiny, silver Slingerland set. Now that she had a full set of drums, we both got a lot of exercise! We would negotiate who would carry the big brass drum every time we'd go into a club to do a show. In retrospect, many women go to gyms to tone up; I was doing the same thing, yet I was getting paid for it! It was amazing what we could fit in our car: a huge set of drums (in cases), guitar, amplifier, mike, trumpet, prop case, garment bag, and four people!

Steven, Bill, Lisa

TO TRAVEL OR NOT TO TRAVEL

Our act was well suited to the '70s. We would work what were considered the "elite" jobs in Pittsburgh: every country club, every "big time" banquet, and every nightclub.

The Holiday House in Monroeville, PA, was considered the tops. We signed to a seven-day contract. We would open the show. The top critic at the time was Lenny Litman who wrote the "Nightbeat" column for the *Pittsburgh Press*. He could be tough on some entertainers. Cindy and I were concerned about how he would critique us. When Lenny Litman came backstage to interview us, the first question out of his mouth was, "Where are you girls from?" He couldn't believe it when we said, "Pittsburgh!" We talked for a while. We couldn't wait to get the papers the next day to see what he would write about us. We were delighted with his review: "Two young Pitt-land housewives who have certainly liberated themselves are Pat Fallon and Cindy Dunn who open the show. They do a fine 20 minutes of songs and comedy and are especially strong on impressions of such stars as Carol Channing, Phyllis Diller and Mae West."

Just a few weeks later, George Claire, the agent for the Holiday House booking, called me at home. George wanted Fallon & Dunn to work some jobs in the Poconos and in the famous Catskill Mountains—dream jobs for many entertainers. When I hung up and told Marty about the booking offer, he exploded! Never in all our years of marriage had I ever seen him so angry. He turned into Rumplestilskin right before my eyes, ranting and raving! He yelled, "You're not going to work THERE!" He went on and on. I told him to calm down and that if it made him so unhappy I wouldn't accept the offer. Cindy and I were working all the time, and she was okay with not accepting the offer. I called George, thanked him, and said we couldn't do it.

I waited a while to ask Marty why he was so upset about the offer. He told me stories he had heard about the area: how men would spike a woman's drink and then "have their way." As I reflect on his reasoning I do believe Marty was afraid that sudden fame would jeopardize our marriage. The many stories I have heard about the effects of fame are not always happy. Agents who handle famous stars take complete control of the stars' lives. I've enjoyed calling my own shots: choosing where I wanted to work, when I wanted to work, what material I did, and what wardrobe I wanted to wear. It's a freedom I cherish.

With the success of our team, we were approached many times to travel. We were on a big show at the Hilton Hotel in Pittsburgh when an agent, Ken Thomas from Variety Attractions, made us an offer. He pressed vigorously to book us on a tour. "We both have children," we would say. And he would say, "Get a tutor!" The big money he offered could have covered this expense. We kept saying "NO!" His last angry remark to us was, "Everyone has got a price!" We really exasperated him—there was no price that could buy us on the idea.

Within that year, Cindy and I would be in another similar circumstance. We had been doing some dates for Syd Marke. He booked us on a show with a very good comic from New York. It took this comic telling Syd how good we were for him to really believe it. Syd had some big-time connections. He set us up for an audition in New York for *The Ed Sullivan Show*. The three of us drove up to New York. With our confident, enthusiastic fervor, we auditioned for Mark J. Ledey, one of the agents for the show. He was very interested in us. In fact, he wanted to book us in all the "big" clubs in the country. And in fact, that was the one condition to get on the Sullivan show: agreeing to be booked in the big clubs across the United States. We were flattered by the offer and, in its own way, it was a happy ending: We found out we were good enough for the Big Time!

That evening we did get to sit in the front row of the theater to see the "live" *Ed Sullivan Show*, which featured Barbra Streisand singing "Happy Days Are Here Again" and the McGuire Sisters.

We came home with the offer in our heads. I didn't even need to discuss this with Marty. It was out of the question. Cindy and I now had three children each. To be on the road for a year? The choice was not a hard one to make. Fortunately Cindy and I were in complete agreement. I never regretted the decision for a moment. Cindy and I still worked as much as we wanted to work locally.

DIRTY TRICKS (THE ONES I FOUND OUT ABOUT)

Most of the entertainers were kind and helpful. Most of them became role models. It would sadden me to hear of trickery!

The Gateway Clipper fleet at Station Square in Pittsburgh has always had live entertainment. I did shows on the Gateway Clipper many times: as a solo, Patti Eberle; with the team, Fallon & Dunn; with my daughter Lisa; and with Lisa and my son Steven. For most of the shows I performed solo as Patti Eberle. Often on the bill was a great square dance caller, Gary Diehl. After one of the solo shows he asked me for my telephone number. He complimented me on what a good show I did! He said he could book me on a lot of Shriner shows. I gave him my number and didn't hear from him. After a couple of weeks, I called him. He hesitated, then mumbled something about a local comic, Nick, commenting on my age. Nick had asked, "Gary, do you realize how old Patti is?" I was forty-nine at the time, and for a long time I looked ten or more years younger than I was. Plus I have been blessed with incredible energy. Gary was probably much younger than me, and so forty-nine must have seemed really old to him. Ironically, Nick, the comic, was my age or older, but he wanted Gary to hire him instead of me.

Every summer the musicians' union had a picnic. It was always well attended. Marty, being a member, and I always went and enjoyed the camaraderie. I couldn't wait to approach Nick. I asked him, "What's the bit about my age when you talked to Gary Diehl?" Nick calmly said to me, "A job's a job!" Backstabbing comes to mind and so does selfishness and greed. Power comes to mind, too, but greed is the reason behind the desire for power. Envy plays its part, too. Being happy does not bode well with any of them. I vote for happy.

Another dirty trick involved an agent named Zeke. What is ironic is how much money Zeke made in booking our young team, The Fun Fillys. Our dear friend Louis Angelo was bidding on a date to book our team. Zeke was bidding on the same job, but offering other entertainers. What he said even baffled Louis. Louis knew what a good act we had and that we had done a lot of jobs for Zeke. Louis told us he had learned that Zeke had said derogatory things about our act: "The one girl just stands there!" I'm sure the "one girl" he referred to was me. It's sad when I think of all the money Zeke had made in bookings we did for him! I never did confront him about this incident...I hate confrontations!

Zeke booked us many times in the beautiful Mountain View Hotel in Greensburg, PA. On one of these dates we worked with a comedian. I'm going to call him B. W.

He was handsome, well groomed, and we presumed, a gentleman. The gig was a huge banquet with an all-male audience. Once again B. W. was considered the star, so would close the show. Cindy and I went over sensationally. (I can brag now; it seems so long ago that I feel like I'm talking about someone else!) When B. W. followed our act, he had a hard time getting any momentum going. He was really struggling. He got so frustrated that he started to swear—REALLY swear—at the audience! He vented all the bad words, including the "F" word. He couldn't get their attention. At least the audience was all men. Cindy and I were never given credit for what a great job we did, but Zeke totally defended B. W. (He definitely favored male acts.) Zeke bawled out the committee for the audience indifference to his comedian—and he didn't want to be accused of a bad booking. As showbiz expressions go, when you go over great, you've "killed 'em!" The opposite happened to B. W. that night: He "bombed!"

The last dirty trick I'll mention beats them all. One particular agent had a hard time swallowing our quick success. It really riled him. I'll call him J. C. Once while we were standing in his office someone called him on the phone and wanted to book us. He stared into our faces and said we weren't available, but we were at the time! We ignored it, thinking it was a petty peeve. That was a prelude to what he did on a Christmas booking. We were already booked with another agent for a banquet in the Roosevelt Hotel in Pittsburgh. J. C. had another booking earlier the same day. His show was in Butler, PA, an hour's drive from town. It was for a Butler Pullman car banquet. We agreed to do it if we could go on first. There were several acts on the show. When the show started, we were dressed and ready. J. C. kept putting the other acts on before us. We were really getting nervous. It was a wintry December night. The roads were getting snowy and icy. We finally went on.

J. C. offered to go outside and start Cindy's car. We thought that was a good idea. We stayed in wardrobe for the drive to the next show. When J. C. handed Cindy her car keys, the ignition key was broken in half. He claimed it was the cold weather! MEAN! GREEN! MEAN! Fortunately Cindy had an extra key. Still, we were late for our second show. Trickery! The "Green-Eyed Monster" had its way with this agent.

When I started my career, there was wonderful camaraderie among the entertainers. Most of us respected whatever talents the others possessed, and the same held true with musicians. In the twilight of my career I realize how slowly, over time, that closeness has eroded.

MORE TRANSITIONS

I have been a volunteer at our MOW (Meals on Wheels) for many years. I had done some shows for the picnics they had for their volunteers. When I was hired to perform for a gathering of MOW from all over the area, it became a case of one door closing and another one opening. The show was extremely well received. On this show Pittsburgh radio personality John Cigna was present. I got him up to do the line "Why is everybody pickin' on me?" from the Charlie Brown song. From this show I was kept busy for a couple of years doing shows for a fee in all the many MOW locations.

The nightclub scene, as I knew it, steadily collapsed. Our show offers would continue, albeit sporadically. As Patti Eberle, I could still pick up solo jobs with my guitar as my musical accompaniment. It was a little more difficult for Cindy. The few gigs that were still running shows could afford only one act.

Steven and Lisa began joining me in shows as "Faloon Family Fun!" We had 8x10 photos made. Lisa was seven years old, and Steven was fourteen. The first show we did together was another of my happily-ever-after moments. I opened the show singing a chorus of "Proud Mary." I introduced Steven, who played his cornet for the second chorus. He and I harmonized the third chorus as Lisa played her drums. The audience loved it, and I was thrilled, even getting goose bumps! All those years of lessons and practice created this happy event.

We continued transitioning and had another set of 8x10 glossies made. This time Cindy was included and we called ourselves "Faloon Family and Friend." We got many great bookings with this group.

In the spring of 1973, the BOOTS group had a picnic. It was held in the Riverview Park Pavilion on the North Side. With Marty joining us, the entire Faloon family— the Faloon Four—put on a show. One of the premiere agents attended this picnic. After our show he talked to us. He wanted to book the family on some "big deal" touring shows. He was very impressed with our performance. I was glad a top agency was impressed with our family talent. Once again, we said, "No!"

Cindy and I always felt we could do a show anywhere, but we were in for a surprise when we were booked to do a show at The Meadows, a popular harness horseracing track in Little Washington, PA, practically a suburb of Pittsburgh. Believe me, this booking placed us in the "Loser's Circle." The setup was impossible. Picture the oval-shaped track with a fence around it, then the wide track. They had a small stage behind the wide track. We performed as if we were on a small island...away from civilization. Contact with the audience (which we loved) was impossible. It was one of those "The show must go on" performances, but it was torture.

On March 2, 1973, there was a huge snowstorm in Pittsburgh. Faloon Family & Friend were booked for a show in Johnstown. Considering the long trip ahead of me, I decided to leave Lisa at home. As we left in the deep snow, I could see Lisa standing on the wide windowsill facing the front of the house. She was crying and banging on the window loudly. "I want to go! I WANT TO GO TOO!" As we traveled along Route 22, the car actually straddled a road divider that couldn't be seen. And then, as if by magic, we entered the flat town of Johnstown and there was no snow! Our agent, Brownie, was pacing in front of the masonic temple. We were late. He was furious. The next day, on the front page of the newspaper, was a picture and story about the big snowstorm. I sent Brownie the whole page. We worked for him again and he never mentioned it.

STREAKING

Streaking became a fad in the early 1970s. A streaker would take off all his or her clothes and run through graduation parties, a football field, or anywhere there was a crowd. Personally, I thought it was a very funny idea.

My own rendition happened at a Tupperware party at my cousin Doo's house. This would be my one and only adult "striptease"! What I always loved about these parties, before the merchandise presentation, were the games that were played.

The guests, all housewives, were sitting in a large living room. A powder room was directly off the living room. What I did was not planned. The set-up (staging) was perfect. Soooooo, I went into the powder room... stripped...and opened the door and streaked! I circled around the room so swiftly, there was hardly enough time for the partygoers to comprehend what happened. Imagine my nerve!

I knew half the audience as relatives and friends, and they were hardly shocked at all. As for some of the women I never met, I can only imagine what they thought! I heard shrieks of laughter. What I could not hear was the expression of stunned disbelief coming from some of the ladies in the room: "What was *that?*" "Did I see what I think I saw?" I dressed and emerged with a little smile— another satisfying audience reaction!

AUDIENCE PARTICIPATION

I can't remember if, during my first years in showbiz, performers had an audience participation component with their acts. Many of the nightclub entertainers came from the vaudeville era where they were separated from the audience by a pit orchestra and then the stage. In the early days of floorshows the customers seemed glued to their seats even if an act tried to get them to be a part of the show. It was a slow, but steady progression toward the audience members wanting to participate. It's only a guess, though. I'm thinking that audiences had so much exposure to variety shows that people became a little bored with just sitting and watching the same type of performer. Eventually TV gobbled up the newness of any type of variety act. Some very exceptional acts began adding comedy to their performances and some audience participation to their usually "straight" routines. Ballroom dancers and jugglers, for example, began doing this.

Most of the time when I involved the audience I did it spontaneously, but once in a while I would set someone up in the audience beforehand. When John Denver came out with his big hit "Country Roads" and I performed this song, I would have an audience "plant" come out on stage wearing one of those huge foam cowboy hats! Pure laughter!

I took classes in belly dancing at a local community college, and utilized it in my act. I would invite a man onstage and put him in a skirt. This wonderful skirt had a piece of material that hung longer in the back than in the front, and I would bring the longer piece up from the back, between his legs, and up to his waist. Then I would

tie the material in front. These maneuvers alone got so many laughs. Then I would put a black, braided loop around his head and have him wear dark sunglasses. He looked something like a sheik! I had him follow my steps and twirl his hips as we danced to "If I were a Rich Man," from *Fiddler on the Roof.* The more serious he was, the funnier it was.

The song "Ride 'Em Cowboy" was a moderate hit. I would pull an empty chair onto the floor and ask a fella to come up. Then I'd put a cowboy hat on him and point to the chair. "There's your horse! Hop on him, and let's get ridin'!" He would straddle the chair, and I would sing. When I got to the chorus, I would tell him to giddy up!

When Willie Nelson came out with the big hit "On the Road Again," I added it to my repertoire. Usually the participant in the chair would hold onto the back of the chair he was straddling and rock back and forth as if he were riding the "horse." He'd slap the side of his leg, raise his hat, and really get into it. Once in a while he would actually travel down the full length of the floor to the delightful whoops and laughter from the audience.

Like Elvis Presley, singer Billy Ray Cyrus is famous for his hip swiveling. "Achy, Breaky Heart" is a silly but catchy song that made Billy Ray a star. I would tell the audience that I was looking for a cowboy. I would get a fella up on stage, then give him a plastic streamer that resembled a lasso when it was twirled. I reminded the fella that Billy Ray moved when he sang. I wanted to see both the lasso and the fella swing! The audience would clap in unison with the chorus. This song is a great action-reaction bit.

Following this bit, I would sing an even sillier song, but one that made a star out of Elvis Presley. The first line of the lyrics went, "You ain't nothin' but a hound dog." I would have the fella "howl" after each line. "You ain't nothin' but a hound dog…(HOWL) cryin' all the time… (HOWL)." So funny!

I would often mosey through a store and find props that I could connect immediately with a song. The best time to find props was during Halloween…all those costume sales! One time I purchased a baby bib and a bonnet. In the show I would put these on a female participant and say to the audience, "I'm going to show you what this pretty lady looked like as a baby!" I've used this bit with different songs: "You Must Have Been a Beautiful Baby," "Baby Face," and "Rock-a-Bye-Baby."

Naturally, once in a great while a participant would get carried away. As soon as possible he (*never* a "she") would be led back to his seat—by me! At one of my solo shows, when I was younger, one man became a total nuisance. He embarrassed me, but REALLY embarrassed himself. He was a showoff. He strutted around doing his own foolish gestures, even pretending he was trying to get fresh with me. No one in the audience was impressed with him and the really sad part was that *he* thought he was being entertaining!!!

I have NEVER tried to make a fool of anyone. My success with audience participation is that the audiences have trusted me to treat them respectfully while still having fun.

Over the years, I have done a couple of shows at Carlow College (now Carlow University) in the Oakland section of Pittsburgh. This is a Catholic school and most of the professors are nuns. Some of the best audiences for fun and laughter have been Catholic groups, but especially the nuns who were like little children ready to have some fun; they enjoyed prancing around with the feather boas. Whenever we involved a priest in the act, that would go over tremendously. The parishioners *loved* their priests. The more a participant is liked, the bigger and better the audience reaction. One priest so enjoyed the response he got that after the show he made a beeline for me to thank me for letting him be a part of the show.

We were very successful with many big outdoor shows. One in particular was the Ohio River Festival in Ravenswood, West Virginia. It was a huge three-day festival with boat races, hot air balloon rides, and live entertainment provided for a range of all ages. The magazine advertising for the event was a full-page photo of the entertainers: Lisa, Cindy, and me, and a group called Booger Hole Revival. (The Fun Fillys would have fit in well with this group!) The featured group was the New Christy Minstrels. The great country music star Kenny Rogers was once with this group. The New Christy Minstrels found a way to continue once he left the group.

Outdoor affairs were not always pleasant because of the heat, the bugs, and the unpredictable weather! We preferred indoor venues, many of which are no more.

M-I-CK-E-Y M-O-U-S-E

October 1976 presented me with another chance to experience the wonderful, infinite variety in the entertainment field. The opportunity came to me courtesy of my friend, the magician Harry Albacker. Greengate Mall in Greensburg, PA, was celebrating its eleventh anniversary by hosting at least three shows a day that were being handled and promoted by the Walt Disney empire. The shows were intended to keep alive the American classic, Mickey Mouse. The mall became a delightful Disney fantasyland.

Cindy and I were booked for a week of shows. Our commitment to this weeklong date meant that we were neglecting our homes and kids. Harry Albacker really had my number, as they say. He once told an agency that was looking for a marionette act, "Call Patti Eberle. She'll put strings on her kids!"

The script that was sent from Walt Disney World noted:

"OUR MOUSEKETEER MC should be wearing the same kind of outfit worn by the original TV MOUSEKETEER personality.

That is: neat open shirt, slacks, and MOUSEKETEER ears.

MC: (LOVABLE, LAUGHABLE CLOWN-TYPE. ABLE TO ENTERTAIN AND SET MOOD OF ENTHUSIASM FOR ARRIVAL OF DISNEY CHARACTERS FOR APPROXIMATELY 10 MINUTES, UNTIL FIRST DISNEY CHARACTER COMES ON STAGE. COULD BE LOCAL TV OR RADIO PERSONALITY, OR CLOWN THAT GENERATES ENTHUSIASM AND CAN AD-LIB QUICKLY.)

I was eager and willing to try another aspect of showbiz. I had a Mickey Mouse hat. I wore a white, full-sleeved, turtleneck shirt. Luckily I had kept a pair of bright-red, tight pants with a big flare at the knees (bell bottoms).

They were perfect. I would be the emcee, and Cindy would be Pluto.

The show was held in the center court of the mall on a large stage, which allowed for the huge crowds we would get at each performance. Each day Cindy and I commuted forty-five minutes one way. The money was good, and the experience was delightful, at least for me as emcee. Although there was a script I had to follow, as the emcee I was allowed some freedom to incorporate my own ideas. For example, I had all the kids and some of the parents imitate me as I spelled out Mickey Mouse with my body. Of course, the "I" was the easiest; "K" was tricky, but got the most laughs.

The Disney characters were Mickey Mouse, Donald Duck, and Pluto. For Cindy, the only good thing about being Pluto was that she didn't have to worry about her hair. "Her "game spirit"—one of her greatest assets—which I always admired, was really needed for this role. The heavy, furry material, however, was like performing in three blankets. When Cindy did the dog "panting," it was for real! I think she lost ten pounds that week, and five pounds of it was sweat!

In the summer of 1977 we did an outdoor fair. It was our "Participation" act with the three of us: Lisa, Cindy, and me. The featured star on this big fair date was Tom Netherton, a regular on the Lawrence Welk TV show. Tom was a tall, handsome fella with a beautiful, mellow voice. What a nice person he was. He posed for a picture with Lisa and her friend Cindy.

This was the year that Disco and the new and exciting music style of the Bee Gees ("Stayin' Alive") were very popular. My cousin Olga and I took classes in disco dancing. I always tried to keep up with the current fad. (I read in the news that 1982 was the year disco died.)

SLINGS AND ARROWS

The year 1979 would be the happiest and the saddest time of my life, going from the highest point to the lowest to which my spirits had ever sunk. The year began with much promise. Lisa was now a freshman at Brashear High. She was doing so well in basketball that she would get a full scholarship to Penn State. She was also doing shows with me. Our son Bill was in Florida on the verge of a grand-scale business venture into the world of vitamins. He would become the co-founder of Life Extension Foundation. Steven was a senior at

Carnegie-Mellon University and doing well in all aspects
of his life. Life was moving so smoothly. I had no idea of
the "rough" waters ahead.

A few years earlier Steven had gotten a starring role
in *Finian's Rainbow*, which was being staged by the St.
George's Theatre Guild at a local church. My 6 foot-3
inch tall, thin son played the part of Og, a leprechaun!
Despite his height, he was marvelous in the role! He
was so well equipped with his background of singing
and performing publicly on shows with me. We had a lot
of fun rehearsing the Irish dialect around the house. A
line the leprechaun had to repeat so often was, "Doom
and gloom! Doom and gloom!" These prophetic words
would live to haunt me.

I would say to Steven, "I'd love to have a small part
in one of the musicals!" Remember, I wanted to be an
actress! Auditions were held, and I got offered a part—and
what a part it was! I got to play the lead character, Reno
Sweeney, made famous by Ethel Merman of Broadway
fame. The show? It was the musical *Anything Goes*, which
is often produced as high school musicals. There was one
problem with St. George's productions: no microphone!
I'd always had a microphone. The Reno Sweeney part
was more songs than dialogue, so I started looking for
a vocal coach. My first phone call was to the vivacious
Dione Patterson. I already had some of the sheet music
for the songs, but the music was almost never written in a
female vocal range, unless for sopranos. As I tried singing
in the high-range key, I was screeching! The first time I
sang for Dione—that is, screeched out the song "Anything

Goes"—I don't know how she kept from laughing! We did become friends. I love kind people, and she was kind.

I was so relieved when I received the music scores because the keys were much lower. Dione helped me so much. For several months I did the scales and slowly obtained more volume. We had the summer to rehearse, as the show wasn't scheduled until October.

As a singer, I'm more of a crooner, singing popular ballads. However, with no mike, I needed to have lots of volume...I had to be LOUD! I would practice the songs riding in the car, the shower, and even while walking on my treadmill at home. I'm so glad I was in shape so that my stomach's diaphragm enabled me to hold long phrases and notes. (That other kind of diaphragm is what helped me plan my family!)

Steven had another starring role in this musical playing Sir Evelyn, Reno's love interest! The stage is a wonderful place where age can stand still on one's face, because the bright spotlights have always been kind to aging actors. I've always looked younger, so that helped, too. The director, knowing I was a tap dancer, incorporated a tap number into the show. When this show opened on October 4 (my birthday), I was fifty years old; Steven was twenty-one. As I was co-starring with my son, I had a very difficult time saying one of the lines in the show: "I've got hot pants for you!"

The show ran for three nights. Dress rehearsal was flawless, but opening night was not! Right from the beginning I had a difficult time unsnapping my white, boa-feathered jacket...but, finally, I did it! Something happened to the stage lights, and we all had to improvise through that snag. A pair of shoes I wore for one number were slippery, so Marty had glued rubber half-soles onto them. During the big production number "Blow, Gabriel, Blow," I had to step up onto a small round table and stay there for most of the number. As I was singing and moving around, so were the rubber soles. The glue was "melting" and definitely not holding. As I reflect on the scene, I'm proud of my effort to keep singing while simultaneously twisting my ankles to align the moving rubber soles. I didn't lose a beat with the song, the dialogue, or the dance.

The next two nights went flawlessly as we performed each time to a full house. All the months of rehearsing had paid off. I was on cloud nine! I had to turn down a few jobs to be in this show, but it was well worth it. It would always remain another one of those happily-ever-after moments in my life. I felt like I was on top of Mt. Olympus, the place of the enshrined Greek gods. I had no idea when I toppled from that mountain that the valley would be so dark and deep!

Meanwhile, one of Lisa's classmates sent an audiotape of Lisa playing the drums to *Kidsworld*, a national TV show featuring talented kids. Lisa was fourteen years old. I remember going into a studio in Pittsburgh to have the audiotape made. Two of the engineers seemed awed by her performance. I thought it was because she was a girl, but they were amazed by her age! The TV show liked the tape and asked us to find a location in Pittsburgh for the shoot. On Marty's mailman route there was a neat little bar called the Suburban Room. Lisa did her drumming there to "Carry on, My Wayward Son" by the rock group Kansas.

We were so excited. We called our friends and relatives across the country. A week before the airing, Pittsburgh canceled the show. I don't know why? However, I did send a copy of the tape to a local TV show on KDKA-TV, *The Trolley Show*. The show's producer was immediately impressed, and Lisa did the show. I was happy that now all those friends in Pittsburgh would be able to see Lisa on television.

On May 14, 1979, Steven graduated from Carnegie-Mellon University. As a student he established a world record for memorizing numbers in a CMU project exploring the power of memory. (He could recall up to eighty-one numbers in the exact sequence spoken to him.)

The University of Pittsburgh made him a fantastic offer to work toward his doctorate in the psychology department. However, Steven was tired of books and earnestly wanted to become a teacher. He struggled with the decision about his future. We would often hear him down in the den playing the piano and singing a Christian song, "Show Me the Way." The faith that he had embraced would prove to be a true rock for him.

Steven became a teacher at Holy Ghost High and was barely into his chosen profession when he began feeling extreme fatigue. We attributed it to his hectic schedule. A checkup with the doctor proved some startling results. After some test results were obtained, the doctor called and said he wanted Steven in the hospital immediately! Shakespeare wrote about the "slings and arrows of outrageous fortune...." The slings and arrows were poised and positioned on their unsuspecting prey. Steven's diagnosis: aplastic anemia, a rare blood disorder that attacks the bone marrow. The bone marrow steadily reduces production of red cells. It was an unthinkable prognosis, forcing us to anticipate a dire outcome. To this day I thank God for Steven's faith. On the way home from receiving this dismal news, Steven tried to grasp the full meaning of the situation. First he said, "But there is so much I want do." Then he said, "I'm not afraid, if this is what God wants." I will be forever grateful for his faith. It helped all of us get through this ordeal.

All family members were tested for a bone marrow match, but without success. Steven would begin treatment with doses of hormones and weekly blood transfusions. Other than being prone to infections, there is no pain with this condition. Steven was tired, though, and doctors advised him to lead a sedentary life. Steven said he simply couldn't do that! He never lost his enthusiasm for teaching and putting on musicals. After Steven's diagnosis, our struggle with reality began. The show had to go on—and so it did.

We fell into a routine, with Steven getting regular checkups and weekly transfusions. Still, he remained extremely active. We proceeded with hope. There is dignity in hope. It gives one strength and endurance. Steven's courage was heroic. I thanked God for the continued bookings for shows that always put me in a happy place… most of the time.

During this time the steroids Steven was getting were not doing what we had hoped for. I found out about a doctor in Galveston, Texas, who was working exclusively with blood disorders. Steven and I made the first of a couple trips to Galveston and came back with a special "trial" serum.

When we had our annual family reunion, Steven fooled everyone with his attitude and up-tempo demeanor.

The Memorial Day parade was a heart-wrenching experience for me. Lisa was playing the triple drums. Each year Steven had played the trumpet in the ceremony at the gravesite. He rode in a convertible with some of the veterans. At the cemetery, as he had done before, he played "Taps." I was filming during the parade, but when I began filming this sad trumpet tribute, I had to stop. The connection between the song and the battle Steven was in was unbearable for me. I asked the doctor after this event, "Is playing the trumpet a strain on someone who has aplastic anemia?" The doctor said that it was.

That summer we were asked to work as a family act at the Allegheny County Fair. I considered it but decided that this year we would just pass.

In September, Steven began his new teaching assignment at South Side Catholic High. Once again he was a whirlwind of action. He was brimming with enthusiasm. I was grateful he was alive. He requested a piano for his classroom. He would play the piano whenever he felt the class was losing focus or getting tense. The students—boys and girls alike—would come to adore him. They had no idea of his serious medical condition. As I said before, there is no pain with aplastic anemia. The battle would be with infections. A wisdom tooth needed to be pulled, but because his blood platelet counts were so low, it couldn't be done. So he developed a sinus infection. He, therefore, had a couple of hospital stays, and the students flooded him with get-well cards.

At this school, he launched varsity cross-country and track teams for both boys and girls. Again, he coached the girls' basketball team. In the drama class he persuaded kids who had never performed to take to the stage.

Steven had only been teaching for four months when he put on his first musical variety show. Since 1910 the passion play, Veronica's Veil, is still being performed on the same stage. Steven came onto the stage to handle the introductions. The auditorium was completely dark except for the spotlight. As soon as Steve appeared on the stage, the students began cheering. The admiration and love was palpable. I began praying, "Oh, God, surely he's going to live. He has so much to give!" The show was great! The students performed with verve.

What wasn't great was that Dr. Garner's serum was not working. The blood counts stayed low. We would return to Galveston on Christmas break of 1980. On our previous trip, Steven had made friends with many of the doctors and the staff. He received a telegram, "Bring Steeler beer next time you come to Galveston. Yea Oilers! Fabian Martinez, Nuclear Medicine." The news must have circulated around the hospital that Steven was returning. We arrived with a case of Iron City Beer (a photo of the Steelers was on the cans) to great excitement. You'd have thought we were passing out gold. The cans vanished like magic!

I had brought along my guitar. On Christmas Eve Steven and I strolled through the hospital singing carols for the staff, patients, and visitors. I believe it was on this trip that Steven said to me, "Well, Mom, I guess I'm still supposed to be here!"

When we returned home, Steven began working with the high school seniors to perform the school's first-ever senior-class play, *The Education of Hyman Kaplan*.

One day near the end of March, Steven told us excitedly that he and Dr. Chase from CMU would be appearing on *The Today Show* in New York. Their appearance was filmed on March 30.

Prof. William Chase, center, of the psychology department and research assistant Steven Faloon (HS'79) appeared on the Today Show on March 30. Chase is a memory expert and under his direction Faloon developed the ability to memorize up to 80 digits in about as many seconds. During the live show seen by millions of people, Faloon memorized a difficult sequence of 20 digits.

We note with deep sorrow that Steve Faloon died on May 14 from aplastic anemia. He was 23 years old. He first became ill about one and half years ago. He had been a teacher of history and drama at South Side Catholic High School in Pittsburgh. He continued teaching until several weeks before his death, even directing the school play until illness forced his hospitalization.

And then one Sunday I had to rush him to the hospital. This time he was diagnosed with pneumonia and a sinus infection. While being treated in his room, he began making arrangements for the play, giving instructions to the piano player he had hired. Whenever possible, he also played the piano in the lobby of the hospital.

As Steven's condition stabilized, his students discovered they could visit. He had a private room. They came in droves. I would always go out into the hall, where I could hear peals of laughter coming from the group.

To Steven's dismay, he had to miss the play. I was able to attend. The young students had worked energetically in the final rehearsal days and pulled off a wonderful show. The play ended with a rousing ovation. Father Sal stood in front of the curtain and gave a speech in which he described Steven as being "like a tree that had life, and the students were like the branches that got life and impetus from him." The next day I was able to give Steven a report on the success of the show and all the wonderful compliments. He was so pleased!

On May 13, in the morning, Steven wanted me to help him walk down the hallway. When we returned to his room he collapsed onto the bed, exhausted. Suddenly he said to me, "I can't feel my legs! Mom, I'm scared!" He had just suffered a massive brain hemorrhage.

Throughout the night the doctors tried everything they could. All day we were permitted to see him. He was not conscious. It was an unbelievable turn of events. A doctor finally came and discussed everything they had tried. He showed me the X-rays and the irreversible damage done to Steven's brain. The bleeding, he said, was simply out of control.

That evening, May 14, 1981, Steven lost the battle he had fought so courageously. He was twenty-three years old. The pain and sorrow cannot be expressed in words. His death was a tragedy, an "honorable" tragedy, *if* there is such a thing. The outpouring of love for our son from others was overwhelming. We had so much love and admiration for him and found that many shared those same feelings.

AFTER STEVEN

And so you have this jigsaw puzzle that is your life, your striving, and your dreams. They've all come together in a beautiful picture—not perfect, but secure in hope for the future. Then one day it begins to come apart, never to be the same. The pieces don't fit together any more. You reach out desperately trying to hold them together and wanting to deny the reality that it will never be the same. Now you must construct another life, one without Steven. However, he WAS, and nothing can ever change that, so you keep that picture in your heart. It's a snapshot of a time in time. You deal with the present, waiting for the pieces of another puzzle to fall into place and then stay together. You seek a life in order. I cry daily. My will power makes me determined to move on, yet I miss him so....

Within the week Lisa and I attended her high school band awards ceremony at the Stanley Theatre (now Heinz Hall). Although we were devastated and sorely bruised by our loss, I felt it important to continue. It was "The Show Must Go On" part of life.

After canceling several shows, Cindy and I performed at a banquet on May 24. I was losing weight; when I'm really sad, I lose my appetite.

In June there was a luncheon at South Side Catholic for a retiring nun, who asked me to do the entertaining. I am amazed at what people ask me to do. More amazing is that I do it! My program was well received.

I helped to keep Steven in my life by doing a special musical show in his honor, with proceeds going to the Blood Bank of Pittsburgh.

In August Steve's running buddies initiated a 5K (3 mile) race along a trail Steven loved to run in Schenley Park. Money was donated to the Blood Bank. It was tremendously successful.

Besides working my shows, I continued to keep occupied in everything from weekly swims at a local pool to piano lessons. I was like the person who spends his life going to school, except that I was going to piano lessons. I would start taking lessons for a while and then quit, over and over again. But I do love the piano and have mastered playing chords so that I can do sing-alongs.

One year after Steven's death, God was good to me by keeping me BUSY! It's pretty presumptuous (ego rationalizing, perhaps), but I have thought about all the good things that have happened in my life since losing Steven. He was such a good and wonderful son. Yes, how could God hurt me so? WHY? I sometimes like to think that God is saying, "I'm sorry! I'm sorry for the pain that Steven, you, and your family have endured. I'm glad there is still some happiness for you on earth!" Thinking this way helps me to endure incredible sadness and to embrace the good things that happen.

For example, there was the phone call from a college wanting to recruit Lisa for their basketball team. They were offering her a full scholarship. All of Lisa's dedication and hard work was paying off. Lisa was a high school junior and wouldn't graduate until the next year. That phone call would be one of many. Lisa was recruited by more than sixty colleges. After a visit to Penn State, Lisa decided Penn State would be her choice. When Lisa got her full scholarship, Marty was able to retire, though his guitar playing would still provide some income.

In 1983 the Warner Movie Theatre in downtown Pittsburgh was renovated into an entertainment complex featuring live entertainment, cafés, and shops. The developers were looking to "shake up" the downtown scene. There was a lot of publicity for this new venture. A call went out for auditions for a Pittsburgh "Millie" for Pittsburgh Millie's Opera House. Both Cindy and I tried out. They were going to choose three females so that there would be continuous entertainment. "Millie" would be on a stage, behind a long bar, with a piano player as accompaniment.

My tryout was at the Parkway Center Mall in Green Tree, a ten-minute drive from my house. The stage was about four feet high. I sang a couple of songs. I started to sing my second song, "Bill Bailey." I hardly stand still for anything, especially a song. With a traveling mike I traveled! Halfway through the song I backed up, and—you guessed it—I dropped off the back of the stage. I got back up right away without losing a beat and finished the song. I didn't get chosen, but Cindy did. The idea of "Pittsburgh Millie" lasted for about a year. It seemed like a great plan, but it wasn't a success.

SEND IN THE CLOWN

One day while talking to Harry Albacker, my magician friend, I commented on how things had slowed down. He had a suggestion. "A clown! Be a clown!" he said. "There is work out there for kiddie shows and birthday parties." I didn't take to the idea...not at the time!

Even before trying out a clown act myself, I had been singing "Send in the Clowns." Eventually in my shows I would ask a man to get up in front of the audience. Then I would put some clown makeup on him and top his head off with a funny hat as I sang the song.

I was still picking up some gigs mainly because I could back myself up with the guitar. The jobs that were still out there could afford only one act; Cindy and I could no longer demand the money for the two of us.

When I told Cindy about Harry's suggestion, she wasn't a bit reluctant. In fact, she liked the idea. Harry with his magic act had been touring a lot during the summer on fair dates. In the cooler months he would do a lot of birthday parties. There were also many "kiddie" shows, especially around the holidays. Cindy decided to try it, and she appropriately called her clown persona "Sunshine." Cindy had a dazzling smile. When Cindy told me how much clown work was out there, I started to reconsider the idea. Harry also continued encouraging me to do it. Once I began, I loved it! Here was a brand-new adventure waiting for me. I've always loved kids, so this was a good match!

The first "free trial" birthday party show I did was for a friend's grandchild. I thought the entrance I made as a clown should be important; I wanted to make a good impression on the children. So I arrived at the house with a dozen big balloons, each with its own string of ribbon. Unfortunately, the strings had gotten so tangled that we had to cut them to separate the balloons. Duh! There would be many mishaps in my clowning journey.

Clowning and creativity make for a dynamic duo. Being a clown opened up an exciting variety of creative choices for me. With my background of singing, dancing, and comedy, I had a good foundation to build upon. I went to any clown seminar in the area that I could. Attending these clown conventions opened up a whole new world of entertainment to me. It was like landing in the Land of Oz!

Now for my clown name! I was pleased that the annual Steve Faloon Memorial Rainbow Run, which was started by his running buddies, was doing well. After the first three-mile run, Steven's buddies teased me and said, "You should run it next year, Mrs. Faloon!" I decided to make the commitment to jog every day for thirty minutes. The

following year I finished the race in close to thirty minutes, a respectable time I was told. I was 52 years old and
I told them I was "running with a full deck!" Four years
later, I would take over the helm. (Most of his buddies
had moved out of town.) My first year, 1986, the City of
Pittsburgh erected a marker on the Schenley Park Trail:
STEVE FALOON MEMORIAL TRAIL.

After I lost my son, directing the race reattached me to
Steven; it was one of the ways I could honor him always.
So Steven's Rainbow Run inspired me to call myself
Rainbow the Clown. Still thinking of Steven, I would
paint a red heart on my right cheek, and on my left, a
rainbow-colored teardrop.

An oil painting by Frank Marcello

From the beginning I was aware that most clowns are adamant about certain rules in costuming. They are VERY
strict about what can be part of the clown outfit. Here are
some of the rules:

1. *Whatever costume chosen as the clown character*
   must be the one and only outfit._(If a clown
   had ten outfits, they had to be identical.)
   I'm afraid that would have bored me to no
   end. I instead chose different colored tops
   and different colored pants with suspend-
   ers. Since I was "Rainbow," I could play
   with many varied colors. I put sequins on
   many of my costumes, too. One of my

goals was to be a "pretty" clown and not frighten children. In fact, I was complimented often on my outfits. The one part of my wardrobe that has never changed is the rainbow-colored wig.

2. *Must wear over-sized shoes.* Anybody who knows me knows this would never work for me. I'm too active, and I would have lots of trips and falls. (If I were younger, that could have been funny!) I wear good Nike shoes. I put shiny stickers on them and they always have rainbow-colored shoestrings.

3. *Wear a big, round nose.* I think I would have gone cross-eyed wearing a big round nose. Instead, I painted my nose red and, with special eyelash glue, attached a red sequin star to the tip of my nose. If the light hit it right, the sequin would shine like a star. When I began clowning, I didn't know that after putting on the grease paint I was to powder it down to hold the colors in place. It was a good thing I didn't perspire too much.

Before I started attending clown conventions, I just stumbled along. Dear Louis Angelo in faraway Kane, PA, booked me on one of my first clown dates. The lady in charge of the event offered me her playroom to use to put on my makeup. It would have been great, but all during the process she and her two kids watched every minute, every second of the procedure. It was excruciating! Being a clown was still new to me, and I was still learning, so trying to appear professional was difficult. I decided right then that Rainbow the Clown would always leave home fully dressed and with makeup on!

As a clown, I'm able to do goofy things without even trying…even without an audience. One time I had just finished a birthday party in the backyard of a lovely home in a housing development with manicured lawns. After the party, as I was traipsing across the front lawn, I ducked under a small tree. Almost like a magic trick, my rainbow wig left my head! One of the branches had caught the wig! The rainbow wig swayed like a bowl of colored fruit. Embarrassed, I quickly looked around and saw no one! Yippee! I snatched the wig off the tree limb and stuck it back onto my head. I was glad the backyard didn't have trees.

To perform for little kids is a delight. When I'm doing magic tricks, the children exclaim, "Oh, how did you do that?" The beautiful, innocent young eyes widen in wonder and surprise. But, for me, the wonder and surprise came when I would begin performing a trick and forget to set up or "load" the main finish for the trick. The neat part of being a clown is that one can cover up the goof by acting silly…as if the goof-up occurred on purpose.

My long experience in doing shows enabled me to do many of my previously successful bits; only now I was dressed as a clown. Being able to play the guitar for the shows was another advantage.

My guitar came in handy for a Christmas kiddies' event at a local department store. The highlight of this annual event was a luncheon with Santa. I was not dressed as a clown, but I did wear happy Christmas colors. While the children ate, I played and sang Christmas songs. While I sang, Santa Claus was seated in a large chair....asleep! When the children finished their meal, I sang "Santa Claus Is Coming to Town" and Santa woke up! This was very effective, going over very well with the children! I did this gig for several years.

For one December show there was a reunion for the Fun Fillys/Fallon & Dunn duo. This was a Christmas kiddies' show at an American Legion hall. We appeared as two clowns: Sunshine and Rainbow!

Alternating between appearing as Rainbow the Clown and as Patti Eberle, musical entertainer, kept me busy and happy.

I was now fifty-seven years old. I felt very fortunate because my showbiz career was still going nonstop. As a clown, I was entertaining children; As Patti Eberle, I was entertaining older folks. Thank goodness many of the older audiences have retained the child inside themselves and are ready to have fun!

One of the things I had to learn to do as a clown was to make balloon creations. I remember telling Cindy, "I can't stand twisting those balloons...I always expect them to break!" But I was intrigued so I decided to give it a try. Many evenings Marty would be watching TV and I would be in another room twisting balloons. First I tried to make balloon dogs. I broke the balloons. BANG! BANG! A couple of months of trying to learn this new skill surely contributed to my hearing loss. Like many other people, I don't want to bother reading directions.

However, I learned that in order to be successful with this, I had to leave one end of the long, skinny balloon deflated (a "tail"), because each time I would twist a balloon, the air would be pushed into that section of the balloon. The air had to go somewhere!

Eventually I got the hang of it with practice, practice, and more practice. I slowly expanded my repertoire beyond dogs to bees, butterflies, fish, parrots, swans, bunnies, horses, octopuses, bears, monkeys, cats, hats, flowers, rainbows, and on and on. The boys always wanted swords, swords, and more swords!

Face painting is so creative and fun. Little girls love the hearts, rainbows, unicorns, and especially, butterflies...with sparkles. Little boys prefer snakes, alligators, skulls, and Batman. In Pittsburgh they love the Steelers' football logo.

I've always loved that children want to share stories with me. One time at a birthday party in a lovely home, I was holding a little "magic" sponge frog in the palm of my hand. I asked the kids, "Did you ever hold a frog in your hand?" The little birthday girl wanted to share her story. She blurted out, "Oh, I did, and it peed in my hand!" The other kids laughed. Her mother was embarrassed. I found it best to comment in an even voice, "I'm sure that can happen," and quickly moved on to the next bit. I figured I could always laugh later.

CHILDREN'S HOSPITAL

Learning magic tricks and twisting balloons sure came in handy while I was a Sunday school teacher for little children, for I was able to hold their interest. At one event at church I twisted balloons into an octopus and gave it to a little boy. He walked around telling everybody, "Look! Look at the testicles!" We all grinned and quietly corrected him. "Those are tentacles!"

For quite a few years, I went to Children's Hospital of Pittsburgh once a month to do two shows. The first time I found it very difficult, seeing all those precious children with so many problems. A little boy said to me, "You're not a clown!" I answered, "Yes, I am!" He said, "You're not funny!" I realized my sadness was showing.

So, after that first day and thereafter, I entertained these children just like I did for all other kids. It worked— for me and for them. I always made one of them a clown. I wasn't permitted to use any kind of face paint on their faces, so I used colored stickers instead.

I would often see the same children on subsequent visits, children who had severe, chronic problems. One of these was a little girl who always came to the shows. She remembered my routines. One day she asked me, "Can I be the clown today?" I was happy to make her the clown with the stickers, the paper party hat, and the noisemaker. I told her, "Now you are the clown for the rest of the day. Smile, and the smile will come back to you!" Within a month this dear little child was gone.

My heart felt the pain of the parents of these children. There were always a few parents present during my performances. One of my greatest triumphs was being a distraction, if only for a little while, for these anxious, caring parents. I might put a Mickey Mouse hat on a daddy or a baby bonnet on a mommy. The kids loved it! I would get everyone in the room laughing, even for a tiny "Camelot" moment.

Another incident at Children's was really fun. I said to a little boy standing with his mother, "I'll bet I can guess your age! Five!" And he said, "How did you do that?" I quickly said, "I can guess your name too! What's the first letter?" He said, "J!" I began guessing, "Jason... John...(and then) Jeremy!" He beamed and said, "Yes!" Suddenly the boy's father appeared. "Now," said the little boy, "guess my daddy's name." I said, " What's the first letter?" He said, "D!" I guessed, "David? Daniel? Darrell? Donald?" Finally the little boy said, "No, it's DADDY!"

The little ones delighted in my "magic" mommy and daddy bunnies who could make five little baby bunnies. I would place two sponge rabbits into a child's cupped hands and say the cupped hands were the bunnies' nest. I would close the child's fingers together and then say, "Now open wide." The child would open his or her hands to reveal seven bunnies. One time one little boy, when I said, "Open wide," opened his mouth, really, really wide, not his cupped hands. His mom and grandparents laughed. I said, "He thinks I'm a dentist." After more laughter, they explained, "His father *is* a dentist."

SPECIAL MEMORIES

Many of the birthday parties and shows I've done have been recorded. For one of my earlier parties, a parent had an extra videotape made and sent it to me. It was the first time I would see myself on a gig. It served a good purpose in that I would know to tell the next "filmmaker" to be sure and scan the audience so that they would be able to see the reaction of their child and invited guests.

As Rainbow the Clown, I would stand on my head, put the microphone on the floor by my mouth, and sing a song. The kids loved it. Eventually my chiropractor told me to quit standing on my head. Darn! Another laugh exits.

Once I was called to do a show for a group of Jehovah's Witnesses. They had rented a barn and called the show a "Noah's Ark Party." It was a wonderful event with live animals. The costumes for the children had to be biblical. (This sect does not believe in Halloween or the Easter Bunny.) I was ready to sing "Here comes Peter Cottontail!"

when a mother came up to me and whispered, "We don't use the word Easter." I replaced the word with "happy day." A group of ladies stood up and gave me a combination of thumbs-up and high-fives.

I once had a note sent to me during my clown show. The note read: "There's a little boy sitting in the back that is afraid of clowns." If I see a scared child, I turn sideways and give a shy little wave of my hand as if to say "Hi." Often, that is enough to win the child over. I once walked into a house for a four-year-old's birthday party, and the birthday girl started CRYING. I did my shy bit and proceeded with the show. She slowly emerged from the back of the room and sat right up front. When it came time for me to leave, she hung onto my leg and cried, "Don't go!"

In the early days of doing clown shows, I seldom went straight home after a show. There was always someone I knew in the hospital or a nursing home, so I would make a stop and hopefully get them smiling.

One time I went to visit a former neighbor in her assisted-living home. When I arrived, she was in bed. Here I was in full get-up, with my rainbow wig, my white face, and my shiny, sequined, ruffled collar. I leaned over her, and when she opened her eyes, they got as big as saucers! I said to her, "No, you haven't died and gone to clown heaven." Then she grinned. We really loved each other.

Sometime later I was summoned to her bed because she was failing. I came into her room and stood near the foot of the bed. She was surrounded by aides and a doctor. Her eyes crinkled and with a twinkle in her eye, she stuck her tongue out at me. Soon she was gone.

It took me a couple of years to feel really secure in my clowning career. My background in show business certainly bolstered my courage. My range of talent had given me an advantage. For shows I would play the guitar. I remember after one of these shows a lady came up to compliment me. She said, "When they announced a clown for the show, I started to walk away. However, when I saw you with a guitar, I became intrigued. I'm glad I stayed, I really enjoyed your show!"

I got a gig appearing at a picnic in Fox Chapel with KDKA's Jon Burnette. He was very friendly and everybody enjoyed the day.

BRICKED IN PHILLY

In October 1987, a reunion of the 253rd Blood and Fire Infantry was held in Philadelphia. It was to be a fabulous weekend. These guys had bravely served our country in World War II. Many of them were together when the war ended. What a bond they had! Several of them had appeared in the *Carmen* show, the GIs' farce about the opera *Carmen*. Marty had directed the band for this show all across Europe.

We had dinner at a hotel outside of town. A lot of the GIs were also there with their spouses and girlfriends. The camaraderie among them was incredible. What is there about a group of men who have lived through hell? Maybe it's surviving and being grateful to be alive to enjoy life.

After dinner, a big, yellow, chartered school bus hauled us to a downtown club where our dear friend Charlie Byrd was performing. Instead of taking the freeway as planned, the driver decided he would cut through the town. It was an extremely dark night. The bus flew through the streets at a fast pace. I sat by a window. I looked out and could dimly see a couple of young males and I remember seeing one raise his arm. In an instant two of the bus windows were shattered by red bricks. One brick hit me in the chest and some pieces of glass landed in Marty's eyes. A couple of rows in front of us another couple had also been injured; another brick cut the woman's face and pieces of glass went into her husband's eyes. (To think our husbands were the guys who had fought to make our world safe!) The woman would need stitches on her chin. I was the lucky one—only my chest was bruised. The window had stopped the full force. Both our husbands kept their eyes open, trying not to blink for fear of further damage. The bus driver drove the four of us right to the hospital. Then he drove the others to see Charlie Byrd's show. Fortunately, the doctors at the local hospital were able to flush the glass out of both men's eyes.

When we were ready to leave the hospital, I approached the main desk and asked if a policeman could take us back to our hotel. The nurse said to me, "Just get a cab, and get out of here as soon as you can!" We called a cab. We missed Charlie Byrd's show, but at least we were alive.

YELLOW PAGES, GOLDEN TEETH

· ·

After a couple of my learning years, I decided to place an ad in the Yellow Pages. Advertising in the Yellow Pages was an expensive leap. I first checked to see if there was another clown named Rainbow. There wasn't. I saw an attorney and, then, for two hundred dollars, had the name legalized. I listened to my mentor, Harry Albacker: "Brag!" So my ad read: "Rainbow the Clown — Multi-Talented — Musical Magical Clown — Balloon Creations — Audience Participation — Spontaneous Surprises!

A friend, Billy Jones, a painter by trade, was also a fine artist. I hired him to do some sketches of Rainbow the Clown for my business cards. I noted that aging entertainers often had sketches instead of pictures for advertising. He also did a sketch of Patti Eberle holding a guitar to be used for business cards. I got many years of use out of these cards; I mailed them out until the computer began to rule the world.

Christmas kiddie shows were still having their heyday! The Yellow Pages ad was really paying off.

As I'm thinking of the word "yellow," I remember that after I applied my white-face makeup, my teeth did not look white. A little one once exclaimed as he looked at me, "Oh, you have golden teeth!" After that, I grinned a lot without showing my teeth! Then I had my dentist order caps. He told me a lot of movie stars had them. With them on, I thought I looked like Mary Tyler Moore, with her big, white smile. This worked fine until one Christmas show in which I opened the show as a clown, singing and playing my guitar to the tune of "Deck the Halls." There are a lot of "Fa, la, la, la, la's" in this song. I think it was at the second "Fa" that the caps flew out of my mouth! (Try it: Put your teeth down on your lower lip and belt out a strong "Fa!") Back I was to my golden teeth. Maybe the audience thought that I had lost a wad of gum! Eventually I had porcelain dentistry. Wow! What a relief! I could smile BIG again.

LENNY LITMAN

. . . .

Over the years I have had close friendships with many showbiz people. Lenny Litman, the showbiz critic for the *Pittsburgh Press*, was one of them. He had given Cindy and me the good review when we worked the revered Holiday House.

Lenny at one time owned the Copa Club, a Pittsburgh nightclub that was a nationally famous "home" of the world's great stars, including Joey Bishop, Frankie Laine, Vic Damone, Christine Jorgensen (the first person to undergo a male-to-female sex change), Mel Torme, Artie Shaw, Cab Calloway, Billie Holiday, Andy Williams, Ella Fitzgerald, Tony Bennett, and Patti Page.

I would become Lenny's source for news of the demise of local performers. I would relay the news to Lenny and he would relay it to New York. It would be printed in the famous showbiz newspaper VARIETY.

Having an active life has its blessings in all its diversions. Just a couple of weeks after my father died, I received an invitation from Lenny's wife. The invitation read: "It's been show time for over 50 years!" The party was to be a big bash for Lenny's seventy-fifth birthday. I had a great time there, reliving the exciting world of nightclub days. Or should I say, nightclub nights?

Lenny wrote me a lovely thank you note with an intriguing postscript: "After talking to you, I will tell Stacy Keach he has a blessing from clown heaven." (Lenny knew I was a clown and maybe Stacy Keach was ill?)

ON WITH THE SHOW

Marty's army/air force band reunion was held in St. Louis in 1991. Marty and I had been doing a show each year on the final banquet night. We put together a brand-new show for each year's performance. In St. Louis that year I especially enjoyed a number I did with sweet Alma Mantese whose husband, Larry, was one of the band members and also a music teacher. The couple lived in St. Louis and hosted the reunion. As a trumpet player, Larry also had a popular band in the area. He was a great, energetic entertainer.

For the show I bought two long T-shirts that were printed with a design of a woman wearing sexy lingerie with stockings and garters. I had Alma leave the room to put hers on. I put mine on and started singing the verse: "I hate to see the evening sun go down..." Then, when I got to the chorus,"...St. Louis woman with all her diamond rings...," I told Alma to walk in "stripper-like" as I continued singing. It went over great!

In St. Louis there was an impressive mall that had been a former train station, much like Pitt's Station Square. In the middle of the mall a clown was twisting balloon creations. Of course, I was fascinated. I could do most of the different balloons that the clown produced. However, there was one that I studied and studied as I stood there watching it being designed; it was a lovely balloon flower with a balloon stem. By the time I got back to Pittsburgh, I still hadn't figured out how it was done. One of the members in our reunion group, Dom Caramagna, always took movies of the events and would send everyone a copy of them. Sometimes being the recipient of dumb luck can be the most unexpected, thrilling experience. Case in point: Dom had been in the mall and filmed the flower-balloon-twisting clown... making the flower. Watching the process over and over, I was finally able to make the flower balloon.

In 1991, after the expense of advertising in the Yellow Pages, a terrible mistake was made in my clown ad. Instead of listing Rainbow the Clown, the Yellow Pages listed Marty's band. To add insult to injury, the band was listed under "Male Exotic Dancers." Oh, the calls we got that year! All the clowns in the area who advertise in the Yellow Pages can thank me. Up until this time, the listing "clown" had never been in the alphabetical listings of businesses. It is now! Thank goodness I had established enough of a reputation that some work did come in despite the snafu. I'm sure an omission like this could kill some new businesses.

The manager at PC-TV, a public cable station, suggested my doing a clown show program. I liked the idea. I was optimistic about the program I scripted. This was a one-shot, nonstop deal. Marty would play the guitar. Our artist friend, Frank Marcello, would do sketches of the characters from the Wizard of Oz. The kids would guess which Oz characters he was drawing. (Frank was a fine professional artist. He wanted to do an oil painting of me as a clown as a gift. From a snapshot he painted, in glorious colors, Rainbow the Clown. The frame is perfect with its circus colors, red and shiny gold.) I had a group of nine children ranging in age from three to seven seated in front of a foot-high stage. There was a platform on which I displayed an array of twisted balloon creations. While I was standing in front doing the introduction for the show, unbeknownst to me, two of the younger kids scattered the balloons all over the place. When I turned around, I was stunned to see the balloons, mostly animals, scattered everywhere.

During the show, I held up beautiful pictures of Pittsburgh scenes for the song about Pittsburgh I had written. Frank Marcello sang the song in his beautiful "Perry Como" style. I did some magic tricks sitting among the kids. If a little one reached up to grab part of a trick, I would calmly move his hand away. I twisted a balloon parrot perched on a balloon circle. Each child got to hold a finished balloon animal. As they held their animals, we sang "Old McDonald Had a Farm." I closed the show with Marcello singing "Somewhere Over the Rainbow" as I performed the song in sign language.

We would not see the film on TV for a couple of weeks. I was truly amazed at my coolness on the film, despite the fact that frustrations were churning inside me. No one would ever know how upset I was during the filming. Guess it's what you call acting like an "old pro." With all my years of experience, the show must go on!

In 1992, once again the Yellow Pages made a major goof that would significantly affect the clown work I was able to obtain. I made the mistake of upgrading my ad. In the process, somehow my ad was omitted. There was no listing at all! Once again the reputation of my work would help me get repeat gigs. Plus, Harry Albacker threw a lot of jobs my way. Some mishaps can be corrected, but once that Yellow Book is printed and distributed, nothing can be done for a year.

I was glad I was still picking up gigs as Patti Eberle. I got a booking for a show at the Edgewood Country Club. Marty's music gigs were really slowing down. I knew how much he loved playing the guitar, and I suggested that he come along and back me up on this show. It worked out fine. I had no idea at the time I would have a new showbiz partner—my husband—at this point in my career!

1993

· ·

St. Patrick's Day in 1993 proved to be a BIG snow day for Pittsburgh. I had a clown birthday party booked in Regent Square, which is normally a twenty-minute drive from home. Marty wanted me to cancel. The entire city is Irish that day. I put the TV on to see if the parade was indeed happening. The snow was coming down and so was the parade...right down Fifth Avenue. I called to see if the birthday party was cancelled. The father of the birthday child said, "No, and I've got a parking spot all dug out for you!" I knew the three side streets near my house would be deep with snow and dangerous. However, I thought that by the time I reached the main street, it would be clear. Not so; it was still deep and untraveled. I felt that Marty was right, and that I had made a mistake by not cancelling my appearance. The one thing I had going for me was that I pretty much had the whole road to myself. When I was close to my destination, though, a car in front of mine almost stopped on a little upward grade. I prayed aloud, "Please don't stop. Please keep moving." If the car had stopped fully, I don't believe I would have made it to my destination. There were at least twenty kids at the party. How were all of them able to get there? Simple. They all lived in the same neighborhood. It was a short walk for them, a walk they probably enjoyed!

On my trip back home after the party, I got as far as a block and a half away from my house. In front of me was a hump over which my car would have to climb. Many times over the years I'd driven home from Penn State University in snowstorms, and yet I couldn't get up and over that hump. I parked my car on a level spot and carried my bags up the final hill to my house. It wouldn't be the last time. My "The Show Must Go On" mantra keeps my guardian angel busy.

My friend Harry Albacker would go south for the summer, but he battled the winter driving like the rest of us. I would have Harry at my house for lunch to discuss show business and bookings, but most of the time we would meet in a restaurant. Harry was like me in that he loved reaction. He had a dry wit that gave me many laughs. For example, before hanging up during a phone conversation with him, I'd say, "I'll call you tomorrow." He would say to me, "Is that a threat?" I'd laugh. We were two of a kind in that we loved what we were doing and never wanted to stop!

I'll admit I'm a softie. If I believe someone earnestly wants some advice and I can help them, I do. Many of us have heard of the expression that when someone helps another and that other person tries to repay them, the originator says, "Pass it on!" I've always been grateful for people like Albacker who have helped and advised me. I've had calls from people asking me, "How do I become a clown?" If they sound sincere and nice (my favorite four-letter word), I will talk to them.

Once I got a call from a fella who wanted to help a girlfriend who wanted to become a clown. The longer we talked, the more I realized they didn't have much money for makeup and supplies. I told him I had some extra supplies, and so we agreed to meet at a restaurant. When I arrived at the restaurant I have to admit I was surprised. The man was white; the girl wasn't. I was able to give her makeup, a wig, and an outfit. I explained how to put on the makeup. I gave her some grease paint sticks in various colors. I gave her some of the white makeup I use as my face color base. I explained, "I put the white on first, then the colors. I told her to be creative with the colors and that a must was the white talcum powder that had to be applied with a quick pat all over the face. (Some clowns put the talcum in a white sock. They tie the sock in a knot and "whack" their face with the sock to release the powder, which "sets" the grease paint, making it last for hours.) Next, I said, "You need to work on a routine, hopefully a funny one! To get started do a lot of free performances to practice, and perfect your act." I never heard what happened to this lady.

I realize that in all the years I've been doing clowning in the Tri-State area surrounding Pittsburgh, I have never heard of or seen a black clown. The funny part about this is that my personal experience has shown that people of African-American descent—at least in the Pittsburgh area—tend to LOVE clowns. Often when I ride to gigs with my clown outfit on, many Caucasian folks ignore me or pretend they don't see me. I've done many birthday parties for persons of color, and the reaction from many of the adults is childlike; young and old alike enjoy the balloons, comedy, and magic.

AUTHOR'S NOTE

When I began writing this book, I had no idea it was going to cover eighty years! So the rest of this journey will focus on the highlights of each year until now.

1994 "A time to be born, a time to die"

It was in this year that my dear friend and mentor, Harry Albacker, died. My last phone conversation with Harry had been prophetically sad. He wasn't feeling well, and the jobs in Pittsburgh were not plentiful. One of the last things he said to me was, "I'm getting the hell out of this town." He died the way most of us entertainers want to "go": He was just finishing a show and collapsed. He was sixty-eight years old. Magicians have a special funeral service for their peers called the Broken Wand. Harry's service was very touching. Oh, how I will miss this human link to all my years in show business.

On a brighter note, this was the year Lisa started her own personal training business, Fitness Techniques, in Oakmont, PA. I now have Bill, with his vitamins, and Lisa keeping me fit and in good shape. Plus I probably have some good genes.

On October 8th my son Bill and Wife Debbie presented us with a baby boy, Chance. Grandparents at last!

1995

I was getting gigs throughout the year. I placed an ad in the *Pittsburgh Senior News*: "Patti Eberle, comedy, variety and musical fun." That ad became a good conduit for obtaining bookings at AARP and senior shows. My ad for Rainbow the Clown was in the Yellow Pages, too. After all the goof-ups with the Yellow Pages in the past, I had learned my lesson; whenever I got called each year to place an ad, I'd say, "Don't change a thing!" So far, so good.

1996

Sixty-seven years old and still performing! Thank you, Lord!

My son Billy gave Marty and me a much-needed vacation: a lovely trip to the Bahamas. This was the first time I would see the "Macarena" performed. I knew immediately it was a good participation number. I was able to write down the dance movements. When I got back to Pittsburgh, I put it in my first show. Even though the tune had not yet caught on in Pittsburgh, I predicted that it would. It did. I tried very hard to learn the foreign lyrics, but finally made up my own.

On August 29th we would become grandparents again to another boy, Chase. So it's now—Chance and Chase, cha cha cha!

Cindy and I as Fallon & Dunn got a job now and then. Our reputation from the past had been that of a "good act." We worked the beautiful, five-star Nemacolin Woodland resort. We had worked at this lovely resort with Slim Bryant and the Wildcats, a popular group from Pittsburgh. What a sweet gentleman Slim was.

I was busy with the clown work and senior citizen events. It had become evident by this time that many of Pittsburgh's finest musicians were not working much. Marty's body, it seemed, was connected to his guitar. He converted a room in the basement into a music room. Hardly a day went by that he was not playing his guitar and taping. After retiring as a mailman, his only exercise was his music. He also bought a banjo. He tuned it like a guitar and was about to pick up some gigs. All the musicians were scrambling with ideas on how to keep playing. One musician picked up a lot of jobs as Santa Claus during the Christmas season.

Patti & Marty

As the demand for live musicians decreased, I suggested to Marty that he do the senior citizen gigs with me. So we became "Patti & Marty." I changed the ad in the *Senior News* magazine from "Patti Eberle" to "Patti & Marty, Musical Fun with Everyone." It worked out great for both of us. We could get a little more money, and I didn't have to play my guitar. I had complete freedom, as I once did when there were live bands to back up my act. Between the two of us, we knew hundreds of songs. One of the features of our shows together was to see if the audience could stump him with a song. I don't remember him ever getting stumped. He knew songs ranging from "Letter Edged in Black" to "Barney Google." We were in the right place at the right time: older us, older songs, older audiences.

1997

I joined Marty in his lifelong dream of taking a long train ride. We took Amtrak to Florida. I was really glad we took this long train journey because about a month later, Marty, now seventy-five years old, had three-way bypass surgery and received a heart valve. Although the surgery was successful, I was traumatized by the way he looked as he lay there on his hospital bed. He was not awake. The many tubes and beeping medical machinery were frightening. I thought I was going to faint, I felt my knees buckling. Thankfully, Marty recovered quickly and came home.

Charlie Byrd came to town and wanted Marty to play with him. Marty would have loved it, but due to the recent operation he couldn't. We did go and see the marvelous genius that was Charlie Byrd perform.

He returned to Pittsburgh later in the year to play at the Manchester Craftsmen's Guild. This time he stayed at our house. We moved Lisa out of her bedroom so that

Charlie had a place to sleep. We kidded him about how frilly and feminine Lisa's bedroom was: white provincial furniture with a covered canopy bed. Charlie had an endearing, easy-to-please persona.

Eventually Marty was able to resume playing his guitar. He had an ongoing gig at Allegheny General Hospital with his trio. Sometimes I would do the gig with him, singing with the group. Playing again, Marty was so happy to be playing again, caressing my rival for his love: his guitar. We continued our AARP shows as Patti & Marty. Our team was getting busy and well established.

Compared to the clown wardrobe and makeup, the "Patti" wardrobe was a cinch. It consisted of a pair of black pants and any one of a number of "showy" tops. As with the clown outfits, I had an infinite variety of tops, most of them with something shiny—either sparkles or sequins. Now, as I'm writing this in 2009, I've seen in magazines and on the television's *Today Show* that sequins are "in" again. My handsome Marty always wore a nice suit and tie. Classy.

In the fall, Cindy and I attended a balloon twisters' convention at the Radisson Hotel in Monroeville. At the age of sixty-eight, I was still learning new stuff. We were interviewed by a newspaper reporter who seemed interested in us "older" ones. We were both quoted. Cindy: "To be a successful clown, one needs to think young!" I got the punch line in the article by saying, "I hope to die with my (clown) nose on!"

1998

January has usually been a slow month for entertainers although the acts "Patti & Marty" and "Rainbow the Clown" were thriving.

Near the end of February I missed my first show in fifty-one years due to illness. My journey this year would be my trial of all trials, centered around trying to answer one question: "What's wrong with me?" I was sick all the time, with a sore throat, phlegm, or nausea. I was continually running to doctors and trying different medications; nothing was working. I started to get depressed. I would have a good day followed by a bad day. On a bad day I would do something like wash a wall in a room of my house. Any kind of physical labor would free my mind of worrying about what was wrong with me. During this period I continued my shows.

"Hallelujah!" was my joyful cry of thanks when I finally got an answer to my chronic sickness problem. I had a bad bacteria in my stomach called H-Pylori. After a course of antibiotics, I felt healthy again.

Around this time, KDKA-TV had a contest for any original tribute to Pittsburgh in the form of a song, poem, etc. I sent in a tape of the song I wrote and got a call that I was one of ten winners. A TV crew came to my house and filmed me singing, accompanied by Marty on the guitar:

I like my city because
It's my very own Land of Oz.
Emerald rivers and trees surround
Pittsburgh, I love you! My neat, sweet town.

Come see a castle of glass winkin' at the sun,
The glimmering glow where the three
rivers run.
Station Square, I declare, shining there.
Incline to Mt. Washington, only me and you.
Hold me close as we toast the marvelous view.
We're up so high, we'll touch the sky, you
and I.

The buildings are so pretty, delightful
sights to see.
Each one seems to say, "Look at me!
Look at me!"
Our many bridges we applaud; see them
smiling up at God.
Come, let my city with a smile, smile at you!

KDKA introduced me as the Jingle Lady! Only a few lines of the song were played when the piece aired on TV. I didn't win any money. It didn't matter. I was proud of my city. I was old enough to have watched it grow and prosper.

We took another trip to Florida, where I did a magic show for my grandson Chance's fourth birthday. Later I was treated to a front-row seat at the Ringling Bros. and Barnum & Bailey "Greatest Show on Earth" circus. The star of the show was a clown named David Larible, known as the "Prince of Laughter." And he truly was the star of this production. He staged two different performances in the center ring. For one of his skits, he brought some audience members onstage and had them put on tutus and perform a ballet. It got a lot of laughs.

I had done something similar twenty years earlier. I had a seamstress make me two very large tutus with special Velcro closures at the waists so that the tutus could fit all sizes. I would bring two men up from the audience and have them don the tutus—and bows for their hair! They would then practice some ballet steps with me. The band would play some appropriate music, and the men would happily "ham it up" to great laughter. At the circus I was watching a world-class act doing the same bit on a larger scale. I still have the tutus, but now, doing the senior shows, it's too strenuous a bit for the seniors. Plus, there's no live music to back me up.

For Larible's second bit, he once again gathered audience members and formed an orchestra, providing each person with a very large instrument and seating them all on a large stage. This bit was a sensation.

I had been doing a similar audience-participating bit for about ten years. I would open the show with a song. Then I would lament the days of doing shows with big bands to back me up. I would talk of the wonderful orchestrations I had. Many in the audience would nod their heads, remembering. Next I'd say, "It's amazing the talent I find wherever I go! In fact, right here in this room are some very talented musicians." I would bring four people onto the stage and give them different instruments: a tambourine, small toy horns, and flutes. They would get to keep these after the act was over. The tune I would have them play was the American classic, "Alexander's Ragtime Band," written by Irving Berlin in 1911. Seeing Larible do a similar bit resonated well with me. Wasn't it Shakespeare who said, "There is nothing new under the sun"? I agree. It's what an individual does to twist an idea that makes for something "new."

1999

Cindy loved her activities director job…everything but the crafts, that is. I told her I'd dream up something for a craft project and come and do it with the group. I did. I hadn't seen Cindy for a while, and I thought she looked ill. I called her afterward and took her to lunch. She was losing weight. She had no appetite. She wouldn't confide in me, and so just let me worry.

I received a telephone call from a man who was interested in my Martin D18 guitar. I had paid $250 for it. He offered me $1,500. We antiques can be valuable!

Marty and I performed at the first home for Alzheimer's patients. We were asked back many times, but the show was a challenge. I was always glad there were family members in the audience. Considering what the residents and their families were going through, it felt great that we could get them to relax and smile for a little while.

In November, Charlie Byrd died—this great American jazz and classical guitarist and our dear, dear friend. Marty and I had a show booked on the date of the funeral in Virginia. Marty attended the funeral, and I did the show solo.

2000

One day my son Bill's wife, Debbie, called and said, "Mom, you and Dad are going to be married fifty years in November. Do you want a cruise or a party?" Without an ounce of hesitation, I said, "PARTY!"

There was constant busy-ness surrounding preparations for our anniversary party. It was to be held at the Churchill Valley Country Club. At one time country clubs were active, booking musicians and acts to entertain at members' parties and banquets, plus corporate clients and many social events. Like so many of the private clubs which had passed their prime, these venues began to tumble with declining membership. There was a change in social habits among people with disposable income. In two more years, nine country clubs in the Tri-State area would have been sold.

Marty and I were pleased that our party would be at this lovely club we had both worked so many times. We weren't able to get the big ballroom, and we were limited to 150 people in the smaller room. It was difficult to draw up the invitation list, having so many relatives, neighbors, regular friends, and showbiz friends. When the RSVPs started coming in and I would receive a "can't make it" reply, I would turn to my waiting list. Deciding whom to invite was both a joy and a frustration.

Marty and I had had a very modest wedding and a very modest reception. That old saying about "starting from scratch" was us! Through good fortune, hard work, and perseverance, we had a good marriage. To quote another favorite song called "All the Way:"   "...through the good and lean years, and for all the in-between years, come what may..."

The morning before our party, nearly a year in the planning, we attended the funeral of my baby brother's lifelong bride. The timing seemed unbelievable. Genny had just turned sixty-five years old. She and my brother had a love for each other that was greatly admired. I had constantly been with my brother throughout the heart-wrenching ordeal. The anniversary party was the next day. If ever there was a case of "The Show Must Go On," we were about to do it big time!

Our two grownup children, Bill and Lisa, were both successful in their careers and wanted to go all out for our celebration. Bill's wife, Debbie, was enjoying planning the party. Marty enjoyed choosing the band, a four-piece group, counting Marty on the guitar. The drummer was our dear friend Bobby Rawsthorne, a drummer for Mister Rogers of children's TV fame, with Bill Bickel's son Ronnie on the piano. We also had a trumpet player and comedian, Ray DeFay.

With all that was going on with Genny, I never got around to planning the entertainment. The party wound up being a spontaneous, lively affair. The evening was a huge success, with a rainbow of friends and relatives and many lifelong musician friends. We had interesting groups at each table. At one table was my chiropractor; our children's pediatrician; Marty's leader from the Army/Air Force Band and his son; a doctor; plus Dr. Pat Benjamin, a minister who went to school with Marty. After we ate, Marty and I walked around the room with a microphone, reminiscing and sharing funny, personal stories with and about the guests. I got an unexpected long laugh when I introduced Dr. Albo. I said, "This is Dr. Albo. He had all my kids!" His wife, Trinka, deadpanned, "Oh, really!" I quickly realized I had not worded that well, but what a great laugh it got.

Cindy and I relived some of our "days of glory" tunes. Many knew us in our prime. The laughter we received for our antics felt familiar and good.

A precious moment for me was having my two grandsons, Chance and Chase, do the song-and-dance routine I had taught them. It was from a Shirley Temple movie: "Have you seen my new shoes, they are made out of wood..."

Chase, Patti, & Chance

Many of the now-grown-up Gladys Avenue Gang were able to attend. What a glorious time we had digging into our reservoir of long-ago songs that we did in our kiddie shows. The Charleston-like routine with the now-grown boys was hilarious; even my son Bill joined in. The girls, now women, did the cutesy "Doggie in the Window," wagging their "tails." We turned the clock back for a few minutes. These kids had all grown up into delightful "hams"!

Bobby Rawsthorne's group, The Steel City Stompers, did a couple of hilarious routines. Marty played a special solo on his guitar just for me—my favorite, "All the Things You Are."

346 • PITTSBURGH PIZZAZZ

To have a room full of people one has known through your life's journey is an overwhelming happily-ever-after moment.

A couple that missed the party wrote us a note of apology. They were really mad at themselves for having forgotten the date, especially since they reported, "We heard we missed the best party of the year!"

2001

What a yo-yo life hands us! A Saturday morning in February was the day of my dear cousin Trina's funeral. That afternoon I did a clown show with Marty. In the evening Marty and I performed at a senior show. How did I do it? I just did it, and still do it!

Marty began a steady series of hospital stays as he was experiencing one problem after another, everything from a cataract operation to adjustments with his medications relating to his heart surgery. He kept coping; we kept working!

After much nagging from Marty and Lisa, I finally went for a hearing test. They were both tired of me saying, "What did you say?" I was stubborn, though, telling them, "I'm okay, my shows are going over great!" In the end I got hearing aids. When the doctor suggested possible reasons for my hearing loss, I admitted I had experienced them all. Had I fallen a lot? Oh, yes. Loud noises? Oh, yes. I recalled loud, mostly-trumpet jam sessions. Then there was Lisa practicing her drums to loud rock and roll music. I do believe the final straw was learning to twist balloons. I broke soooooo many balloons right next to my ears.

The last time I saw Cindy alive was during a visit to her in the assisted-care facility where she was now living. My friend Claire and I were both startled to see how small and weak Cindy looked. She was sleeping, but she awoke and sat up on the edge of the bed to talk with us. She sat between Claire and me, both of us wearing hearing aids. This partner, whose biggest asset was a beautiful, big, contagious smile, managed a little grin and commented, "This is the first time I've ever sat between two hearing-impaired people!" We laughed, just the response Cindy wanted.

On December 8 Cindy died. She was seventy-one years old. She never told anyone, including her husband, that she had breast cancer. I notified the newspaper and sent them a photo of our team for the following write-up about her:

Half of duo that spread music, laughs in region, Fallon and Dunn delivered a double whammy of laughs and music throughout the Tri-State area for 15 years…Together the two young mothers made the rounds of the Pittsburgh area's nightclubs, hotels, and lodges of the 1960s and 1970s. They traveled as far away as Toronto, making sure they made it home in time to tuck in their children Sunday night.…

A bright student, Cindy received a scholarship to Duquesne University, but her parents didn't have enough money for the incidental college costs. She wanted to entertain and loved the limelight and loved to make people laugh, said her son.…

In 1984, almost 40 years after her high school graduation, Mrs. Slone earned an associate degree in health from Community College of Allegheny County. She then became activity director at several local nursing homes.

I had been blessed with a wonderful partner and friend. We had shared so much. We never had a single argument. We loved and respected each other.

Once again I would get through an unbelievably trying day. Cindy's funeral was in the morning. That afternoon, Marty and I did a show. Our Christmas bookings were full. We were mourning, but still believed that "the show must on"!

2002

The team of Patti & Marty was kept busy with shows. However, Marty's health was in constant jeopardy. It was one thing after the other. We were living happy, sad, and bad days. I begged him to take the therapy that was offered to him after his successful heart operation. He wouldn't do it. All those good years of on-the-job physical therapy—carrying mail—were over. The most exercise he did nearly every day was playing his guitar. At least the guitar playing was less strenuous than playing the banjo. What bothered Marty the most was the painful rheumatoid arthritis that developed primarily in his hands. Still, he didn't, wouldn't, couldn't stop playing his beloved guitar.

The last show Patti & Marty would do was at a Lutheran church. It was a celebration for Bishop Donald McCoid. The audience was joyously enthusiastic. The evening was significant in many ways, one of them being that Marty and I had been married in a Lutheran church. Here we were doing what we loved. It seemed appropriate that our finale would be in in a Lutheran church.

Marty died the first day of May. Someday I may write about the terrible and trying moments associated with his death. I did get to talk with my dear, struggling husband before he underwent a medical procedure on what was to be his last hospital visit. I stood outside the door, and the door was ajar. Something went awry with the procedure, and I saw a nurse put her hand up to her mouth in a fearful manner. Suddenly doctors were surrounding Marty's bed. They blocked the view of Marty's last breath, which I didn't realize had occurred at the time. It took quite a while for a doctor to come out and tell me that Marty had died.

I have a copy of the last answering machine message from Marty, and I treasure it. The most important part of the message was, "I love you."

Nate Guidry, a *Pittsburgh Post-Gazette* staff writer, wrote a long and lovely tribute to Marty's life. It was titled "As Jazz Guitarist, Letter Carrier Met and Played with Greats." Many friends were surprised to read about Marty's awards for bravery in World War II.

The memorial service overflowed with friends and family. Marty's fellow musicians came and played with heart and feeling for their friend. The band grew throughout the service. Bill and Debbie had purchased an oversized replica of a guitar made with brown and yellow chrysanthemums. Marty had requested a small memorial service, but the funeral home was jam-packed. No one had anticipated such a large gathering.

After the funeral, the business of getting papers and bills straightened out kept me very busy. This was a good thing at the time. As far as fulfilling the dates that we had already booked, I did. The bookings required two people, so I hired the best piano-playing musicians I could and paid them well. Several of the dates were repeats, and many of the people who booked Marty and me together were truly shocked to hear that Marty had died. I was doing fine when I was busy with paperwork and the shows. However, slowly I began to feel the loneliness of being one. Entering our house became excruciatingly difficult. Thank God for our dog, Whisper—another heartbeat! She, however, was not another person. Never in my life had I lived alone.

My daughter, Lisa, worried about me. She insisted we take a one-day trip to Berkeley Springs. It was good. We saw some Hobday relatives. I especially enjoyed meeting an older lady who remembered my mom so lovingly.

I spent a good deal of time planting flowers at Steven's marker in Schenley Park. Lisa and I spread Marty's ashes along the trail as we had done with Steven's. This is what I want to have done for me someday.

One evening, quite late, I began experiencing heart palpitations. I had such a rapid heartbeat that it frightened me. I called Lisa, asking for some advice since she is an excellent personal trainer. Instead of giving me advice, she and her friend Ann came to my house. They insisted and I resisted, but I finally agreed to go to the hospital. Just lying in the emergency room and feeling foolish for bothering them, I started to calm down. I even started joking and acting silly. The one time the two left the room, a great "reaction" bit came to me. I pulled the sheet up over my head. I did get the reaction I hoped for, and all three of us started laughing after the joke was revealed. The doctors at the hospital wanted to keep me overnight, but when I promised I'd see my doctor the next day, I was able to go home. I had some testing done, and physically all was okay. Emotionally, though, I needed to heal. I can only figure that the heart palpitations were triggered by overwhelming thoughts, and panic set in. Healing would take time.

Six months later, when I was ready for my six-month perm, I got a surprise. My hairdresser asked me, "Did you know your hair is breaking off?" I had been in such a whirl that I hadn't noticed. A doctor prescribed an intense series of hair treatments. These worked, but it took a while. Interestingly, the doctor commented, "This often occurs beginning about six months after someone loses a mate." It was exactly six months since Marty's death! I know I confessed earlier that when I'm sad I lose my appetite. I lost thirty pounds this year. Oh, the mental, emotional, and physical changes our bodies endure in the face of drastic life changes, including losing a loved one.

2003

At the last minute, my piano-playing partner cancelled a booking of Patti & Friend, so desperation gave the "gift" of invention.

I had been using a large, soft, furry, white puppet that resembled some kind of bird. I called him Louie. The kids loved him. The seniors at the assisted-living shows I did loved him, too. I had the puppet sit on their laps, and they would pet him lovingly. I remember standing in front of a full-length mirror practicing a routine with Louie. It was a little song-and-dance number performed to the tune of "Ball and a Jack," that wonderful "oldie" tune that I had seen the great Danny Kaye perform in person. The first time I sang the song, I made the puppet dance until I realized a certain action in the routine was not possible. One of the lines in the song goes, "You spread your lovin' arms way out in space..." Arms? This puppet did not have any arms! I went on to do the number anyway, telling my audience about the time I realized that Louie didn't have arms. They always laughed. This routine has consistently been a crowd pleaser.

For this show there was a big poster in the hallway of a veterans' "special" hospital show announcing "Today's Show: Patti & Friend." There was a huge crowd with patients and their family and friends. I told the lady in charge that my piano player had cancelled at the last minute and that I was unable to get another one. Thank goodness I always played my guitar on these shows. I suggested that Louie the puppet could be my friend that day. She was fine with the idea, and Louie was a big hit. When I introduced him, I said, "He's quite a Romeo...he loves the ladies!" I would seat him on a lady's lap and then give her a candy Hershey's kiss!

I had come full circle with my single name and performances. I was seventeen years old when I started in showbiz, and now, at seventy-three, I was Patti Eberle again. With Cindy and then Marty, I had had two totally dependable partners. Now, once again, my act was self-contained and I only had myself to rely on. I continued performing as Rainbow the Clown. I still have lots of energy and ideas. I often count my blessings.

Whenever I run into old friends I haven't seen for a long while, they always ask, "Are you still entertaining?" The question is asked as if they already know the answer. When I tell them, "I am," they say in disbelief, "You couldn't possibly be!"

2004

· ·

Almost two years to the day of Marty's death, I had my first date. Actually there had been widowed male friends who had taken me out before this and who wanted to get serious, but I was neither ready nor interested.

This handsome fella suddenly appeared at my church. He looked familiar, but I didn't know his name. He was sitting with two very dear friends of mine. Above the altar, sparks began shooting out of the fluorescent ceiling fixture. The church custodian rushed downstairs to turn off the electricity. The handsome fella, who I later learned was a retired plant engineer, stepped up to the altar to check it out. He turned to our minister, Sherry Sparks—Yep, that's her name!—and said, "You sure know how to put fire into your sermon!" As the congregation left the church after the service, he approached me. We chatted for a few minutes, but I was in a hurry to go somewhere. I found out later that my friends had told him I was now a widow.

A week or so later this same man popped his head into the kitchen at Meals on Wheels where I was working. He asked me, "Are you going to church Sunday?" I said, "I expect to be there." In the meantime, I called a couple of my lady church members and asked them what they knew about this man. One remembered he had recently donated quite a sum to help fund our church's new roof. As I probed, one said, "I don't know if he's married." That was an important piece of information I wanted to know. At least I did find out his name. I found out later that he had lost his wife six years earlier.

That Sunday he did come back to my church. He approached me again, and we talked for a few minutes. As the service began, I told him I liked to sit up front because I could hear better. So he sat up front with me. This was the start of a new chapter in my life. When Jack and I shook hands during the greeting—typically my church members hug a lot—it was amusing to see the expressions on the faces of some of my friends. One friend winked at me. Another whispered, "He's cute." I just gave a little smile and shrugged.

Jack and I found out that we share many common interests. Aside from going to different Presbyterian churches, we both love music and we love to sing. On our first date we went to a concert of the River City Brass Band. We have since become loyal fans of this talented group. We go to dances, and have even attended a couple of square dances. Jack accompanies me on some of my shows. For senior citizen groups we sing and harmonize an old song together: "I'm a Lonely Little Petunia in an Onion Patch." Overall, we are both in remarkably good health. We both have lots of energy and enthusiasm for life.

•••

An interview I did for the Heinz History Center two years earlier was finally printed in its magazine. I had given the writer many photos I had used for publicity over the years. She was excited because the magazine editors were considering putting my legs—I was wearing fishnet stockings in one photo—on the cover of the magazine. They didn't, but a full page of my legs appeared on the opening page of the article. The young fellas on the staff who were choosing the pictures thought I was really gorgeous and wanted to meet me. The writer exclaimed to them, "Don't you guys realize some of these pictures are more than fifty years old!"

The article was entitled "Showstoppers—When Local Women Entertained Pittsburgh Audiences." Here is a quote: "They sang for us, played for us, and dazzled us in the decades when people went to clubs and hotels to be entertained. And they called their own tunes, no small thing when our 'place' was in the kitchen. They set the pace—until television dropped the curtain on the golden age of live entertainment."

The nine-page article featured two other local female performers: Regina Peterson, with her accordion, on the cover; and Delsey McKay, pianist and singer. Regina had submitted a photo of a musical trio appearing at the William Penn Hotel. It's a picture of Regina with her accordion, Adam DiGasperi on bass, and my husband, Marty, with his guitar. Marty did not live to see the article, a fact that might have some bearing on the misprint I will mention in the next paragraph. I couldn't believe how many theatrical pictures they printed of me, and Cindy, too. Cindy wouldn't live to see this either. I was glad I could get copies for her four sons.

This was written near the end of the article: "The women are confident, resilient, and independent to this day...Patti and Marty Faloon lost their son Steve at age 23 to aplastic anemia. Patti wrote a book, *A Tale of a Trail*, about her son and the running trail named for him.... She performed as Rainbow the Clown with a tear painted on her check *until her passing in 2002.*" When I read this I was shocked: It was Marty who passed on in 2002, not me! It was like reading my own obituary. The magazine staff was deeply embarrassed. We came to an agreement: they agreed to put a picture of Rainbow the Clown in the next issue and clarify that I was still alive!

2005

* *

Pittsburgh Senior News is the monthly newspaper/magazine in which I have been advertising for several years. When the owner/publisher Lynn Webster first started the paper, she wanted to do a story about Rainbow the Clown. I didn't want to do it because articles about a person usually include the person's age. I was about sixty years old then. I didn't believe anyone would want to hire an old female clown. The irony here is that in 2005, fifteen years after she started the paper, I'm seventy-five years old and still active as a clown.

In February, I finally agreed to do an interview for a story in the publication. The title of the article was "A Life Worth Living: A Life Worth Remembering." It began: "There's Dick Clark, and then there's Patti Faloon. Although the irrepressible Dick was sidelined by a stroke several months ago, nothing so far has prevented Patti from bringing her unique style of entertainment to hundreds of folks every year." In the article I was called an "ageless performer." There were a couple of pictures and quotes from me, including: "If you want to keep going, you've got to keep going!" The article mentioned how much I love seeing the reactions I evoke. I told her, "It's been one adventure after another!"

At the end of the article the writer wrote: "Everyone's life holds sorrow and pain, happiness and laughter. Perhaps Patti's greatest talent is the ability to transcend the sorrowful times and keep joy and love in her heart. And, for that extraordinary, perpetual performance we simply say, 'Bravo!'" (She didn't mention my age in the article, but perhaps by using the word perpetual she gave her readers a clue!)

This year brought a neat surprise. I could never had imagined that the adorable "Chrissy" character I saw on TV's *Three's Company* would become a close friend of my son Bill. He had become acquainted with Suzanne Somers through his Life Extension Foundation. The two of them became allies in the quest for anti-aging therapies.

•••

I had been training my dog, Whisper, to do many tricks. Whisper is a Jack Russell terrier, and Jack Russells are bright. One thing she learned on her own was how to bounce a ball, or should I say, drop a ball from her mouth, let it bounce once, and then catch it in her mouth. I had never seen a dog do this before. I encouraged her constantly, and she became very good at it. Whisper could perform other tricks too: walking on her hind legs, dancing in a circle, and twirling around while holding in her mouth a long paper roll tied with colorful scarves on both ends. So I sent a videodisc of Whisper's trick with the ball to the *Pet Star* TV show, which featured talented animals, mostly dogs, doing tricks.

I was thrilled to receive a call from the show. The producers wanted me to teach Whisper how to bounce or dribble the ball and drop it into a little basketball net on a stand. They also wanted me to keep in touch.

I worked with Whisper for a few months, getting her to learn the trick. I made another videodisc for the TV show and called the show producers. I was informed that *Pet Star* had been cancelled! However, there was a positive outcome from all this: Whisper learned how to pick up her toys at the end of the day, and drop them into her toy basket. I had taught her a useful trick!

2006

What an exciting time in Pittsburgh! The Pittsburgh Steelers won their fifth Super Bowl—"one (ring) for the thumb!" I wrote a parody of the song "Tie a Yellow Ribbon" and called it "the Jerome Bettis Bus Song":

I'm coming home, I've done my time.
And with this great event it feels divine.
This Bus has been on schedule, getting bumped
and bruised, but
Gee! I'd do the same all over again,
for we made history. We made history...

Tie a gold towel around this Bettis man.
Oh, there's nothing like a Pittsburgh fan.
And when the final curtain was here at hand...
you stayed with the Bus,
You did make a fuss,
As we pursued our dream!

With Ben we'd win,
and we'd become the Super Bowl team.
Oh, the terrible towels are waving, and I can't
believe I see
Thousands of fans are cheering the
Steeler family!

I had lots of fun with this song. One time I had a phone conversation about a bill with a woman in Texas. She said she was a Steeler fan, so I sang the song to her. She asked me to email the parody to her because her mother, who lived in Texas, was a huge Steeler fan. I used the song during my senior citizen shows for the entire year. The Steeler team fans are fiercely loyal down to their bones. I always got a great reaction from the Steeler fans, lots of cheering and hooting!

A small group of us neighbors went to a little club in Bloomfield that had an "open mike" night. We elders were a bit conspicuous. All the young Steeler fans were brimming with excitement. We were, too! I was about to do something I had never done before: sing at an open microphone for a show that I hadn't been booked for in advance. I love doing things that I've never done before—as long as they're legal! We were seated in front. When I got up on the little stage and told the emcee that I had a Steelers song, I could see he was dubious. However, he was also polite and curious. I sang the song to great applause and appreciation. Our group only stayed a little while. As we exited the long walk through the crowd, I was hailed like a super star. The Steeler fans howled and applauded! It was another heyday moment.

I had been working on a "Walk on a Trail" event on Steven's memorial trail (where like always, the proceeds would benefit The Steve Faloon Bone Marrow Fund at Children's Hospital) when Brian O'Neill, a respected journalist in Pittsburgh, wrote about the trail in his column:

> ...We walked the trail together and talked. Pat finds that her work as Rainbow the Clown keeps her nimble. Her bright blue-and-white sneakers flecked with multicolored hearts got a little muddy on our two-mile hike, but she had no trouble balancing on logs to cross puddles. As we walked, Mrs. Faloon asked me not to mention "Killer Hill" as her son and friends called it because she was afraid it would discourage participation. Then she climbed it deftly, without ever breaking our conversation....

2007

It was this year, 2007, when I noticed a definite change. My bookings became less frequent. The slide made me think we were heading into another Depression. There were fewer "at-the-house" birthday parties. I often did birthday parties at daycare centers instead. Parents would tell me they had a hard time vying for a child's time; the weekends would have planned activities of all sorts: sports, dancing classes, etc.

Despite the downturn, I got enough gigs to keep in shape. I performed shows I repeated every year, and I continued to get excellent references from my bookings. All my performances were successful. I've always promised myself that if I weren't entertaining, if I didn't really "sell," I would stop entertaining.

The Internet is an enormous change that has occurred and has become a necessity for small businesses like mine. I began using the Internet to land jobs. It continues to amaze to me that I can set up a date and finalize a contract without ever having to meet or sometimes even speak to a human being. Aw, shucks, there goes some more "live" stuff!

As in any business, I'm caught between purchasing a Yellow Page ad or an Internet ad. Doing both costs more money. Eventually, I suppose, the Yellow Pages will become extinct.

At Christmas I particularly noticed I had more senior citizen shows than clown kiddie shows!

2008

One day a man from Community College of Allegheny County called and asked for permission to print an essay I had written for their newsletter. I had written the essay in a writing class at CCAC before beginning this book. The man thought my essay might benefit others. I wrote about all the many classes I have taken over the years and how they have helped me in my showbiz career. For example, art classes have helped me when I do face painting on my clown jobs. Disco dancing and belly dancing classes have kept me up with the times. Elements of all those classes have become incorporated into fun audience-participation bits.

Also at this time, I got a call from a M.J. Mandler, a lady in charge of lifetime learning at the Community College of Allegheny County. She had read my essay and wanted me to teach a course in clowning. I told her I would think about it.

For the third time there would be a goof-up in the Yellow Pages ad. I first became aware of this when I got a call for a birthday party. I usually ask first, "Where is the party going to be?" Usually the distance is ten to fifty miles. I got surprised when the caller said, "Philadelphia!" Darn it if the Yellow Pages didn't put my ad in the *Philadelphia* Yellow Book! I had many calls from the City of Brotherly Love.

Performing as Patti Eberle, I did a show at an assisted-living facility, which went over very well. I memorized some piano chords for the tune that went, "I don't know why I love you like I do." It's an old-time favorite that most of the seniors know. I used the guitar to accompany myself, made some balloon creations, told some jokes, and incorporated lots of audience participation. Many of the residents participated beyond my hopes. I had hundreds of song sheets for community sing-alongs titled "Sing Along with Marty." The songs are genuine oldies. I told people, "Please keep these and sing a song each day." On this show I would say my usual, "Choose three songs, and we'll sing them." This group did not want to stop singing. There are about thirty songs on the song sheets, and this group sang every song. I got a compliment from a lively lady who was an asset to the show with all her enthusiasm. She said to me, "Great show! You should have insurance for all your talent!" I said, "You mean like actress Betty Grable had for her legs?" It was a lovely compliment and greatly appreciated.

2009

• •

I'm still alive and though it's been twenty-eight years, so is Steven in some form or another. Recently I emailed Peter Leo upon reading his column about his retirement from the *Pittsburgh Post-Gazette*. I wrote that I would miss his informative and often amusing writings. His reply was spiritually rewarding. He thanked me for my kind words and added, "If you're related to Steve, I'm doubly honored." My heart was full of gratitude for that line.

I was asked to do an Irish program for Saint Patrick's Day, performing as Patti Eberle. The show was in an apartment building in Mount Pleasant and the residents requested lots of familiar Irish songs. I had a grand time using sparkling confetti whenever we sang *"...and they dotted it with silver just to make the lakes so grand, and when they finished, sure they called it 'Ireland.'"* I had a large shamrock flower made out of green balloons. For the first time ever on a show I sang "Danny Boy," hitting all the high notes. Everybody was Irish that day.

March 20 was a very cold day. I was booked as a clown for the grand opening of an insurance office. When I arrived, I couldn't believe I was supposed to perform outside! The gig was from noon to four. It was too cold to twist balloons, even though the office had advertised that helium balloons on strings would be passed out. If I'd only worn long underwear under my outfit, I wouldn't have been so cold. There was little sun that day and it was a record cold for that time of year. It certainly kept the crowds away. Everyone was wearing winter coats and bracing the wind. I kept moving to keep warm and went inside every now and then, too. The office management seemed pleased with me. I was amazed I didn't get sick.

April 4 presented the same dilemma. This time I was prepared and wore long underwear. It was the second year I would twist balloons for a Western Pennsylvania Trail Association race, held along the Allegheny River Wharf. The event was called "River Walk on the North Shore." When it's cold outside to begin with and then the event is near water, the temperatures by the water are even colder still. Once again I didn't get sick.

My friend Jack invited me to a neighborhood block party in Mount Lebanon. I brought my little hand pump and some balloons to twist. The kids were enjoying them. A lady came over to me and said she handled the entertainment at a facility called The Covenant at South Hills. She thought the residents would enjoy the balloon creations. I told her I had done many shows for seniors and so she booked me. I had a grand time with these people. I got to do something I had been working on for months. There was a grand piano in the room, and I passed out copies of four familiar oldies: "If I Had My Life to Live Over," "Ma, He's Makin' Eyes at Me," "Love Me Tender," and "Let the Rest of the World Go By." I played the chords and the background on the songs as we sang. It was the first time I had sung these songs with an audience while playing the piano and I was thrilled. Something new, something new, always something new!

I'm now in my seventy-ninth year and still getting personal notes and emails of praise. This email is from a clown party: "Hi Patti, Thank you so much for the wonderful show you put on for my daughter Charlotte's party yesterday. She talked about you all afternoon and gave us a good fight when it came to removing her clown makeup. I will happily be recommending you to all my friends. Thanks again for a wonderful afternoon of fun!" —Susan F.

•••

My kids had been working all year on plans for a celebration of my "Big 80" in September. From the very beginning of the party planning, Lisa wanted us to do a "show spot" as part of the entertainment. Fine. I'd been working; I was in shape. Then she said, "Mom, we can do the tap-dancing challenge with drums!" I was flattered that she felt I could still do this after all these years! However, I hadn't had my tap shoes on for more than twenty-five years. We were at lunch in a Chinese restaurant when Lisa mentioned one of my twirls. I promptly stood up, attempted one twirl, and lost my balance for a moment. "You mean that one?" I said. We both laughed, and she said, "Yeah!" I found two pairs of old tap shoes. One pair had two-inch heels and the other had flat heels. I decided on flat heels, which gave me more balance!

Oh, what a party! My family put so much time and effort into this glorious celebration. The colorful rainbow and Mylar balloons were generously displayed; there was even a rainbow-colored balloon arch. The rainbow-colored floral centerpieces were beautiful. My daughter-in-law, Debbie, had arranged them with her characteristic flair, and also scattered rainbow sequins spelling "Patricia" and butterflies on the tables.

Lisa put together a collage of pictures of me and my friends from my life to display on a huge screen. Later a video was shown as well. My cousin Trina's daughter, Trina Mae, stood at the microphone and read a beautiful poem she wrote about me entitled "The Love of Pat." I felt she wrote it from her heart, and I truly appreciated it.

Once again Bobby Rawsthorne's band would provide the music. Bobby got one of the biggest laughs of the evening. I have another dear magician friend, Jahinie. He came to the party after having had foot surgery the day before. The pain got too bad and he had to leave. During the show I mentioned his name and said, "Jahinie, where are you?" I'm glad I said what a great magician he was because when I called out again, "Jahinie, where are you?" Bobby Rawthorne said, "He disappeared!" What perfect timing!

I shared memories with my guests about my many years in showbiz and becoming Rainbow the Clown. I sang "Send in the Clowns." Then, I brought two men from the audience to join in. And they did, having put on a big bow tie, a red clown nose, and a clown hat. I talked about Marty and what a great musician he was. I recounted how Jack and I met and then Jack and I sang "Lonely Little Petunia in an Onion Patch." My grandson Chance played a guitar number. I said how happy Marty would have been to see his grandson's love for the guitar. Next, Lisa and I performed the barbershop number "Coney Island Babe" with Marty's niece's son-in-law chiming in with the "Boom-Boom" on cue.

Lisa had her chance to chime in; she spoke as I put on my tap-dancing shoes. Yes, we did the tap/drum duet. I did the one spin as Lisa did the drum roll. When I ended the tap, Lisa did her drum solo. As she has done so often before, she blew the audience away. Following her solo I sang a chorus of the lovely "I Wish You Love" to the audience. I rewrote the bridge of the song and sang: "This birthday bash has all come true, my friends and family all in view, and so my wish, my honest wish, for all of you....I wish you love."

Because we had opened our show with a line of dancers, we also closed the show with a line. I requested some of the ladies to come up on the "floor," and we quickly had a lineup for the classic "Proud Mary!"

Music to the ears of an entertainer is rave compliments. Compliments heard were everything from "Wow!" to "Fabulous!" to "The best birthday party I've ever been to!" to "What a talented family!" I especially enjoyed several guests saying to me, "Whatever you are taking, I want to take!" The show was everything I have loved in my entertaining career. There was the "reaction," and it was live!

FINAL THOUGHTS...
FOR NOW

With the new electronic revolution, changes are evident in all phases of the entertainment business. However, I still believe nothing beats live entertainment. The spontaneity, the humor, the mishaps, the intimacy and my favorite, the eye contact, are all part of live entertainment.

I became an entertainer doing what I loved. Not only did I entertain, but I felt like I was being entertained. Action...Reaction!

I'm still doing senior shows and clowning. Fortunately, many of my shows have been repeat or referred jobs. That's the easy part of booking. Most of the gigs are scheduled over the phone without the caller ever seeing me perform. Sometimes I am asked, "Where are you performing so I can see your act?" I can understand their apprehension in booking someone they've never seen before. I enjoy watching their reaction when I start my show. They usually sit in the audience on the edge of their seat, sometimes crossing their fingers and saying a few prayers. As the audience responds with enthusiasm, I can actually see the tension being lifted from their face. I can see the gratitude and almost hear the sigh of relief from the person who will be held accountable for booking the show.

In the beginning of my career, I wasn't always so confident. When you are young, doubts naturally occur. However, with experience and genuine love for what you are doing, in time, you will learn to hone your skills. Each success breeds more confidence. I've been fortunate knowing what will sell. I seem to have a knack for knowing what an audience will like, whether it is a dance routine, a song, or a joke.

When I was seventeen, I wondered why there were women in their thirties still dancing in clubs. Of course, when I reached thirty, I was still dancing. When I got older, I thought to myself, *I can't be doing this anymore.* To my pleasant surprise, working with the older audiences, such as the senior AARP groups, I found that men can still flirt and so can I. On one of my senior AARP shows, someone said to me, "You're the Betty White of Pittsburgh!" That's a nice thought…I can live with that.

To accomplish the feat of being a "live" entertainer for more than six decades has been a thrilling experience for me. The joy that comes from winning an audience over has never subsided. The sheer intensity of a live presentation is a "high" that often leads to hilarious and unexpected results. Mishaps give the laughter an extra boost in those spontaneous moments. In my private and showbiz life, I have never tired of the "reaction" that has created joy and laughter.

American author William Saroyan summed it up nicely for me: "In the time of your life, live...so that in that wondrous time you shall not add to the misery and sorrow of the world, but shall smile to the infinite variety and mystery of it." My life has been filled with immeasurable joy and immeasurable pain. No matter what life brings, I have always believed that "The Show Must Go On!"

I've been privileged and lucky. The odds of still entertaining have been on my side. Here I am, an octogenarian and still doing what I love! Call me spunky or spry, I'm fine with that. I say to those still able to do something well that they love, DON'T EVER STOP!

Musical Fun with Everyone

Shows • Parties
Special Occasions

412-561-7161

Patti Eberle
Show Time

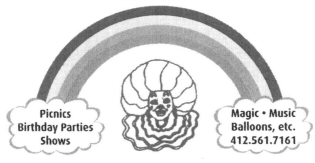

www.rainbowtheclown.net

Picnics
Birthday Parties
Shows

Magic • Music
Balloons, etc.
412.561.7161

WA